Child of
Promise

CHERYL GREEN

Child of Promise

ONE WOMAN'S JOURNEY
FROM TRAGEDY TO TRIUMPH

BROADMAN
& HOLMAN
PUBLISHERS

Nashville, Tennessee

0-8054-2440-70

Published by Broadman & Holman Publishers, Nashville, Tennessee

Dewey Decimal Classification: 277
Subject Heading: BIOGRAPHY
Library of Congress Card Catalog Number: 00-068881

The names of the persons in this story have been changed to protect their identities.

Most of the negro spirituals quoted were found in *The Books of American Negro Spirituals,* J. W. Johnson, J. R. Johnson, and R. Johnson, eds. (Da Capo Press, 1988).

Unless otherwise stated all Scripture citation is from the Holy Bible, New International Version, © 1973, 1978, 1984 by International Bible Society.

Library of Congress Cataloging-in-Publication Data
Green, Cheryl, 1970–
    Child of promise : one woman's journey from
tragedy to triumph / Cheryl Green.
        p. cm.
    ISBN 0-8054-2440-7 (pbk.)
    1. Green, Cheryl, 1970– . 2. Christian biography—United
States. 3. African American handicapped—Biography. I. Title.

BR1725.G74 A3   2001
277.3'0825'092—dc21
[B]   00-068881

1 2 3 4 5 6 7 8 9 10 05 04 03 02 01

This book is dedicated to Anne, Jerome, and Antoinette.
God has blessed me with incredible nieces and a nephew whom I love more
each day we spend together. You three children remind me of God's promise
to heal the wounds of the past. Remember the history of your family.
Always remain faithful to your heavenly Father
who broke the stronghold of abuse in our family to raise up a new
generation of children grounded in faith. You are children of promise.
Never forget your roots or forsake your Father.

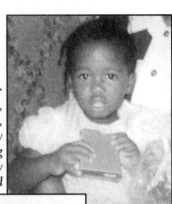

Cheryl K. ▶
Green, age 2,
in a hospital,
one of many
stays during
her early
childhood

▲ *Age 6, enjoying*
family after being
released from a
hospital stay

Today Cheryl is ▶
president/CEO
of Green Oaks
Foundation for
Mental Health

▼ *With Bob Dole at*
his birthday party on
Capitol Hill in 1992

Visiting the Great Wall of China ▶
while in Beijing for the UN World
Conference on Women in 1995

"For I know the plans I have for you," declares the LORD, "plans to prosper you and not to harm you, plans to give you hope and a future. Then you will call upon me and come and pray to me, and I will listen to you. You will seek me and find me when you seek me with all your heart."

JEREMIAH 29:11–13

Contents

Foreword

More than seventeen years ago, I announced to the U.S. Senate that I had established the Dole Foundation to facilitate the economic independence of Americans with disabilities. On that day, I spoke of my experience as a young soldier in World War II and the injuries I sustained in Italy; but more importantly I remembered my neighbors and friends in Russell, Kansas, who provided me with the support I needed to go to school and begin a new career. It was their assistance and confidence in me that allowed me to develop my capacities and to enter public service. Over the years, I have met people with disabilities throughout America who only needed the kind of opportunity I had to develop their talents and contribute their skills to our economy.

It was that generous spirit of the people in my hometown that sparked the idea that eventually became the Dole Foundation—a generosity born not of pity, but of confidence and belief in individuals' abilities to reach their full potential. The Dole Foundation became a philanthropic leader by dedicating itself to sponsoring programs that gave people with disabilities greater opportunity to play a vital part in the workplace and to become full members of the economic and social fabric of the country.

When Cheryl Green came to the Dole Foundation in 1992, she told us that she knew very little about disability policy or the laws that were passed to ensure her right to enter the mainstream of society in spite of her disability. She was dismayed that she actually knew few other people with disabilities. Through her work with us, she blossomed and gained a deep commitment to the disability community. She regards her time at the foundation as her "coming of age."

It was during that time when she discovered the power and potential of being part of a community where people were not ashamed of their disabilities and used their political power, intellect, and passions to ensure equality for all people with disabilities. I am deeply pleased that Cheryl, who began her career in philanthropy with us, has grown into a philanthropic leader in her own right, perpetuating the values which are so important to me and to the well-being of our country—giving people with disabilities the opportunity to bring their many talents into the mainstream of society and providing them with the tools to stay there. It is a source of pride for me to have had a role in sparking a passion in Cheryl for a vision that has guided me in much of my life.

People with disabilities share a common bond of struggle, adversity, and hardship. These shared experiences fuel a common vision and hope for the future. Cheryl's book is a riveting account of a battle with doubt and despair—about a future fought for through numerous obstacles in a still-young life. Ultimately this is a book about an indestructible optimism and a life full of promise. I have learned, as Cheryl has learned, that obstacles are only impediments when you permit them to be. They can be overcome. With her heart full of hope and faith, Cheryl exemplifies triumph over tragedy and is further proof that America is a land without limits.

BOB DOLE
Former Majority Leader, United States Senate

Acknowledgments

I thank you, God, for my life, including my past. I am honored to be called your child and am forever grateful that you infused me with purpose, faith, and hope. Words are not enough to express how much I love you.

This book would not have happened without the love and guidance of my sister, Gayle. Through it all, I always knew you and I had each other's support forever.

R. J., I thank you for being the big brother I always wanted and for keeping my nieces and nephew occupied while I spent many hours holed up in my room writing.

Anne, Jerome, and Antoinette, you are too young to understand why Aunt Cheryl could not play with you all those months while I was writing. One day, I pray you will understand how much of a blessing you are in my life.

Mom, I thank you for your openness and honesty in your struggle. Although describing your unhealthy past has not been easy, I thank you for being willing to share your mistakes so that God can change the hearts of others.

Todd, thank you for being the most steadfast friend in my life. You have been my constant encourager, and I thank God daily for our strong friendship.

Jeanne, words cannot express how much your love, acceptance, and guidance have transformed my life. When we met, I was a beat-up girl struggling to accept my disability. Under your mentorship, I have blossomed into a proud woman with a disability. I profoundly thank you.

Thank you, God, for John, Steve, Robin, and Mary Ann at Heart of a Champion. I am grateful that you introduced my story to Broadman & Holman and for your constant encouragement. Robin, profound thanks for praying with me.

Diedre, Brenda, and Corbett, thank you for taking your little "sista" underneath your wings and encouraging me to fight.

Lynn, Scott, Murray, and Paul, I thank you for the spiritual wisdom, counseling, and prayers as I have grappled with suffering and accepting God's mercy and love.

Many thanks to the Preston Road Church of Christ and Northland Church of Christ for all of the prayers and support I have needed along the way. I especially thank God for the worship team and singles ministry and how much everyone has loved me so deeply.

Karen and Allison, thank you for being by my side during my darkest moments battling the beast called depression. You stuck by me when I could not live up to the nickname "Sunshine." Thank you for your unconditional love.

Tom and Beth, thank you for giving me the opportunity to realize my dreams by leading the Green Oaks Foundation. I appreciate your excitement, support, and encouragement.

Thank you, God, for Gary and the whole Broadman & Holman team. You guys took a chance on a first-time author, transforming my story into something better than I could have imagined. Gary, thank you for your patience and guidance while I tried to find my voice.

I thank God for many of the other people in my life, my "angels," whom I have not mentioned. I love all of you.

Finally, thank you, Lord, for making me who I am and blessing my life with an unshakable faith and hope in you.

INTRODUCTION

No Ways Tired

I don't feel no ways tired,
I've come too far from where I've started from.
Nobody told me, the road would be easy.
I don't believe He brought me this far just to leave me.

JAMES CLEVELAND

The first time someone called me a woman of great faith, I recoiled. I am reluctant to accept the praise because I did not seek this spirit. Early in my life, I wished I never had it. Holding on to faith is hard work and, most of the time, unglamorous. I always thought people of faith sailed through life, fighting the good fight, smiling and laughing through adversity. These people never moaned, never trembled, and above all, never questioned God.

My faith is largely raw and unpolished but no less powerful to shield and save. It always surfaced at times when my life seemed certain for destruction or even when I consciously decided to give up. Unlike the gospel singer in the powerful hymn above, I do feel tired. I have always been tired of fighting the world. The list of battles is long—disability, racism, sexual abuse, poverty, homelessness, and mental illness. Crisis was my way of life. I could always count on some crisis to knock me down, then this thing called faith would always will me back to my feet—or at least to my knees. My acts of faith were not graceful; they were more like stumbling. I would stumble to my feet and then stumble forward. Yet I grew stronger because of the battle. Even in the midst of screams inside my mind, the gentle whispers of God would will me forward. My faith journey is a search to find the source of the indestructible force that gives me the hope to keep straining forward and pressing on.

SHACKLES

I grew up in Houston, Texas, which for many poor, rural African-American laborers like my parents, represented a "promised land." Mom and Dad were raised in living conditions similar to their slave ancestors'. My parents lived in overcrowded wooden shacks. They raised their own food, which ranged from vegetables and fruit to pigs and chickens. They spent most of their time toiling the land of wealthy whites in the oppressive Texas heat. They lived during the time when African-American men were lynched—or disappeared—for merely looking at a white woman. Little white kids could call them "boy" or "nigger" with impunity.

My house was full of storytelling about racism and the lives of slaves. Most stories were variations of how my parents and slave ancestors worked hard in life. Mom and Dad were born in the early 1940s, yet they picked cotton like slaves. The fields of cotton, the "king" of the South, were full of little African-American kids who should have been in school. Mothers had month-old babies strapped to their backs during the never-ending task of filling their sacks with cotton. Mom described how they were paid by the pound and had to work quickly, yet carefully, because there was a premium for clean cotton with no stalks, seeds, bulbs, or specks in it. The hands of the skilled cotton picker could pull cotton from three or four plants at a time. Mom and Dad described how their hands grew raw from picking the prickly cotton plants and how the straps on the sacks dug into their skin as they grew heavier throughout the day.

I was raised to know that I was a descendant of slaves, living in a society bent on shackling the spirit and potential of African-Americans. Through stories, my parents transmitted "our people's" collective experience with oppression and suffering. Mom and Dad emphasized the Civil Rights movement because they lived it, and the era was a shining example of our people's acts of defiance. Segregation. Church bombings. Rosa Parks. The lunch-counter sit-ins. The Freedom Riders. Dr. Martin Luther King Jr. Malcolm X. The March on Washington in August 1963. The water hoses. People screaming. The marches. The singing. My sister Gayle and I knew the stories intimately and were challenged to research anything we did not know. I remember how my parents declared a family holiday to watch *Roots* on television. To commemorate the assassination of Dr. King, Mom and Dad bought the "I Have a Dream" speech on an LP and played it whenever they needed inspiration.

Whenever we watched the news, Mom and Dad would analyze every act of perceived racism and explain its historical significance. My sister and I were children of parents who had limited choices and grew up under segregation. To them, we, the next generation after the Civil Rights era, had a responsibility to honor the people who fought and died for our rights to freedom and equality in America.

I identified strongly with the slaves and freedom fighters because of their dignity and strength despite horrific living conditions. The songs during the marches and rallies revealed a quiet strength that mesmerized me. The Negro spirituals and Civil Rights movement freedom songs were anthems of struggle and dissent during intense oppression and suffering. Through their plaintive sounds, my heart transcended history and joined with those of my ancestors to draw strength—and to first encounter the God of hope. These songs introduced me to God, faith, and salvation. Through the music, I cried out to this largely unknown God for deliverance and freedom from the shackles of hopelessness that always seemed to bind my soul. However, despite Mom and Dad's nostalgia, racism would prove to be the least of my problems.

LOST THEIR WAY

> *"[God] has allowed me to go up to the mountain.*
> *And I've looked over. And I've seen the Promised Land.*
> *I may not get there with you.*
> *But I want you to know tonight,*
> *that we as a people will get to the Promised Land.*
> *And I'm happy tonight. I'm not worried about anything.*
> *I'm not fearing any man. Mine eyes have seen the glory*
> *of the coming of the Lord."*
>
> DR. MARTIN LUTHER KING JR., APRIL 3, 1968

Even Dr. King's speech could not inspire Mom and Dad enough to make it in the promised land. They got there and saw it—they even experienced briefly the opiate of success. The fine brick house. Two cars. Vacations. Children. Money. It was a long way from picking cotton and cleaning the homes of white people. They were educated African-Americans. Mom had a master's degree in dietetics. Dad's degree was in biology. They had good jobs. Mom was a dietitian in a major hospital, and Dad was a chemist in an oil refinery. They had everything they needed. At least they thought they had everything.

Then tragedies came in swift succession: Dad's mother died. His best friend died. Mom had a blood clot in her lungs. They began to have marital problems. Dad had an affair. I was born with a disability. Mom lost her uterus to tumors. Within several years, they both lost their jobs. We lost our house. Lost the cars. They lost their careers. For reasons I'll never understand, they never got other jobs in their chosen career fields, and nothing prevented us from spiraling down the socioeconomic ladder into poverty and homelessness. Mental illness crept into their lives and seized control of our family, and my parents were never able to find their way back to the promised land. Not knowing the God of the real Promised Land, they spent their lives grasping for everything powerless to fulfill the longings of the soul.

I was seven when I began to recognize that my parents were losing their way. The house was full of screaming, cursing, and slamming doors. At the same time, a male cousin began sexually abusing me. Gayle was enduring her own hell of Mom's verbal abuse. "Hussy" and "whore," among other words even less tasteful, became Gayle's nicknames. As our possessions dwindled, my parents grew more paranoid and insular. They had to preserve their faith in a previously unquestioned tenet held by post-Civil Rights era, educated African-Americans: that education was the ticket to the better life they dreamed about for years while toiling the fields in rural Texas. Other African-Americans in their college class were successful doctors, lawyers, teachers, and sports celebrities. My parents had been part of the rising self-made elite of descendants of slaves. They had worked hard for their success, and they fought hard to hold on to it.

Fighting only delayed the inevitable. My parents would lose everything, and the foundation of their entire belief system, their orientation to life, would crumble in the sinking sand. They were failing with all the tools they thought they needed to remain in the promised land. To the end, they believed they were being denied their birthright.

BEHOLD

Newly born in 1970, I was a sight to behold. A mess. Perfectly normal from the waist up and a mangled mass of flesh from the waist down. Something went horribly wrong in my development, and there were precious few explanations. I was born in a time when sonograms were not routine. No one knew that something was wrong inside the womb. Mom had suspicions because I did not squirm around in the womb like my older sister had. Back in those days, the medical profession routinely relegated women's concerns to histrionics. My birth caught everyone off guard. I was two months premature and well into the birth canal in a breech position. Blood was everywhere, and the birthing room became chaotic.

"Mrs. Green, you had a bad baby this time," Dr. Knight told Mom as nurses whisked me out of the birthing room. I can't imagine what was going through Mom's mind. The most exciting day of her life plunged to agony in a matter of minutes. I was the dread of all expectant mothers: a defective child. There would be no jubilation. No pats on the back. No smiles. In their stead were chaos, screaming, and averted eyes.

It was three days before Mom saw me. Doctors were holed up examining me and searching for the diagnosis. A nurse wrapped me tightly in a blanket and took me to her. Mom began her inspection with my face. First, she touched my skin and ran her fingers through my curly black hair. My eyes opened, and she saw clear, healthy, large eyes. Peeling back the blanket, she ran her fingers over my chest toward my shoulders and my arms. Inspecting my hands, she saw and kissed all ten fingers.

She struggled to open the bottom half of the blanket—it was caught. Tugging harder, Mom pulled free the blanket. She took one look and fainted. My lower limbs looked as if I had barely survived a bomb blast. My legs were curved grossly in a bow. No amount of tugging could straighten them. I had no ankles; the area where they should have been was turned inward, and my legs were lying on top of each other. I had no toes; the bones were all there, but all anyone could see was a ball of flesh.

I was defective—less than perfect. The culprit had a sinister name: arthrogryposis multiplex congenita. To this day the term causes a gasp in those who hear it. Doctors attending my birth had barely heard of the condition, let alone seen a child with it. Jerry Lewis would hold no telethons for it. There were no foundations for it and no celebrity pushing for awareness and a cure.

I was born at the wrong time in my parents' lives as well. I came along as they were clawing to stay on top. Life was full of contradictions. My parents transmitted their belief in the power of education to my sister and me. They told us the history of our ancestors so that we would always understand the collective right we shared in enjoying the fruits of America on equal footing with whites. They imparted our people's history of strength, dignity, and determination. Yet my parents were also the bastion of dysfunction. The verbal assaults. The physical beatings. Using their children to destroy each other. Finally, their inability to protect and provide allowed predators to slither in and wound the souls of two children lost in the wilderness with them.

My family lost more than possessions and social standing: we lost our souls. My parents had no other hope to transmit to their children. We were left on our own to find the will to continue. I remember saying to them, "Why is there no love in this house?" Though my parents could not answer me, gentle whispers always protected my soul:

My dear child, you do not know me, but I know all about you. I will always love you. Soon you will hear my voice and see my face. Do not be afraid, my dear, because I am here to guide you along your way home to me. Your perfect Daddy is here and will never leave you. Soon, my love, you will hear my voice and know that I am here.

JOB

The first time I opened the Bible, I was almost twelve. Dad had been fired from his job, and life for us was about to get very stressful. Dad was fired at the worst possible time—Houston's economy was dismal and jobs were scarce. Because his employer fired him for insubordination, Dad could not find work in his professional field. A twelve-year career and list of accomplishments were worthless if the company was always going to give a bad reference. Dad blamed racism for the way the company treated him. He called a family meeting and shocked everyone by pulling out his Bible.

"God has revealed to me that you girls need to read the Book of Job. I don't want to get into the details about it, but I won't be working for a while. When I was let go from my job, some very racist men made it their mission to destroy me and stab me in the back."

Dad's voice rose with anger. His hands clenched in fists. My sister Gayle and I backed away from him while he ranted. "When you are educated and an African-American man, there are many white people who spend their whole lives trying to destroy all that you have built. All they want to do is tear you down and try to make you feel inferior to them. I am educated and worked hard for twelve years for nothing. Then I had to train all those white kids with nothing but a high school diploma only to see them promoted over me every single time. That is racism."

Dad's eyes filled with tears. He stopped talking and looked away. He was in pain but was not going to continue until he gained control of himself. He told us to believe in him but also to know that our lives would be like Job's. "Job was a righteous man, and Satan sought to destroy him. So Satan took everything from him—all his wealth, his children, his health, everything—just to see how far he could go before Job cursed God," said Dad.

When Gayle and I were alone, we struggled with the Bible. It was a foreign object to us. In our family, the Bible was used to record family history, deaths, and marriages. We never read it. I felt illiterate. Dad had told us earlier that God had to anoint us to understand the Bible. Gayle and I thought Dad had forgotten that we were not that special to God.

My first introduction to the Bible was devastating. Job was not an easy read. I was offended from the beginning that God and Satan destroyed an innocent man's life over a bet. The God of hope turned into a whimsical God who played around with a man's life with reckless disregard for his suffering. I struggled to keep reading. I could not understand why God would remain silent through Job's cries and moans. When God finally spoke, I was appalled. He seemed cold, heartless, and distant. Instead of consoling Job, God seemed to bully him. Dad would later tell us that we have no right to question God, and Job was yelled at because he dishonored God. I could not accept this God as my God of hope. I angrily closed the Bible and would not open it again for three more years.

Job left more of an impact on me than I cared to admit at the time. Job and I were kindred spirits. "Lord, what did I ever do to you to deserve this suffering? Are you making a bet with the devil about my life too?" I asked God variations of this question all my life. I desperately wanted to talk to God, to plead my case as well. My only crime was to be born. Gayle would always say, "I didn't ask to be born."

God's silence always bothered me as well. I did not understand how the God of love could remain silent while people suffered. Why did he never speak to me? Why could I not hear him? I needed to know which God was real. Was God a distant bully, or was he my God of hope and deliverance? I needed my silent God of hope to speak to me. I grew up with a soul begging God to make his presence known to me and to tell me himself that he knew what he was doing.

THROUGH IT ALL

Though my journey has been one of limping and crawling, it has been no less honorable than a journey in which one runs. This book is about the battles and victories, large and small, I have encountered along the way. Mostly, however, these stories are about the development of faith and hope in a person with little reason to believe in God. From the beginning, the God of hope revealed himself in whispers to a broken heart and carried his limping child toward home. This is a story of defiance, not victimization. Faith and hope mix in a mysterious way to create a defiance that may not be attractive, or even wise, but serves as an indestructible shield provided by a God with the infinite power to salve the deepest wounds of the soul.

PART ONE

Soul Cries

Nobody knows de trouble I see.
Lordy, nobody knows my sorrow.
Nobody knows de trouble I see,
But, glory hallelujah.
Sometimes I'm standing crying,
Tears running down my face.
I cried to the Lord, "Have mercy."
"Help me to run this ole race."
Oh, Lord, I have so many trials.
So many pains I've known.
I'm asking for faith and comfort,
Lord, help me to bear this load.
Nobody knows de trouble I see.
Lordy, nobody knows my sorrow.
Nobody knows de trouble I see,
But, glory hallelujah.

NEGRO SPIRITUAL

CHAPTER ONE

Defective

> "Disabilities themselves cause problems, and those physical problems, too, form who we are. I don't like the idea of ignoring that. That's also a potent force in our development. No matter what your disability is, it has an impact on you. To say you're just like everyone else, except you accidentally have this little difference, is really to deny your experience."
>
> DR. CAROL GILL, DISABILITY RIGHTS ACTIVIST

When I was young, I loved watching the Jerry Lewis telethon. Although I did not have muscular dystrophy, I held out hope that one day someone would find a cure for my disability too. As the years passed, the economic hardships my family faced became more serious than my preoccupation with one day being normal, so I stopped watching the yearly television ritual.

Then something caught my eye one day. People with disabilities began protesting Jerry Lewis. They were screaming, "Tune out Jerry!" and "Boycott the telethon!" I could not understand why these people were protesting something as noble as trying to raise money to find a cure for a horrible disease. The telethon supporters were irritated, lashing back with, "Don't you want to be cured? Don't you want to be like everyone else? Don't you want to be normal?"

The activists retorted, "We are whole people. We don't want your pity. We are not helpless and pathetic people. You are raising funds by emphasizing what we can't do, by perpetuating hopelessness, and by reinforcing the stereotypes that devalue us." I was twenty-one, and this was the first time I heard the argument that there are times when helping can harm.

The rhetoric of disability politics was foreign to me. Despite my discomfort with the growing tensions, I listened to the protesters' concerns with interest. They were rejecting the paternalistic and negative attitudes that underlie the telethon. *Handicapped. Lame. Crippled.* They argued that these words automatically elicit images of helplessness, a life less than whole and definitely not something to be displayed with pride. One of the former poster children described the humiliation she felt during the fund-raising appeals. People told her when to smile and when to look sad, while others constantly described the devastation her parents felt at her birth and her pitiful life.

Wading through the rhetoric, I reflected on the many times my parents would emphasize my helpless state when they applied for food stamps and welfare. They used me to appeal to the generosity of the government workers. My disability was guaranteed to pull on the heartstrings of those devoid of compassion. I could relate to being a poster child.

Protesters targeted the telethon's emphasis on a cure. "A person is more than a condition!" "I am somebody even if there is no cure!" They argued that by overemphasizing the cure, a message was sent to millions that a person with a disability could not have a life worth living. According to the telethons, disabled people could rely only on the power of the medical profession and charitable people to make them whole again.

"Wake up and accept this fact: most people with disabilities won't be cured." The spokesperson paused for effect. "Emphasizing our supposedly pitiful state may raise money, but at what cost? Your efforts to help us are stripping us of our dignity. We are moving on and embracing all of who we are, which includes celebrating our disabilities. This is who we are, and most of us are proud of our disabilities. We are proud of who we are."

Protesters argued that more money should be channeled to removing structural and attitudinal barriers that were the true culprits in the hardships faced by people with disabilities. These barriers include buildings with steps and no elevators, transportation systems without wheelchair lifts, and employment discrimination.

I barely heard these arguments. The activists' assertion about being proud of their disabilities stumped me. Some said that they would reject a cure even if one was found. Surely these statements were solely for shock value. My parents raised me to discount my disability: "You are not crippled or handicapped; you just walk differently from others. That is all," Mom and Dad used to say to me. We talked about my disability only if we were applying for government assistance. I could not understand how anyone could be proud of being deviant.

The protesters reminded me of African-Americans during the Civil Rights era shouting, "Black is beautiful!" They were seizing control of a stigma and redefining its meaning. I saw disability activists with posters saying, "Disabled and proud!" and thought, *These people have an uphill battle trying to convince others to think of a disability as anything except a mark of deviance and a source of shame.* I felt that most people with disabilities were like me—they did not want attention drawn to a stigma. I thought, *Who wouldn't want to be just like everyone else?*

"I don't sit around all day hoping and praying for a cure. I have a life—one that is whole and worth living," said a severely disabled protester. With that statement, I was stunned. Although I felt I had a life worth living, I was far from feeling whole.

I had a tough time listening to the protesters because of their preachiness and abrasiveness, but their words touched a nerve. I agreed that my problems had less to do with my disability itself and more with how people reacted to me because I had a disability. The message I received was that I should be ashamed of not being able to do anything like a normal child. My parents would vacillate between telling me that the word *can't* was not in my vocabulary and then appealing to the disability stereotypes to raise money from welfare. I could not believe that it was possible to be proud of something that caused so much pain, hardship, ridicule, and ostracism. These activists achieved pride through political means. I would later try their methods for achieving wholeness, and fail.

Coming to terms with my disability, including people's reactions to it, required me to seek answers beyond protests, speeches, debates, and rhetoric. I would become active in disability politics and struggle to reconcile my activism with my faith. After being a Christian for three years, I began searching for the reasons behind why I still did not feel whole.

My dear child, I know you want to feel whole. Your disability has little to do with the emptiness you are feeling. Be patient and keep on trusting in me, your Daddy. I promise to fill the depths of your soul with joy and peace. My plan is for you to have a soul that is overflowing with hope. Trust me, my love. I promise to make you feel whole.

SPECIMEN

Soon after birth, I became a medical celebrity. Maybe I was more like a laboratory rat. My case was glamorous. I always imagined doctors took one look at me and started to scramble to be the first one to discover the cure. To figure out what I had would guarantee an article or two in the medical journals. To discover how to cure me would guarantee fame. My family called the doctors and researchers Jonas Salk wannabes—scrambling to the medical library, calling colleagues, and jockeying to be the first to crack the mystery of the rare deformity. The textbook case came alive in a small Houston hospital, and I was to be an unwilling subject of twelve years of research.

Although the doctors knew little about my condition, they came in portraying themselves as gods of knowledge. They spoke with authority yet were void of compassion. "Cheryl has arthrogryposis multiplex congenita. It is a rare deformity of unknown causation." So began a doctor's soliloquy that sucked away the hope my parents had in my future.

The term *arthrogryposis* comes from combining *arthro*, a Greek prefix meaning "joint," and *gryposis*, which means "abnormal curvature." For some reason, while I was in the womb, I did not move my lower limbs, and, therefore, my bones formed a bow. The joints in the affected area were severely limited in movement, and the surrounding joint tissue was abnormally connected.

There is no known cause for arthrogryposis. The prevailing theory holds that the condition is related to the lack of movement of the fetus in the uterus, thereby leading to limitations in movement of the arms and legs. Other theories speculate that the muscles did not develop properly. There may not have been enough room in the uterus. The spinal cord could have been damaged. The tendons, bones, and joints could have developed abnormally. Testing on the condition had just begun. Dad conducted his own research and showed Mom pictures of other babies with my disability. Some children had elbows stuck in the straight position or had their arms twisted around their bodies.

"Cheryl's hips, knees, and legs will not develop or move normally," one of the doctors said. "You should prepare yourselves for the possibility that she may never be able to walk. We can't rule out the possibility that she might have some cognitive problems. We just don't know enough about this disorder. What we can tell from the literature, however, is that Cheryl is a very lucky girl because her condition could be worse."

Lucky? Mom felt that I was anything but lucky. All she saw was a little African-American girl born in the South without her physical health. In her mind, there was little hope that I could possibly make anything of my life. The seeds of her hopelessness were sown by the well-meaning doctors. I understand now why many disability activists reject what they call the medical model. Medical labels are frightening and intimidating; they negatively focus on the impairments and relegate the person's abilities to a secondary status. All my problems in life, under this view, would be derived from my disability. To accept this view logically meant adhering to an all-out pursuit of a cure. A cure would guarantee that I could be normal.

After hearing the bleak news about my condition, Mom started crying and grew more depressed; Dad began drinking. As I grew up hearing Mom repeatedly tell me the circumstances of my birth, she would always cry at the doctor's pessimistic prognosis. She would remind me that the doctors were wrong and did not know everything. Mom's happiest moment occurred on the day when, at two years old, I pulled up on the side of a couch and began walking, despite wearing casts on both legs. My parents saw my walking as a sign of hope that the doctors were wrong and I could possibly live a normal life one day.

There would be no cure. I overheard one of Mom's friends asking, "What's going to happen with Cheryl? You have to be strong to be an African-American woman in this country. It's hard enough for those of us with our health to cope with oppression on two fronts. This poor child is African-American, a woman, and a cripple. Who's going to take care of her when you are gone? Bless her heart."

Mom put on her brave front and told her friend that I would grow up to be somebody in spite of my disability. Yet I often caught Mom crying alone in her room. She would rock herself, moaning, "Why did this have to happen? What's going to happen to her? Why are you doing this to me? What did I do wrong?"

Mom could not hear God reassure her: *That precious child of yours is precious to me also. Raise your head and know that she is not a mistake, and I am not punishing you. I love her with a powerful, everlasting love that knows no boundaries. Be encouraged, mother, because I have plans for that precious little one. I promise that she will have a hope and a future.*

BLAME GAME

Disability guarantees a quest for someone to blame. Something or someone has to have caused this anomaly of nature. Fingers start pointing, tears flow, tempers flare, and marriages are strained. The pursuit of culpability is as old as time. The prevailing thought has been that disability is the result of somebody's sin—it can't just happen, and nothing good can come from it.

Mom and Dad were never close to their families after leaving rural Texas for a better life in Houston. Relatives called my parents "Uncle Toms"—African-Americans who were accused of trying to be white. Regardless of the backbiting, Mom and Dad thought it was their duty to maintain the extended family unit. Their children must know their history, and the only way to achieve that was to interact with the keepers of our history. My extended family was also the preserver of the family's tradition of abuse.

Many of my relatives practiced a hybrid religion with elements of Christianity and voodoo. On the outside they looked like other mainstream Christians. They went to church on Sunday, prayed to God and Jesus, sang hymns and slave songs, baptized new believers, and participated in communion. In private, the darker elements of their religion would surface. Dad told us many stories about the evil elements of my parents' families. I heard stories about animal sacrifices, potions, dolls, and spells. I never wanted to believe these wild stories, but they kept me from wanting to visit my relatives. I was terrified of evil and never wanted to develop firsthand knowledge of the interaction between voodoo and Christianity.

When I was seven, Mom and Dad's marriage was failing, so they decided to head to Mexico for a vacation alone. To them, this was a perfect opportunity to introduce their children to their heritage by forcing us to spend the summer on my grandparents' farm in rural Texas. In their romantic notion, we would help Grandmother harvest fruits and vegetables, learn how to tend the chickens, pigs, and cattle, and experience life without the corrupting luxuries of the big city.

Gayle and I were not close to our extended family. Most of them had never seen us before. My parents were forcing Gayle and me to spend an entire summer with strangers. This would be the summer of my confrontation with the blame game.

When we reached Grandmother's house, she was standing outside waiting for us. Having never seen us in person, she began her inspection. She doted over Gayle, complimenting her on her pretty, light skin tone and good straight hair. Grandmother turned to me and stared at the casts on my legs. She spit on the ground next to me and concisely expressed her disgust: "This is one ugly baby."

"Don't talk like that. She's not stupid. She can hear you," Mom said.

"Why is she crippled?"

"How should I know? It's just one of those things."

"What am I supposed to do with a cripple? I'm too old to be dealing with her needs."

"Look, she has Gayle, and they won't be too much trouble. We said that we would pay you for your trouble," Mom said.

"You realize that she has the mark of the devil. What did you do wrong for God to punish you with a demon child?"

"Will you shut up, already?" yelled Dad.

"Do you want to keep these kids or not?" Mom asked.

"Give me my money. I'll keep them. They had better not eat too much. They look like they can eat, especially that ugly one."

I spoke up. "I have a name and I'm not ugly."

Grandmother slapped me. "You don't ever talk back to grown people. What are you city folk teaching these youngsters? I won't put up with disrespect. You girls are going to learn the value of hard work. If you don't work, you won't eat. Nothing is free here. Now scram. I have work to do, and I don't have time worrying with you." Grandmother turned to my Uncle David and told him to figure out what to do with me.

Uncle David battled paranoid schizophrenia for many years; he was also a drug addict and had spent time in jail for drug use and theft. At over six feet tall, he was an imposing figure. He hardly ever smiled and rarely spoke. He was my grandmother's last child and the least wanted. During their frequent arguments, Grandmother always reminded him that she never wanted him. Nevertheless, Uncle David adored her and would do anything to earn her love. When he saw me, I'm sure he saw his opportunity to prove to Grandmother that he was worth something. She was distressed by my disability, and Uncle David must have thought that cleansing me of my sin would alleviate that distress.

When I overheard them talk about the "cleansing ceremony," I grew anxious over the uncertainty of what they intended to do to me. Uncle David would spend hours staring at me as if he were searching for evidence of the specific evil spirit that was tormenting and disfiguring my body. Gayle caught him staring at me one day and heard him mumbling incoherently. She told me, "I don't know what is happening, but if I were you, I'd get lost. Don't even get caught in the same room with them."

"I want to go home," I said as I started to cry. Over the next few days, Gayle and I spent most of our time outside, hiding from my uncle and grandparents. I thought they had forgotten about the cleansing ceremony.

My uncle, however, never forgot about his mission. One day he jumped me from behind and wrapped his arms around my neck. Easily overpowering my flailing arms, he began dragging me across the field and gardens. "It's time to cleanse you."

He stopped dragging me when we reached a spot near the chicken coop. My uncle went inside the coop to pull out a chicken. My heart was racing, and tears streamed from my eyes as I saw him wrap a string around the chicken's neck. He began to whirl the chicken in the air. After chanting something, he placed the chicken on a tree stump, pulled out an ax, and chopped off the chicken's head. In spasms, the beheaded chicken bolted off the tree stump and started running around wildly, heading toward me.

I jumped up from the ground and began to run away as best I could with the casts on my legs. My uncle bolted after the chicken and me.

"Come back here, girl! I need to use this blood to cleanse you. I need to get this devil out of you."

"Somebody help me! Please somebody help me!" I screamed.

"Don't you ever run away from me. When I catch you, girl, I'm going to beat you silly. Come back here!"

God must have heard my cries because the beheaded chicken started to run in a different direction, and my uncle went after it. My sister jumped from the bed of a truck and pulled me inside to safety. I was hysterical. We knew we could not continue to live with our grandparents. To them, disability was a mark of sin and of the devil. They would be constantly trying to cleanse me as long as I lived there. I was the embodiment of evil, and only the blood of the chicken would make me whole.

In gentle whispers I could not hear, but were powerful enough to direct us, God said, *Do not be afraid. The blood of animals has no power. Do not listen to them. They do not know me. You are not a mistake and you are not evil. I promise I will take care of you.*

Gayle spotted a bicycle in the shed and suddenly remembered the directions to our aunt's house. So two kids, ages seven and nine, cycled fearlessly for eight miles in the setting sun to a place and people they barely knew. We lived the rest of the summer with our aunt and her family. Living there was no better—her son sexually molested me the entire summer. But more about that later.

CURES AND HEALING

I will never forget the day I stopped longing for being normal. The price of normalcy had risen too high and discouraging. I was twelve, sitting in the hospital for crippled children and waiting for my all-too-familiar turn at being gawked at by the stream of eager new residents assigned to my case. The nurse handed me the shorts and halter top I had to wear during my examination. The outfit was too small, but I had to wear it anyway. When my name was called, I walked into the large examination room to face fifteen doctors. I knew the drill. I sat on a chair in the middle of the room, and the head doctor brought the other doctors up to speed on my case.

"This is the arthrogryposis multiplex congenita case. . . ." I had become a condition, not a person.

Residents began to close in on me and inspect my legs, feet, hips, and back. As each set of cold hands began poking and pulling at my body, I grew angrier. One of the doctors asked about my prognosis, and they sat down in a huddle to talk about me. I heard one of them say, "This is as far as we can go with this case. If she was younger, we could attempt normalization by—" I tuned out.

I was tired of their trying the latest and greatest trick to make me normal. Now the medical celebrity was getting too old, and they were losing interest in my case. I had been to enough medical circus shows to hear the shift in the tone of their voices. They were finally realizing that they could not cure me. I asked myself what was the point of putting up with the freak show if there was no hope for a cure. I started to choke back tears because reality hit home at that moment. I was always going to be disabled, so as Gayle would say, "If you can't change it, then move on. Ain't no sense in whining about it." I was not about to allow those doctors to hurt me with their decision that there was nothing more they could do for me. When I dressed and met my mother in the waiting room, I made a preemptive strike.

"Mom, I'm tired of coming to this hospital. They can't fix me, and I'm tired of feeling like a freak. I don't want to come back here anymore. I'm tired of wasting my time." Mom and Dad surprised me by not protesting my decision. It was too painful and exhausting to base any more hope on the illusive cure. I was always going to have a disability, and I felt it was time to move on.

The quest for a cure started when I was a few days old. The unquestioned course of treatment for my disability included physical therapy and multiple surgeries. The goal of surgery was to increase the likelihood that I would walk by straightening and realigning my hips, knees, and ankle area. The only way to straighten and align these joints was to break them and use staples to force them to heal together. Over the course of six years, I had surgeries to break and remold the legs in a straight form. Surgeries to shape the flesh into toes. Surgeries to create a functioning ankle by fusing and stapling bones together to form a solid mass for feet. I was in and out of the hospital so frequently that my parents and Gayle rarely saw me. Hospital rules only allowed family visits for one hour a week and excluded visits from children under eighteen.

In between surgeries, the doctors decided to treat me with serial casting; that is, stretching my joints and using the casts to keep them immobilized in the proper position. The goal was to force the bones to grow straight. The casts would typically go on and come off in two-week time spans. Then I had physical therapy and clinic visits to monitor my spine, hips, and legs. I hated clinic visits more than physical therapy. I was tired of being the center of unwanted attention. I was fed up with hospitals and doctors.

I think the seeds of doubt in a cure for my disability were sown during my last set of surgeries when I was seven. I was older and more aware of my surroundings at that time. The hospital seemed big and imposing. All the adults had smiles chiseled on their faces as if they had on permanent masks. My father held me while my arms were wrapped tightly around his neck. My eyes grew larger as we moved through the halls. It was as if I was trying to etch our movements in memory so I could remember my escape route. When we arrived at my bed, my father put me down and helped my mother put my clothes away in the dresser. No one talked or cried.

My home for months at a time would be a fifteen-bed children's ward in the hospital for crippled children. The ward was a strange mix of cheery kid images—balloons, primary colors, cartoons—in a sterile institution full of IV machines, steel-frame beds, and grates over the windows. The children in the beds nearest me did not speak English. My surgery confined me to bed, where I spent most of the day waiting for volunteers to come play with me. Once or twice during the night, volunteers would stroll by with cookies and milk for children who were awake. I was bored, immobilized, and miserable. After the pain medications began to wear off, I would lie in the bed staring out the window. I had no television or video games. At night my entertainment consisted of identifying the images created in the sky by the lights of the offices and the antennas on top of nearby buildings. Every now and then, a helicopter would land on top of the building next door and give me something to watch.

No one told me how long I would stay in the hospital. Medical personnel and my parents told me little about my medical condition or my hospital stay. At that time, many experts believed a child's ignorance would aid in recuperation. With every passing day, however, I felt that my parents had forgotten about me and were going to leave me in the hospital forever. I began to resent my sister because she was receiving all my parents' attention at home.

After a couple of weeks, I began to struggle with my feelings. Everyone tried to cheer me up. Nurses, volunteers, and my parents noticed my refusal to eat. I stopped playing with my stuffed animals. I stared at the ceiling or out the window most of the day. I started wetting the bed, sucking my thumb, and pulling out clumps of my hair. It was clear to everyone that this little girl was on the road to destroying herself.

Though the loneliness and fear were eating away at my spirit, I could not let go of the hope that one day I would be normal. In the hospital I developed one of my most effective coping mechanisms—daydreaming. Full-length movies played in my head—movies about life at home, life in other countries, and life with cartoon characters. All my dreams included a version of me that did not have a disability. In my dreams I was running and jumping. There were no tears or pain, and I was beautiful. I stopped hurting myself when the dreams started. Nevertheless, physical therapy, blood draws, and other intrusive, painful procedures would slam me back to reality. I started to grow tired of balancing fantasy and reality. Bouncing back and forth became too hard. I continued to dream, but it brought an insufficient and inconsistent measure of peace.

One day I awoke to another gentle whisper. A new girl was wheeled into the ward and placed next to me. Toy was a little seven-year-old African-American girl. I never knew what was wrong with her, but she was covered in a body cast all the way to her neck. She had a beautiful smile. We took one look at each other and became instant friends. I do not remember much about our friendship except the sense of peace it brought. We spent the evenings talking about the shapes we saw in the clouds. We shared our daydreams and recounted them like soap operas. Toy made me smile so that I grew oblivious to the needles, the pokes, and the pain. I do not know how long Toy and I were together in the hospital. I felt we had a brief friendship. I never saw Toy again after the hospital discharged us, but I never forgot about her either.

I remember asking Mom if Toy was a real person; she seemed like a character in one of my dreams. Mom remembered meeting her parents. Nevertheless, when I look back on that time, I consider Toy an angel. Our relationship was too short, and I was too young to remember anyone who was merely ordinary. Toy was special. When I was with her, I felt the peace of being normal and accepted. To know that I was not the only one of my kind in the world was liberating. I can almost see God squatting down to hug his frightened little child and smiling as he placed that gift of friendship in my hands.

My precious child, you are not a mistake, and I love you just the way you are. To show you how much I love you, I'm giving you a gift from my heart. Enjoy yourself, my love, and one day you will come to understand that the peace and acceptance you feel now is nothing compared to how you will feel when you come home to live with me. I will always love you and will never leave you. I promise.

As I came of age, I would have more struggles with my feelings about having a disability. After my experience with Toy, however, I began to stop thinking about a cure. I would soon learn that there are problems far worse in life than having a disability.

CHAPTER TWO

Daddy Wounds

The father wound is the deepest wound on earth.

ANONYMOUS

I received a call in 2000 from my father's mistress. After Dad's affair with her and subsequent divorce from my mother, I vowed I would never talk to the faceless woman. I never wanted to see the person who had caused so much grief in my already dysfunctional family. Their affair, which began shortly after I was born, was the source of many of my parents' most heated arguments. Dad and the "faceless one" lost contact as we plunged into poverty and homelessness. Then, fifteen years later, they saw each other again at my uncle's funeral. Their decision to rekindle forbidden love was one of the horrible choices Dad made.

"Your daddy went home to be with the Lord this morning," she told me.

"What are you talking about?"

"I went in to wake him up this morning, and he was gone. Your daddy is dead."

I hung up the telephone feeling nothing. Nothing? How could a child feel nothing at the sudden news that her father had died? Even worse, I decided that I would not go to the funeral. What had happened to the little girl who adored her father? What happened to God's command to honor my father and mother? Surely my feelings were in violation of some commandment of God.

I sat on the edge of my bed trying to comprehend what I had just heard. My father was dead and I felt numb. As I began to process my feelings, I felt a strange sense of relief. The source of many nightmares was gone, never to hurt me again. I could begin to deal with the damage Dad had caused, for my father was an abuser.

Uncle Gene called me late that night after I heard the news. The rest of Dad's family had gathered at my aunt's home to plan the funeral. "Cheryl, you know that we lost Uncle James too. He died in an accident at the same time I told him about your daddy."

I never was close to my aunts and uncles, and although I liked some of the memories of Uncle James, such as his laughter and wit, he was still a stranger to me. "I'm sorry to hear that. What do you need from me?"

"Cheryl, we want to know that you and Gayle are coming to the funeral. It will be a joint funeral to bury both your daddy and James."

"No, we won't be coming."

"No matter what your daddy did to you and how he treated you, you must honor him by being at the funeral. I can't tell you enough how God will not bless you if you don't honor your daddy by being here. In fact, Uncle James had decided not to come to the funeral and ended up running off the road and into a pole while he was on his cell phone with me. He was killed instantly. See, God won't bless you and will punish you all your life if you decide not to come to the funeral."

Anger swelled inside of me, but I kept my silence. Uncle Gene sounded just like my father. He twisted God's fundamental nature to suit his own arguments. God would punish me for not attending the funeral of my abuser? I knew a different God. I was tired of religious-sounding people trying to manipulate me. I was tired of their misrepresenting God to push their own selfish agendas. I was sick of everything that reminded me of Dad.

"No, I'm not going to the funeral. I vowed long ago that I did not ever want to see the face of his mistress. I decided that I would not allow her to hurt my mother or me again. I am also not a hypocrite. Dad and I had an awful relationship, and I'm not going to pretend otherwise. I won't sit there listening to people who barely knew the real him portray him as a saint."

Uncle Gene would not take no for an answer. He kept pushing and threatening that God would punish me. I decided to close the chapter for good, so I hung up the telephone. It was time to put the past behind and heal the numerous wounds Dad had inflicted. The feelings that were held inside for many years have now begun to surface. I have a long way to go on my journey to forgiveness, but Dad's death marked the beginning.

VISIONS

Dad was the best example of a person who took the concept of being special too far. He reminded me of the cult leader Jim Jones whose control and spiritual abuse sealed the fate of thousands of people in Guyana. Similarly, Dad was a persuasive speaker who clothed his words with the authority of God. Dad started out harmlessly yet ended in a blaze of misery. After he lost his job and began to lose his way, he grew sinister. We were never a religious family. We rarely went to church—only for Easter and Christmas. What I knew about the Bible came mainly through my love for Negro spirituals, gospel music, and African-American history. What I knew about God came from Dad, who proclaimed himself to be God's "anointed one."

Dad described his relationship with God as special and divine. The sign of his anointing was a birthmark on his forehead. As God's special son, Dad received heavenly insight through visions and miraculous signs. Kids are preset to believe their parents, and I not only believed Dad, I feared him and his power.

Dad would typically transform a simple trip to the grocery store into a battleground between God's anointed one and the forces of evil. I remember seeing Dad in action when I was ten and he took Gayle and me to the store. While we were waiting in line, an African-American woman, possibly from Haiti, stood behind us. She smiled at me and asked me my name and age. Dad always told us to be wary of strangers because some of them were predators. I told her my name and looked to Dad to make sure that everything was OK.

He was staring at the woman. It was an intense, piercing, and cold stare. Then he extended his hand. When she took it, both of them began to tremble. Then Dad pulled away from her and raised his voice. "Get thee behind me, Satan!" The woman looked at him, stepped backward, and hastily moved to another line ten rows away. Dad turned to us and said, "God told me that she was evil, and when I touched her hand, I felt it. But I protected you." I am sure the woman thought Dad was a nut.

I will never forget when Gayle and I saw *The Exorcist* on television. Dad made us watch it so that we would know the face of evil. After my experience with Uncle David involving the chicken and all of Dad's stories about voodoo, I was terrified to watch the movie. Dad pointed out scenes as proof that if we did not believe in God and in him, this was how the devil would infiltrate our bodies.

Then I saw Linda Blair's character levitate off the bed. I saw her head twist 360 degrees. Whenever she spoke with the malevolent voice of evil, I grabbed Gayle's arm, wishing the movie would end. Dad said that he could spot that kind of demon possession in others and that God had anointed him with the power to rebuke evil. Dad warned us to be on guard for evil because *The Exorcist* really happened.

Gayle and I shared the same bedroom. After watching that movie, I stared at her all night. If she started to levitate, I needed a head start to run and find Dad. When I look back over those times, I realize that fear was Dad's first tool in establishing unquestioned control over us.

Dad's distortion of the image of God was the most pervasive and destructive legacy he left me. When he started revealing his visions to me, he relayed them in the authority of God. "God has revealed to me, and you must believe in me to understand. . . ." To understand God's will and to even communicate with him, I had to go through Dad, God's anointed. Dad said that God only spoke to and heard the prayers of his anointed. The God my father revealed played favorites and ignored everyone else.

For some reason, Dad chose to share his visions with only me. Maybe he excluded Gayle from his trusted inner circle because she hated him and had rejected his authority. She never forgave him for allowing Mom to abuse her. Ironically, her hatred of them protected her from the spiritual abuse I suffered. I still adored Dad. Maybe I feared him more than adored him. Nevertheless, I believed in him and his divine authority. When the visions started, however, something in my spirit compelled me to begin to question his status with God. Dad's visions from God were justifying his wrongdoings.

"Do you still believe in me, Cheryl?"

"Yes, Daddy."

"I had a vision that God is going to bless us tremendously. He's going to make our lives much better than before."

"A vision?"

"God has blessed me with visions into his thinking. He has shown me his plans for us. It will be tough a little while longer, but we will be blessed in the end."

"Does he talk to you?"

"Yes, all the time."

"Why can't I hear him? He doesn't talk to me," I complained.

"Everybody is not blessed with these visions, and you have to be special to hear God. See this mark on my forehead. Everyone told me that this birthmark was a sign that I had a special relationship with

God. I've been running away from my calling all my life. I am called to explain my visions to others. Have you wondered why we haven't been blessed like Job?"

"Yes."

"I had a vision about us on the other side of this mess. We were laughing and playing together. There was a big, pretty house with everything in it that we ever wanted. There were only three people in my vision—you, Gayle, and me."

"What are you talking about, Dad?"

"It is clear from my vision that your mother is holding us back from receiving our blessings. You know she had a job last week at a nursing home, and she just refuses to go back. I begged and pleaded with her, but she won't go back. Remember, I told you that God said we must follow my visions before we can get out of this mess. God is testing us. He told me to tell you that as long as you believe in me, your daddy, we will be fine. God said that you need to always trust in me and believe in what I say. If you do that, then you will be blessed. If you don't, then you will be cursed. Do you believe in me?"

"Yes, Dad." With authority from God, sealed with threats and intimidation from above, Dad's words penetrated my soul. Little did I know that this vision coincided with the start of an affair he was having with a coworker. Within five minutes of his speech, Dad sent me on a mission to kick Mom out of the house. I was sixteen years old.

This vision and command are not from me. I would never send you to dishonor your mother this way.

My anger and frustration over living in poverty overpowered my ability to hear God's whispers. Dad had lit a fuse. I was tired of being evicted. Tired of never having enough food to eat. Tired of the lights being turned off and tired of burning up in oppressive Texas heat. Maybe Mom *was* holding us back. I was torn because I felt that our horrible living situation was both my parents' fault, but Dad seemed to be the only one who could keep a job. I needed him, so I reluctantly accepted my role as his disciple. I needed to keep him happy so that he could keep a roof over my head. Mom, however, was dead weight. If she was standing in the way, then she had to go.

When I finally reached Mom, I was livid. There she was, sitting at the kitchen table reading the paper. I felt a wellspring of anger toward her. I wanted to believe Dad's simplistic vision; it seemed logical that Mom was keeping us from our blessings and happiness.

"Mom, have you found a job yet?" I demanded.

She turned to me. "What are you talking about?"

"I want to know if you have found a job yet!"

"What's wrong with you?"

"I want to know if you have found a job yet!"

"No."

"Dad said that you had one and got yourself fired."

"He said what?" Mother frowned.

"He said that you don't want to work."

"Where is your dad?"

"He said that you are standing in the way of us receiving our blessings because you don't want to work."

"I'm not going to sit here and listen to this. I'm still your mother, and you will change your tone."

"If you were my mother, then you would take responsibility for this family and get a job. If you don't want to work, then you just get out of this house! We don't need anyone here who is going to hold us back. Get out!" I shouted.

I cursed at Mom as I stormed out of the room and slammed my bedroom door. I could hear her crying. Deep within I could also hear, *This was wrong and not from me.* I was confused, still years away from discerning God's voice. If Dad's vision and mission came from God, then why did I feel so bad?

Mom was gone by the morning. She packed her things and left the house during the night. Although I did not know it at the time, Mom checked into a psychiatric hospital. In the morning, when Dad was sitting at the kitchen table and would not look up at me, I decided not to ask him where she was. I felt awful, dirty, and guilty. I began to wonder if Dad had been wrong. I began to wonder if he was using me. I held my head in my hands and closed my eyes. "I wish I knew what to believe. If I can't trust my own father, then whom can I trust?" I wondered.

I know you are struggling to hear me, so I will continue to call your name. Come to me, and I will teach you my ways. Those who do not know me are teaching you false things about me. Soon you will recognize my voice.

WANDERING

Gayle often called Dad a hopelessly irresponsible parent. Everything he touched seemed to crumble in disaster. Every decision he made seemed to plunge us further into a deep, dark hole. Coupled with his other abusive actions, his pattern of poor decision-making made it hard for me to respect him. His job as the father of the house was to provide Gayle and me with a stable, loving, and healthy home environment. He failed repeatedly.

To Dad, respect meant we must never question his commands, never voice our needs, and never show anything other than total belief in his authority and ability to lead. I still struggle to define *respect* or explain what honoring my father actually means. For a long time I wrestled with the idea that respect and honor meant an unquestioned acquiescence to Dad's frivolous, ill-conceived, and intrusive commands.

For so many years, Dad led me to believe that God's command to honor my parents was a global pardon for all of their wrongdoings. It was the parental version of the divine right of kings. Dad always told us that it was not our job as children to question or disobey parental authority. God had ordained them with absolute power over us, and they answered only to God himself.

We were indoctrinated with the idea that each time we disobeyed or dishonored our parents, God would shave time off our lives. I was afraid of Dad's God. I remembered Dad's story of the man who merely tried to catch the ark of the covenant when it was falling off a moving cart, and God struck the man down on the spot. Dad would look at me and say, "God's punishment is swift and severe." Afraid of him or not, I was still ashamed of my father. If Dad was God's anointed, why did he fail in all of his decisions? Why did his actions always pull us further into the gloom and despair of the wilderness?

I learned the art of eavesdropping. Gayle and I needed to know where the land mines were. We needed to know what topics were the triggers of the day. Therefore, we began to listen and examine my parents' arguments. We would dissect every word and vocal inflection to ascertain how we should talk to or avoid Mom or Dad that day. Sometimes I overheard too much. A major blow was learning that Dad had borrowed money from the parents of two of my best friends and could not pay them back. Mom called him a coward for avoiding them and for knowingly borrowing money when he did not have a job.

When I heard that, everything made sense. I had noticed that my friends were suddenly too busy to hang out with me. They had stopped calling. Teen girls tend to be moody; knowing that, I had dismissed their behavior. Now I was angry with Dad because he was ruining what few friendships I had.

Mom was also furious at Dad because he secretly took their life savings and "invested" the money in a start-up insurance company run by a parent of another one of my friends. The company failed, and we lost all our money. Mom was screaming at Dad, calling him stupid for falling for the con. Mom called my friend Tabitha's father a con artist. This was hard for me to hear because I saw Tabitha's father regularly, and he even bought me lunch or dinner whenever he saw me. I liked him mostly because he was obviously close to Tabitha. He always took his children on cool vacations and bought them nice clothes. How would I interact with him now? How could I face Tabitha, knowing that her father stole money from us? Dad's actions had now cost me three friends.

Gayle and I also discovered the true reason Dad lost his job. Racism may have played a part, but his choices played a bigger role. Dad's boss ordered him to attend a meeting, and he refused to go, citing personal reasons. From what we could hear, Dad had been placed on probation several times over the course of a few months. Mom screamed that he was stubborn—if he knew that the white people there did not like African-Americans, then he should have made doubly certain they could not find fault in him. Dad, however, refused to comply with a direct order, so his boss immediately fired him.

MURDER

The day I saw murder in my father's eyes marked the first time I saw Dad's capacity for evil. I knew we were having more serious financial problems when he started hiding our car. He would never park it in the driveway. He either parked it in the garage or on another street. Gayle was at the store when Randy, a police officer, came to visit. He was one of Dad's best friends. I knew something serious was up because Randy had a grave look on his face. My decision to eavesdrop allowed me further insight into Dad's complex character.

"Man, you just need to hide the car from them. I mean, I can stash it at my place and you could use my car. They wouldn't ever find it then," Randy told Dad.

"Yeah, I know. Jim told me to torch it and have the insurance pay the car off before they can repossess it," my dad said.

"That's a good idea. I could also find someone who could lift it from you, then the insurance money would pay it off, and selling the parts could get some money in your pockets. I would do it if it were me."

"Man, keep your voice down. My wife and kids are home."

Both of them looked toward the kitchen where I was hiding. I ducked.

"Look, I'll set it all up, and I won't tell you a thing so you can deny anything if something goes wrong. But I know some good folk who owe me," Randy said.

"All right, man. Let me think about it, OK? What about this house? What do you think I should do?"

"Torch it. I mean, get a professional that would ensure it would look like an accident. Insurance would pay it off, and you'd be set. You could start all over. I could set that up too."

Dad hesitated. "I don't know about this, man. This would be some hard time if we were caught. I don't know."

We would never find out what Dad would have done about the car because Gayle forgot to hide it after she came back from the store. She came in screaming, "Dad! Dad!"

Dad and Randy bolted toward the door. Mom came running from her bedroom. When I reached the front door, I saw our car attached to a wrecker. Dad had his hands around the driver's neck. "Man, you better let go of my car!"

"I—I'm sorry, mister. I can't let it go once it's hooked up." The man's face was red, and his eyes were as big as silver dollars. Sweat was pouring down his face. His whole body was shaking. He was a white man in an African-American neighborhood. He was "the man" caught stealing from a "brother."

I knew this afternoon was not going to be pretty when people started coming outside their homes to applaud Dad's standing up to "the establishment." In the corner of my eye, I saw Randy slip away in his cruiser. I braced for the worst because the only cop on the scene had run away.

My mother began to scream and hit my father in the back. "Let him go! Let him go! You are going to kill him! Let him go!"

"I know what I'm doing!" Dad shouted. My mother backed away as my father raised his hand to strike her. "Now I'm going to give you one last chance to let my car down." Dad tightened his grip around the man's throat. I began to shake, seeing the wellspring of hate rise up from my father's heart and pour out through his eyes, his hands.

"I—I'm sorry, mister. I can't," the man choked out, closing his eyes.

Dad looked over at me and I put my hands over my eyes. "Please don't let him kill anybody." I prayed. "He'll go to jail, and we will be left alone. Please don't let him kill that man. Please. Please."

Dad released his grip on the man's throat and said, "Where's my gun?" He started searching the car as if looking for it. I felt some relief because I knew Dad did not own a gun. At least I hoped he had no gun. I felt he was bluffing now. Nevertheless, for the first time in my life, I had seen murder in his eyes.

I looked toward my sister and saw her crying. I am sure she was feeling guilty and afraid because her lapse in memory set up this horrific moment. I could tell she was planning to get lost until Dad calmed down.

Mom came up from behind Dad and touched him on the shoulder. "It's not worth it. It's just not worth it. That is all these white people want—to lock up another black man. It is not worth it."

Dad dropped his head and walked toward the man. "You are going to give me a chance to clean out my car?"

"Y—yes, mister. Take your time."

Dad cleaned out the car and silently took his belongings into the house. He paused when he walked past Gayle, clenched his fist, then went inside. Gayle, Mom, and I stood together as the wrecker drove away with our car. None of us wanted to go back inside the house. When we came through the door, Dad raised up his head from his lap.

"I'm tired of white folks taking away my stuff. Enough is enough. Gayle, you listen to me next time. You just listen to me—" His voiced cracked; he got up and went into the bedroom.

My dear child, I heard your cry even though you do not know me. I was working this situation out for good before you even recognized the problem. Continue reaching out to me. I promise to never let you down. I promise I will always go before you and fight for you because I love you.

I did not realize that I had prayed that day. Nor was I conscious of God's response. I was glad the car was repossessed; Dad would not have a chance to do something illegal now. I did realize that something unusual had happened to diffuse the escalating hate that day. It was as if someone up above knew that if Dad went to jail, Mom would have a nervous breakdown and my family would have been destroyed. Living with my parents was bad, but the thought of living in foster care, possibly separated from Gayle, was terrifying.

Dad's bizarre behavior continued. Mom caught him plotting to rob a store. When she confronted him, he confessed that he had hired an accomplice who had the gun. He tried to convince us that he would never have been caught because he had designed a brilliant plan. He backed out of it because he had a vision that showed him if he had robbed the store, the accomplice would try to kill him for the money. When he showed no remorse, my loss of respect turned to disgust. My father had stooped so low as to willfully plot to disobey the law and jeopardize the welfare of his children.

Later, he began to rationalize his actions. "How else am I supposed to feed my family? The system is racist and is designed to hold me down. I have to do what I have to do to survive." To Dad, God allowed him to survive under a corrupt system by whatever means necessary. The command to provide for his family superseded the laws of society. Dad was desperately trying to cover his actions with divine authority. Nevertheless, he could not look us in the eyes when he said this.

I am your real Daddy, and I say that no one shall steal.

Somehow I knew that what Dad was plotting to do, and was now attempting to justify, was wrong before man and before God. I could not have a neutral attitude toward him though. What I lost in fear and respect, I gained in anger. I could not understand how a college-educated man with years of work experience could so hopelessly lose his way.

The next morning Dad came into my room, presumably to walk me to the bus stop. "You still believe in me? I don't know what I would do if you ever stopped believing in me."

I felt sorry for him and nodded.

"Things will get better. You know your sister has given up on me. I know you will not give up on me. You remember me telling you about my vision?"

I nodded.

"Well, the three people I saw, I can see more clearly now. It's you, your mom, and me. Gayle doesn't believe in me anymore. She has left me. You won't leave me, right?"

"No," I lied again. I was too afraid to tell him the truth.

"Good, because God told me that our blessings are not too far off."

"Why doesn't God talk to me? Why does he only talk to you?" I asked.

Dad stared at me. I guess he was shocked at the question and afraid that I was losing faith in him. "Why do you ask?"

"I just have some questions to ask him. He won't talk to me and I want to know why."

"You don't believe in me anymore?" Dad asked.

"It's not that. I just want to talk to God myself."

"Are you going to leave me like Gayle did?"

"Dad, it's not like that. . . . Oh, never mind." I walked away and locked myself in the bathroom.

I am sure that Dad was panicking because he was losing his disciple. I was trying to bypass him to reach out to God myself. For some unknown reason, I was growing more confident that Dad's visions were not from God. I no longer believed in his divine authority. I was still too afraid of him to tell him that I rejected his special status with God. I felt God had yet to speak to me. I was still waiting for my own vision or some thunderous voice from heaven. I felt I was missing something important in my quest to talk to God. Maybe there was a secret code I needed before God would speak to me. In the meantime, I would have to sit quietly and watch my father destroy himself, pulling all of us down in the process.

My child, I'm here to take care of you. You are so close to me; soon you will be able to hear my voice. Oh, how much I long for you to hear me and rest in my care. I know you are angry, but do not let yourself be consumed by that anger. I don't want you to hurt yourself. I offer you more than your father ever could because I am the perfect Daddy. I promise to meet all your needs. I promise this because I love you. Soon you will rest in my love.

SURROGATE

I was twenty-five, struggling with depression, and sitting in my therapist's office crying. While waiting for my session, I was reading a poem that knocked the wind out of me.

> *Hush, little baby, don't you cry:*
> *Close your eyes, don't breathe a sigh.*
> *Don't pay no heed to what we try;*
> *Ain't no one at all on whom to rely.*
> *Good little baby, you didn't cry;*
> *You did what we said, even stifled*
>   *your sigh.*
> *Beg again, you can go, by-and-by,*
> *We'll just say that you're telling a lie.*
> *Poor little baby, guess your mind went*
>   *awry;*
> *You still can't never, ever even cry.*
> *Sure don't know why you didn't die;*
> *Instead, spent a lifetime asking,*
>   *"Why?"*
>
> ANONYMOUS PATIENT

Jackie, my therapist, called me into her office and immediately noticed I was struggling with my emotions. Before she could ask me questions, I asked her who wrote that poem. In the typical therapist fashion, she asked why I was interested in it. She was probing. For some reason, the poem resonated in my soul, and I wanted to know why.

"Cheryl, that poem was published in a book called *Courage to Heal.* Have you heard about that book?"

"No."

"The person who wrote the poem was an incest survivor."

Silence overtook the room. Jackie was no doubt waiting for my response, and I dreaded opening my mouth. I was not ready to talk about the years of sexual abuse by a male cousin. "OK, Cheryl, we won't talk about anything you don't want to talk about. Why don't you tell me a little bit more about your family? Start with your parents."

I started describing my relationship with my father. When I ended my session, I had a deeper understanding of incest. It encompasses much more than the sex act.

As far back as seven or eight years old, I recall being the person Dad turned to when he and Mom were having marital troubles. He would come into my room or call me to sit on his lap and typically say, "I have to get you another mommy." Then Dad would pour out his heart to me. He would say that Mom was killing him because she could not find a job or would nag him about something. He always looked me in the eye to say, "Now, when you get married, don't be a wife like your mother."

Being afraid and in awe of Dad, I always took his side. Blind devotion. Whenever Mom and Dad fought, I automatically assumed it was her fault and hated her. I was Dad's disciple and felt I had to be there for him—no one else understood him as I did. Dad always told me that I was "special" and our relationship was too. In reality, the term equated to something forbidden. I was responsible for my father's happiness, even at the expense of my own. Such a huge burden on the soul of a child.

By my junior year in high school, I began to feel dirty and ashamed of our special relationship. Dad had been struggling to get us out of poverty. Although he had a bachelor's degree in biology and had spent over a decade as a chemist in the petrochemical industry, once he was fired, he could find work only in fast food restaurants. He was moody and irritable. He and Mom fought constantly. He began to have more visions about Mom's not being in the picture.

Moreover, during this time Dad's talks with me grew sexual. I began to know more than I ever wanted to know about my parents' marriage. Supposedly, to make me a better wife when I got married, my father began verbally teaching me how to be a good sex partner. He graphically catalogued every detail of the sex life that he always wanted in his marriage. God told him to prepare me to be a better wife than Mom had been to him. When he invoked the authority of God, he took away my choice in listening.

He began to show me pornography to demonstrate what a good wife does. My biggest and growing fear was that one day I would be forced to model what I had learned. I began to live in a state of battle readiness. I was always on guard for the time when I would be called to become more to my father than just his daughter.

Dad and Mom were secretive people. The family rule was, "Don't tell anyone our business." No one was to know what happened behind our doors—not that Gayle and I felt anyone would believe us anyway. Mom and Dad cleaned up really well. When we went out in public, there was no hint of the filth that happened in secrecy. No one knew Mom was verbally abusing Gayle. No one knew that I had become a surrogate wife for Dad. The code of silence was seared deep within us. The legacy of the loss of trust in your parents is that you lose trust in everyone else. I trusted no one, yet still wondered if trustworthy people existed in this life. I kept the code of silence mostly, however, because I felt ashamed. Maybe if I had been born normal, all the bad things would not have happened to me. Maybe if I had a stronger faith in Dad and his god, then I would not feel so bad. In the eyes of a child, everything is her fault.

By sixteen, I was incapable of repressing the pain and pretending that all was fine at home. It is hard work faking. It was harder on me to remain in battle mode. At school, I was preparing for a Black History Month celebration. My friends and I decided to dress like slaves, sing

Negro spirituals, and recite some speeches and poems by famous African-Americans. I had an album by Mahalia Jackson, a famous African-American gospel singer, so I started to listen to it for songs that I could sing—this after enduring one of Dad's "special" talks that left me feeling so dirty and ashamed.

I began to sob, muffling my cries and constantly looking over my shoulder. The rules of the house were to never cry or show weakness. I also wanted to be left alone. I knew no one in my family could fix what Dad had broken in my spirit. Then Mahalia started singing the Thomas Dorsey song, "Precious Lord, Take My Hand." I heard it once and knew that this was my song.

> *Precious Lord, take my hand.*
> *Lead me on, let me stand.*
> *I am tired, I am weak, and worn.*
> *Through the storm, through the night,*
> *Lead me on to the light.*
> *Take my hand, precious Lord,*
> *Lead me home.*
> *When my way grows drear,*
> *Precious Lord, lead me near,*
> *When my life is almost gone.*
> *Hear my cry, hear my call.*
> *Hold my hand, lest I fall.*
> *Take my hand, precious Lord,*
> *Lead me home.*

I could not finish the song before I collapsed to the floor weeping. For a split moment I thought I felt the presence of God. The rush of hope and peace overtook my soul and weakened my knees. Although I did not know it, I had prayed to the real God. I had told him that I could no longer stand under the burdens of my life. Foreshadowing my future suicide attempt, I was telling God that I could no longer take the pain, shame, and guilt I felt in my life. I was asking him to lead me home. Yet I still did not know who he was or how to reach him. I did not know what home was.

Wanting that feeling of peace back, I sang the song repeatedly to relive the experience. But I could not get it back. I knew I did not want the god my father had revealed. That god caused me nothing but sorrow. He sanctioned a vile behavior in my father that served no other purpose but to maim. The gentle whispers to my soul from the true God had been beckoning me toward him. In feeble attempts, I was stumbling and reaching forward, but I still did not know to whom I was reaching.

Researching the song, I discovered that Thomas Dorsey wrote it after losing his wife and unborn child suddenly while he was away performing. I learned that at the time of his greatest sorrow and anger at God for taking his family, this song came to him like a rushing waterfall. God restored his hope and blessed him with a new family. The song was also Dr. Martin Luther King's favorite spiritual and was sung by Mahalia at his funeral procession. I wondered if he stood so bold and strong in the face of death because the God appealed to in the song reached out to hold his hand. I wondered if that same God would do that for me.

When I sang the song at school, again the brief rush of soothing peace swept over my body and "Precious Lord" became the spiritual that best represented my soul's deepest cries. However, Dad had sown a seed of doubt within me that would sprout to overpower hope and take years to purge. What if I discovered that Dad's god was the true one? If that were the case, I was terrified that this god and Dad would punish me for my lack of faith. The legacy of child abuse includes a fear that rules the heart and drives behavior. "Hush, little baby, don't you cry," my father's god seemed to say. "Question again and I'll make sure you die."

There I was, sitting in Jackie's office over ten years later, recounting for the first time my incestuous relationship with my father. Although

I was a Christian at this point and knew the real God, I could not let go of the shame of the past. Until that moment, I had never spoken of the abuse to anyone. I felt so ashamed that I never spoke about it to God. My biggest fear was that once I talked about it, I would cry. It would be a cry so fierce and crippling, I would never be able to stop. I was tired and weak from carrying the burden on my shoulders, from trying to heal from the wound in my soul. Even Jackie could not heal the daddy wound. There are some hurts that only God can heal. Despite my efforts to ignore the pain of Dad's legacy, God gently whispered that it was time to learn how to trust my real and perfect Daddy.

My dear sweet child, I love you with a love that is not bound by time. My love for you is richer and purer than your earthly father could ever express. I am the perfect Father, here to meet all your needs. I am Daddy and will always rush to comfort you in your sorrows. I promise to heal your soul. I promise to wipe away your tears. I will never let go of your hand. And no matter how long it takes for your healing, I will always be here hugging your soul. Trust me, my precious child. There is no wound too deep for me to heal. I will never leave you, and I will never fail you.

CHAPTER THREE

Motherless Child

Sometimes I feel like a motherless child.
Sometimes I feel like a motherless child.
Sometimes I feel, I really feel, like a motherless child.
A long way from home.

NEGRO SPIRITUAL

Mom is among the millions of people who are chronically mentally ill. The experts still cannot agree on her diagnosis. The short list of suspects includes paranoid schizophrenia, major depression with psychotic features, and bipolar disorder. The psychiatric hospital has increasingly become a revolving door to her. Her commitments for mental health treatments are growing more frequent and lasting longer. Mom is among the people who hear voices, are sometimes a danger to themselves or others, and tend to have needs that overload the family support system.

People like Mom usually end up in state hospitals or nursing homes. Children of severely mentally ill parents often reverse roles with the parent. I started taking care of Mom when I turned twelve. She had been struggling long before her breakdown in 1982, but most people dismissed her angry and hostile behavior as a personality trait.

Lately Mom's slips into insanity resemble plunges off Mount Everest—they are sudden, swift, and severe. She falls onto me like an outcropping and hangs on, and then I have to struggle to hold on and not fall too. Whenever Mom slips, she becomes paralyzed. When I was taking care of her in my home, I had to tell her when to wake and when to sleep. I made her meals and managed her diabetes. My house became a hospital in which I made rounds throughout the day, assessing her vital signs and monitoring her mental status. I brought her daily cocktail of twelve medications and made her take the pills in my presence. Whenever she grew agitated, I monitored the danger she posed to herself or others. Whenever she heard voices, I monitored what they told her to do.

Years ago I became proficient at determining the point at which I needed to take her to the psychiatric facility for professional help. I am single, without children, but caring for Mom exhausted even me. I do not understand how adults with young children take care of dependent parents as well. Even as a Christian psychologist, I sometimes forget to rely on God's strength. As a result, I grow frustrated and burn out.

Coping with the role reversal between Mom and me carries additional baggage. She has severe hypertension and diabetes, so some of her hospital stays are for emergencies associated with her physical health. She is unnecessarily old at fifty-seven. The rapid deterioration of her physical and mental health has sapped the life out of her. I can always tell when she is about to lose hold of her sanity—she starts talking about slavery and chanting, "Cry freedom!" In her own way she is asking for help against the slavery of mental illness.

Mom and I both feel mental illness is like slavery in its inhumanity, but for differing reasons. Mom feels the shackles of the illness. I identify with the families that were routinely broken up and assigned to plantations in different regions, sometimes different states. Slave owners ripped babies from the arms of mothers, stripping slaves of a sense of family. An intense and demoralizing suffering comes when a child is stripped of a relationship with his or her mother. If the daddy wound is the deepest wound on earth, how can one describe the mommy wound? Slaves expressed similar anguish through another Negro spiritual:

> *Lord, how come me here?*
> *Lord, how come me here?*
> *Lord, how come me here?*
> *I wish I never was born.*

The relationship I have with Mom is as complex as the one I had with Dad. She and I share a tumultuous history. At times she would fight for my rights to an equal education with normal children, yet turned around and used my disability to invoke sympathy among welfare employees. She would tell me that I was special and that I would grow up to be something, yet she grew increasingly depressed and guilty about having a child with a disability. When she suffered her first breakdown, her paranoia fueled an attempt to kill me.

After becoming a psychologist, I began to understand her illness enough to have profound compassion for her. Nevertheless, I struggle with resentment when I sometimes allow her problems to overwhelm me. Although my relationship with Mom is difficult, it is an example of divine restoration. When she tried to kill me when I was twelve, I killed her in my heart as my mother. Living each day with her now is a process in forgiveness and an act of faith in God's power to heal.

SLAVE MASTER

When I turned twelve years old, Mom had her first battle with schizophrenia. Her descent into slavery was gradual. No one knows what causes schizophrenia. According to the most popular theory, a person has a genetic predisposition for mental illness, and stress or trauma triggers the full-blown disorder. Dad always told us that she could not handle the stress in her life. Could the culprit have been giving birth to a child with a disability? Dad's affair? Her hysterectomy and blood clot in her lungs? Lack of a job? No one knows what triggered her illness.

At the time, Gayle and I did not know how bad things were getting. We did not know we were about to lose the house or that our parents' marriage was in trouble again. We also did not realize that Dad was about to lose his job and that his boss would blacklist him from the industry. All we knew was that Mom was frequently going through fits of rage and increasing her verbal assaults on Gayle. We quickly learned that we just needed to stay out of her way.

Gayle and I always thought Mom was a strange woman. We simply accepted her paranoid personality and saw nothing abnormal, at least for Mom, about her thinking someone was following her or listening to her conversations over the telephone. Since she was so mean, we understood why she never had many close friends.

"Everyone is out to get me. They are trying to persecute me and destroy my family," Mom would say.

"Who's trying to destroy you?" Dad would ask.

"Don't you hear them plotting against me? Everywhere I go the government is out there spying on me and trying to destroy this family. They have even bugged our phones."

"No one cares enough about you to plot like that."

"I don't care if you believe me because I have proof!"

"What proof? You need to get over it. You are not that important for anyone to waste time worrying about what you do," Dad would say.

"Someone broke into this house and stole my plants. See, I had five plants and now there are only four. I know that Ronald Reagan sent a spy into this house." Mom began to blame President Reagan for everything that negatively affected the family. She spent hours collecting newspapers; she searched for proof of a conspiracy against her. None of us recognized that her growing paranoia was a symptom of something more serious. She had always told Gayle and me never to tell anyone about "our business." We simply thought she wanted to hide the family secrets of child abuse and dysfunction. In her own reality, Mom was at war against the spies trying to destroy her.

Although she was once a brilliant student in college, Mom began having trouble organizing her thoughts. She could not concentrate long enough to read. Whenever she talked, her thoughts would trail off in sentences that did not make much sense.

"Mom, can I go to a football game tonight with the West family?" Gayle would ask.

"What time is the game and I want you home by ten. . . . What is civil rights? Where is the justice in . . .? I'm sick of Ronald Reagan abusing me. . . . I wonder how many people are named Ronald. . . . I picked cotton and the helicopters came and we hid in a ditch. . . ."

"Mom, what are you talking about?"

"I earned all *As* in college."

"Mom!"

"What? Oh, yeah, go. Just be back by ten."

I began to notice that Mom was growing more quiet and detached from the family. It was strange when she stopped yelling at Gayle. I thought she was ill, but I enjoyed the silence in the house. Little did we know that this was the beginning of her battle with schizophrenia.

One day when I was twelve years old and I arrived home from school, I noticed Gayle leaning against the car with her head on the hood. I thought she had locked herself outside the house.

"What's up?" I asked. No answer. "Is the door locked?"

"No." Gayle was acting strange, so I thought that she and Mom had had another fight. I was happy about earning a good grade on my math test and wanted to cheer Mom up with my good news. I went inside to look for her. The house was dark and silent.

"Mom?" I called.

I found her in the kitchen. Mom was staring blankly at the ovens. She looked like a zombie. Her hair looked as if she had not combed it in several days. She wore an old, torn nightgown. She had not bathed at all that day. One of her hands was balled in a fist.

"Mom, are you all right?"

No answer. No recognition that I even called her name.

I touched her arm and pushed her lightly. Mom did not respond. I knew something was wrong. Mom's behavior was strange, even for her. Since I could not take my eyes off her, I walked backward toward the front door.

"Gayle, what is going on? Why is Mom looking like that? She's spooky."

"I don't know. She was like that when I came home," replied my sister.

"Well, what are we going to do? I'm not going back in the house with her looking like that. Where's Dad?"

"He's at some funeral. I called him, and it's going to take him about five hours to get back home," Gayle said.

"Five hours! It'll be dark by then. I'm not going back in there."

"We have to, Cheryl. What if she hurts herself?"

"Man, I hate this family. What is wrong with her?"

We went back into the house. When we reached the kitchen, we noticed a puddle of urine around Mom's legs. "Great. She used the bathroom on herself. Who's going to clean her up?" Gayle asked.

"Why are you looking at me?" But I sighed as I pushed Gayle aside. I threw some paper towels on the puddle. Gayle touched Mom's arm.

"Mom, you need to go take a bath," Gayle said, but Mom did not move. Her face showed no recognition that Gayle had talked to her or touched her. It was my turn.

"Mom, we need to go to the bathroom and get you cleaned up. Is that OK?"

Mom's body was dead weight, and I struggled to get her into the tub. I began to resent Gayle for leaving me to take care of Mom by myself. After I bathed Mom, Gayle helped me get her dressed and back in bed.

"How much longer before Dad comes back?" I asked.

"Another two hours, I think."

I sighed. I wanted this nightmare to be over. Little did I know that I would revisit this scene many more times in the future. I realize now that Gayle and I were in a position of power over an abuser. Since Mom was helpless, we could have taken revenge on her. I have no doubt that if I were not there, Gayle's hatred would have compelled her to ignore Mom and leave her to stand in her own urine, at the very least. I did not like Mom either, but her helplessness moved me. I could have crushed her, but for some inexplicable reason, I felt moved to show her mercy.

Listen to me, my dear child. Your loving and merciful Daddy is talking. I know that it is difficult for you to understand this right now. I am here to help you to honor your mother in a way that pleases me. Sweetheart, this is a lesson you will understand more as you grow up and come to know me. There are many times when I could crush somebody, too, but instead, I show that person love and mercy. Keep looking up to me and model my behavior. Daddy wants you to be the best that you can be. I promise to help you along the way.

FIGHTING DEMONS

Later that day, Mom began to grow worse when she started to hear voices.

"It's the television, Mom. No one is talking to you and telling you to do something." I held Mom down and calmly tried to reassure her that no one was talking to her through the television.

"Who's that yelling at me?"

"Mom, no one is yelling at you."

"Make them stop yelling at me. Make them stop. Make them stop." After several attempts to get up from the bed, Mom stopped talking and stared blankly at the ceiling. Her body became rigid again. There was no life in her eyes. The voices in Mom's head were growing louder and more frightening to her. The constant clamoring made her agitated, then she would suddenly collapse into a rigid, inflexible position. It looked as if her body had reached its breaking point and suddenly shut down.

I went looking for Gayle, who was outside waiting for Dad. Ms. Kitty, our neighbor, came outside. She waved and started to walk toward us. My mother never liked Ms. Kitty. We thought Mom kept her distance because Ms. Kitty talked about God all the time. Mom always said that Ms. Kitty thought she was better than we were. Gayle and I did not know that Ms. Kitty had a strong resemblance to one of Dad's former mistresses. I groaned when she started coming over. Ms. Kitty was one of those preachy types whose every word sounded like a Sunday morning sermon. Since she was also a nosy gossip, she could hone in on a juicy story like radar.

"God bless you, girls. Why are you outside by yourselves on this glorious evening? Is there anything wrong?"

"Everything is fine, Ms. Kitty," my sister replied.

"Then why are you out here in the dark looking so sad? Where are your parents?"

"Dad is at a funeral, and Mom is sick inside," Gayle said.

I flashed a mean look at Gayle for revealing that something was wrong inside.

"Oh, your mom is sick? What's wrong? Maybe I can go and pray over her."

"I don't know about that, Ms. Kitty. She just wants to be left alone," I replied.

Ms. Kitty walked toward the house. My sister and I looked at each other. Once this woman got inside, our family secret would be out. Everyone in the neighborhood would know about Mom.

My mother was lying in bed looking blankly at the ceiling. Ms. Kitty gasped and dropped to her knees to pray loudly over her: "Oh, Lord Jesus, there are evil spirits all around here, Lord—"

Mom snapped her head around toward Ms. Kitty and started yelling at her. "Who let you in here? Get out of my house!"

"Now, Mrs. Green, I'm here to pray over you for healing—"

"Reagan sent you to spy on me! You have been trying to destroy me for years! I will not stand for this!" Mom shouted.

"Mrs. Green, what are you talking about, dear? You have to let me pray these demon spirits out of you."

"You are here to steal my husband again. I won't stand for this. Get out of my house!" Mom began throwing things at Ms. Kitty and cursing at her. I tried to calm Mom down, but she was extremely agitated. I left the room to look for Gayle. When we returned, Gayle took Ms. Kitty out of the house. Mom was furious. She jumped out of bed and started throwing everything around the room. She was pacing wildly and mumbling. For the first time since the situation began, I felt I was in danger. I backed out of the room and went outside to wait for Dad.

"What is going on now?" Gayle asked.

"I don't know. Ms. Kitty made her very mad. She is throwing stuff all over the place. She's screaming something, but I can't understand what she is saying."

Ms. Kitty said, "All I did was pray over her. You know the devil is around; that's why she got so upset about me using the Word of God. Your mother has evil spirits in her. Her voice even changed into something evil right before me. Oh, Lord Jesus, what is your pastor's name? You girls need to get a holy person over here to deal with your mother."

Gayle yelled at Ms. Kitty. "That's stupid! She is not possessed. She just had a breakdown. You better not go around telling folks anything like that about my mother!"

"Who's your pastor?" Ms. Kitty asked again.

"We don't go to church, and Gayle is right. Don't start saying that weird stuff about my mother. She's not possessed. She just doesn't like you," I said.

I was relieved when Dad's car pulled in the driveway. Dad would know what to do. Ms. Kitty told him that he seemed like a praying man, so he could understand that Mom was possessed by evil spirits.

She told Dad to get the church over to our house to pray for Mom. Dad yelled at her to mind her own business.

Dad wrestled with Mom all night. He told us to lock ourselves in our rooms for our own safety. The next morning he told us that Mom was not possessed by a demon. She had a nervous breakdown because she was not strong enough to handle the stress in her life. Dad called her weak and said she needed to go to the psychiatric hospital where they treated other weak people. "Your mother is not the strong, African-American woman I thought she was. That's why I'm going to get you guys a new mommy."

Dad had attacked Mom repeatedly with that statement. One of the most enduring and celebrated stereotypes within the African-American community is that of the "strong black woman." African-American girls embrace the image, but both Mom and I had disabilities that were incompatible with the perception of strength.

It wasn't until I majored in psychology and began working in disability politics that I began to understand the pervasiveness of the theories of demon possession and the weak personality as causes of mental illness. I learned about the biological bases for mental illness and heard the rhetoric that mental illness is no different from diabetes or hypertension and people should not be stigmatized because of their medically verifiable illnesses.

Alternately, I heard many religious arguments that mental illness is a spiritual sickness that signifies a weakness in faith. Some religious people believe that evil spirits cause mental illness. I cannot explain mental illness, particularly the one my mother has. I have seen many other people like her who are strong in their faith, yet still battle this slave master.

DELUSIONS

Sometimes mental illness can turn deadly. Being dangerous is not synonymous with mental illness, but it is a possibility in some cases. Mom was one of those special cases. In the midst of her first breakdown, Dad decided to take her to the psychiatric hospital. Gayle and I went with them. Although Mom was calm, I saw fear on her face. My father was practically dragging her by the hand toward the car. She tried to wrench free.

"You—you are trying to kill me! You want to get rid of me so you can be with that woman!" she screamed.

"I'm not trying to hurt you. You need help. We are taking you to the hospital."

"You are trying to kill me!" she screamed as we drove down the street. Mom turned toward the car door to open it. My father pulled her hand away and held it while he drove.

Gayle and I were silently watching Mom grow more agitated as we neared the hospital. When we drove up the freeway ramp, she began to wave her hands wildly to get loose from my father's grip. "You are trying to kill me! You want me dead!" Screaming, she managed to open the car door.

Mom lunged for the open door without regard for our speed. Gayle and I grabbed at her and screamed for her to get back in the car. My father pulled her back in the car by her clothes, then turned the car around. As we started to drive back home, Mom calmed down. When we reached the house, she jumped out of the car and ran down the street. My father leaped from the car and sprinted toward her. All I could hear was her screaming that he was trying to kill her.

Gayle and I were embarrassed. The entire neighborhood would know that she had a nervous breakdown. We were also angry about being stuck with her since she refused to go to the hospital voluntarily. Dad was growing more impatient with the deteriorating situation. It was obvious to us that he had found somebody else he wanted to marry. I felt that he wanted to close the chapter on Mom by committing her to the hospital.

We had to live with this tension for several more days because Dad could not figure out how to get Mom to agree to go to the hospital. Then Dad called one of his brothers, Robert, who was a police officer, for advice. Dad wanted Uncle Robert to pick Mom up against her will, but Mom had not been declared legally dangerous to herself or others. Dad asked him to come over anyway and scare her into going to the hospital. My uncle declined, saying that the trick would not work. The hospital would learn that she was not coming voluntarily and would not keep her. We had to wait until Mom either admitted herself voluntarily or hurt herself—or one of us.

Mom lost her ability to do anything for herself. She would stare at a fork as if she had never seen one before. She spent hours shifting and reshifting a stack of papers. Somebody had to watch her at all times so she would not hurt anyone. Mom's sleep cycle was off, and she began to mix up the days and nights. She experienced insomnia, sleeping for no more than two hours at a time. No one else could sleep because she was constantly roaming the house or going outside.

"Mom, where are you going?" I asked after catching her with a suitcase.

"I need to go to the store for some baking powder. Don't you want some biscuits?"

"Mom, it's 2:00 A.M. It's not time for breakfast."

"If I don't cook some biscuits, they are going to be mad."

"Who's going to be mad? Is someone talking to you again? Are you hearing voices in your head?"

"What's that noise?" she started.

"I don't hear anything, Mom."

"What's that?"

"Do you mean me tapping my fingers?"

"Oh, I thought they were after me."

"Who's after you, Mom?"

"What's that?" Mom was pointing at the driveway. She looked terrified.

I looked. "Mom, that's a newspaper in the driveway."

"You better go to sleep because you have surgery in the morning. They will take the cast off your legs. Don't cry now."

"Mom, they took my casts off years ago. Do you know how old I am?"

"Who are you, sweetheart?"

I woke Dad and told him that Mom no longer knew who I was. He told me to go to bed; he would handle it. The voices in Mom's head were growing stronger. She could no longer look at television or listen to the radio without thinking that someone was talking to her through the airwaves. The voices were commanding her to do things like leave the house in the middle of the night.

She began to vacillate between rage and depression. None of us knew what triggered either emotional state. Life boiled down to looking out for the emotional land mines in the house. We knew something would trigger Mom; we just did not know what the triggers were or how to avoid them. Looking back, I can only imagine how difficult it was for her to cope with voices screaming at her all day, every day. Soon her irritation moved to uncontrollable rage. Mom had reached her breaking point, and no one was prepared for what would happen next.

AT KNIFE POINT

When I received a telephone call from my friend Tabitha, I pretended that nothing was wrong in my house. Because I turned my back toward the kitchen to talk on the telephone, I never saw Mom enter the room. She was in the grip of delusions; instead of seeing me as her daughter, all she saw was an enemy trying to harm her. I did not know that she was dangerously paranoid now. She screamed, "You are plotting against me, aren't you?"

I turned around and saw her coming toward me. "No one is plotting against you, Mom. I'm talking to Tabitha."

"Tabitha? I knew it. You, that girl, and her family are trying to destroy me. I will not have it. I will not stand by and let you destroy me!" Mom ripped the telephone line out of the wall. She turned toward a drawer, grabbed a knife, and started to charge toward me.

Although my head was screaming orders for me to run, my body would not move. I was too terrified. As she was coming toward me, all I could do was close my eyes. The tip of the knife reached my neck, but it never pierced my skin. I opened my eyes to see that Gayle had tackled my mother to the floor and was wrestling the knife from her hand. Gayle punched her, slapped her, and screamed at her. "Mom, that is Cheryl! You were trying to kill your daughter! Mom! That is your daughter!"

I slumped against the wall and slid down to the floor. I could not move or cry. I was numb. Dad rushed into the room and used another telephone to call my uncle. Mom was now legally dangerous. If necessary, the police could use force to take her to the hospital. Without incident, my uncle led Mom outside and placed her in the back seat of his squad car.

For some reason, Dad never brought home our new mommy. Gayle and I figured that he felt too sorry for Mom to leave her. Part of me felt pity for Mom, too, because she could not live on her own. We were stuck with her.

"How do we deal with her when she comes back home?" I asked Gayle.

"I don't know. It's not as if she can command us to respect her anymore. Not after all the stuff she pulled."

"She's still your mother, and you still treat her with respect. God said that you have to do that," Dad said.

"How am I supposed to respect someone who tried to kill me?"

"Cheryl, she wasn't in her right mind. The doctors say that the medicine will bring her back to normal."

"What is normal? All she ever did was talk weird and yell all the time. Will she go back to that or be really normal?" I asked.

"We just have to wait and see."

The hospital released Mom after a couple of months. I barely recognized her. She had lost over forty pounds and looked as if she had aged ten years. She walked painfully slow. Every step was deliberate, and she would sway as if she were about to fall. She slept through most of the day. The doctors assured us she was no longer dangerous. They told us that most people with schizophrenia were not dangerous and we should resist stereotypes. I did not care about other people. My mother tried to kill me, and that was a fact, not a stereotype.

When the months passed without many incidents, I grew less afraid of Mom. Instead, I pitied her. It was clear that she was not going to be the same again. Even with the medication, Mom was still paranoid. She had trouble keeping up a normal conversation. Although she was intelligent and educated, Mom could no longer hold a job. She always complained of the stress, of people persecuting her. She continued to push people away and never developed close friends. The only people in her life were Dad, Gayle, and me. None of us wanted to take care of a grown woman. We were ashamed of her. I never realized how angry I was at Mom until I found myself telling people that she was dead.

I made a huge mistake when I told that lie to my choir teacher, Mr. Jones. He was looking for help with a bake sale and asked me if Mom would volunteer. I did not want people at school to know that she had been in the psychiatric hospital. Mr. Jones was a gossip, and I felt that if he knew the truth, my entire school would know. I was sick of having to cover for Mom, sick of her problems interfering with my life. So instead of simply saying that she was ill, I told Mr. Jones that she was dead.

I was amazed at how easy it was to lie. I felt a fleeting sense of relief when I heard myself tell Mr. Jones that Mom was dead. Nevertheless, I was afraid of being caught. I tried to rationalize what I had done by saying that my real mother was dead, that the woman who had tried to kill me was technically not my mother.

Just as I feared, the news of my mother's "death" spread throughout my school and my neighborhood. I tried to intercept all the mail to weed out sympathy cards. When people started sending flowers, I told Dad that people knew Mom was sick in the general sense of the word. After several weeks, my lie fell apart. My grandmother called.

"I can't believe that you people would not call me and let me know that my daughter died!" Grandmother cried.

"What are you talking about?" asked Dad.

"I just heard from a stranger that my baby is gone. Why didn't you tell me? Is she already buried? Where is she?"

"I don't know what you are talking about, but she is not dead. She had a nervous breakdown and was in the hospital," Dad told her.

"Everybody said that she's dead."

I was shocked that my lie could spread hundreds of miles to the backwoods of Texas and reach my grandmother. I knew that Dad would trace the rumor back to me. Grandmother told Mom that everyone thought she was dead, and Mom saw it as more proof that someone was out to get her. My lie only served to strengthen her delusion of persecution. As a preemptive strike, I told Dad that Mr. Jones misunderstood me when I told him that Mom was sick and I felt as if she was dead. He was satisfied with that.

As Mr. Jones soon discovered that I had lied, he wanted to discuss the matter with me. So I had to tell him that Mom had spent time in the psychiatric hospital. I confessed that I was ashamed of her. After that, each time I saw him I wondered how many people knew my shame because of his gossip. It became too painful to take a class with people I felt were snickering at my shame. I dropped out of choir.

Mom had violated a fundamental moral law: mothers are not supposed to harm their children. I was so angry with her that I started to believe Dad when he said that she was too weak to be a real mother to Gayle and me. My mind could not comprehend how my own mother had tried to kill me.

Resentment quickly turned to hatred. After all the mercy I had shown her, she showed me nothing but contempt. As time passed, however, my hatred for Mom subsided. My attention was diverted to other more pressing matters, like homelessness. I learned early that I needed to conserve my strength and resign myself to the fact that Mom was not going anywhere. I would not revisit my anger and hurt again for another five years, when I became a Christian. Then I was shocked at how much venom had pooled within my soul toward my parents. Today, nineteen years later, Mom's mental status is the same, but my faith has changed me and our relationship.

My dear child, what your parents have done grieves me. It was never my intention for them to hurt you. Forgive them because they do not know what they are doing. Do not focus on what almost happened with your mother. I am here and in control. I have plans for your life, my child. I know you are confused and angry. I know you are hurt, but do not wallow in the anger and start to hate. You cannot grow into the person I want you to be while harboring hate. I promise to work this out for good, and my power to heal will be displayed through your life. You do not have to be afraid, my love. I will keep reminding you of that until you hear me. Trust me. I have not, and will not, let you down.

CHAPTER FOUR

Survivor

There is a balm in Gilead
To make the wounded whole;
There is a balm in Gilead
To heal the sin sick soul.
Sometimes I feel discouraged,
And think my work's in vain,
But then the Holy Spirit
Revives my soul again.

NEGRO SPIRITUAL

I was twenty-two and at college when my best friend, Todd, invited me
to a rally at the Women's Center on campus. I would never have
attended the rally had I known that the topic was sexual abuse. Todd,
however, thought I needed to go. He had sat with me many hours in my
dorm room as I cried and struggled with my past. Although he knew
much of my story, I could not yet talk about the sexual abuse. Todd had
his suspicions and knew I needed to finally talk about what happened
to me. I was miles away from my abusers and had successfully frozen

my feelings. I felt nothing. No pain. No joy. Nothing. My carefully constructed emotional wall came crumbling down when a woman started to speak about her own experience with sexual abuse. Other women were crying and hugging each other.

I looked around, feeling threatened. I did not want to go back to that time in my past. I did not want to remember. The more I listened to the woman's story, the more my own memories started to overwhelm my thoughts. I only allowed one tear to fall in front of those strangers. I put on my stone face and left the rally. Todd followed me to ask why I was leaving. I lied and told him that I could not relate to all that whining and crying. I walked away. He knew I was not ready to address the abuse and backed off. The next day, he left a tape of Mariah Carey's song "Hero" by my door with a note simply telling me that I was his hero and that he would be there for me no matter how long it took for me to recover.

For the next two years, I struggled to tuck the feelings and memories back inside. By sheer will, I tried to stop feeling again. I failed miserably. I know now that God wanted to relieve me of a major emotional and spiritual burden, but I wrestled with him to keep my life the way I had it, with everything in neat emotional boxes. I could not change the past, so why relive it?

But one day, the nightmares came back and I began to feel dirty again. I was powerless to make the memories go away.

The summer of the cleansing ceremony by my Uncle David marked the beginning of my loss of innocence. Gayle and I escaped that harmful living situation by riding a bicycle to our aunt's house eight miles away. We lived the rest of the summer with her, during which time her son John sexually molested me. John and I were both seven at the time. He was learning how to be a man from my Uncle David. The two of them were inseparable.

"No one will ever love you like I do," John would tell me.

My early memories of these incidents are fragmented, so I do not recall if I told John to stop. That gap in my memory would fuel guilt and shame for years. I remember him calling me ugly and crippled. He told me that his love would be the only love I would ever receive because nobody would want an ugly cripple. At the time, the most confusing part for me was the tension between the physical pleasure of his touch and the shame I felt. I felt dirty because I could not prevent my body from responding.

He and Uncle David would tell me that it was all my fault, that I was a bad girl, and I wanted it to happen. John was well schooled in the techniques of fear. He told me that if I ever told anyone, my parents would kick me out of the house because it was my fault. When I look back on this, I am amazed at how readily I believed John and Uncle David. I am amazed at how starved I was for someone—anyone—to make me feel loved.

Most nights my cousin would slip into my room. Whenever the door opened, I would start sobbing. Deep down I feared that his touching and kissing would lead to something else, though I did not have a clear idea what that was. When morning came, I would spend hours in the bathroom scrubbing my body until it was raw. Nothing I did could cleanse me of the dirtiness I felt.

I began to run away to the cornfields where I spent hours dreaming about a better life. I wanted to start over again and have God make it turn out right. I wanted to start life over without a disability. I started wetting the bed, sucking my thumb, and crying all the time. My aunt ignored all this, attributing my sudden change in behavior to the quirks of being crippled.

The molestation continued for years. Everyone dismissed my strange behavior as my inability to cope with my disability. No one suspected child abuse. Soon, a great uncle started becoming more "friendly" with me. It began innocently by his offering me money for a kiss on the cheek. Everyone, including my parents, thought it was cute that this little old man was showering me with attention and affection.

I would strenuously resist going near him; his touches made me feel the same dirtiness I had felt with John. Despite my cries of protest, my relatives always pushed me toward my great uncle. As a child I had no choice. Soon the hugs and kisses grew more protracted, and his hands started to roam. John and my great uncle would resume their lewd behavior whenever either of us visited the other's home.

When I was eleven, John came to visit us for Christmas. I was angry and tired of him. As in previous years, when it was bedtime, John crept into my room. He was shocked when he opened the door to see my sister staring at him. I had asked Gayle to sleep in my room because John was looking at me funny, but even then I was too embarrassed to tell her the truth.

She told me I could never show weakness around our relatives because some of them were animals. I was shocked to hear that John had tried to molest her, but she had beaten him up. Gayle told me that boys would always try to take advantage of me because of my disability—it sent a message that I was a weak person. As my reliable protector, Gayle helped me develop a story to tell Mom and Dad to ensure that we would never have to see our relatives again.

Gayle came up with a brilliant story that appealed to my parents' pride as progressive African-Americans struggling for a better life. She and I told them of all the times our relatives called us Uncle Toms and how we had to talk as they did, downplaying our education so they would not be mean to us. Although we told them the strict factual truth, we lied about the impact. Truthfully, we did not like many of our relatives. They were abusive strangers, and Gayle and I wanted nothing more to do with them or their way of life. At that, Mom and Dad were livid. They said they would not allow the jealousies in their families to undermine all they had worked so hard to build. I never saw John again.

AFTERMATH

Ten years later, I was seventeen and was still reliving the years with John, my great uncle, and Dad; I felt the same shame and guilt I had felt as a child. I did not understand that time could only dull the pain, not heal the wounds. Even after I had been a Christian for nearly five years, I still felt ashamed of the sins of my abusers. I had learned how to control my emotions, channeling them into constructive efforts that would help me break free of my parents. I was trying to gain control of my life.

When the old emotions started to resurface, my carefully controlled new life was threatened. I had to be in control. I had to be perfect. If I allowed my emotions to surface, I would become powerless like my parents. I hated feeling powerless because feelings of worthlessness were not too far behind. I also felt betrayed by my parents. Since it was their job to protect me, who protected me from them? I heard that childhood sexual abuse is a betrayal of trust. As a result, I trusted no one—I was even struggling to trust God. I felt betrayed and unloved by God because he did not prevent the abuse. A battle raged within my soul because I craved and hungered for true love and intimacy yet felt that no one, including God, would love me.

"Dear God, I know you said that you love me. I know you said that you would work all things out for good. How can any good come from my past? I don't want to remember. I don't want to feel this pain again. I am struggling to understand why I can't just forget about it. I know what the Bible says about how much you care for me—sometimes I do feel that you care. Dear God, I feel so dirty and unloved that I'm afraid I will never feel clean again. My heart is breaking, and I am struggling to keep my life together. I don't know what to do anymore, Lord. Please help me."

In the outpouring of my fears, I was too agitated to hear God's whispers in response. But he was there.

VENGEANCE

My feelings of powerlessness soon gave way to anger and hatred. I wanted all my abusers to die, go to hell, and suffer eternal punishment. Immediately I felt guilty, knowing that God was not pleased with my anger turning to sin and wanting vengeance on my terms. I went to a support group for survivors of sexual abuse at the Women's Center on campus but stopped going after two meetings. I was relieved that I was not the only one who had been stripped of her innocence, but I found no soul-satisfying answers there. All my life I felt God had abandoned me, and I needed to know why.

I remember going to church, wading through the people to find someone willing to listen to my story and help me to make peace with the past. I talked with one woman, Sister Griggs, telling her only that I was struggling with childhood sexual abuse. I purposely avoided telling her too much. Sister Griggs panicked: "Child, you need to go to the Lord with this problem. I can't help you, but I'll pray for you."

After that, she avoided me for weeks. I remember seeing her almost fall over herself to get out of the church building when she saw me coming down the aisle. Maybe I picked the wrong person to confide in and should have looked for someone else, but at that point I stopped trying to find a Christian to talk to about my past. One of the women in the campus support group told me, "Church folks are the worst. They are too dignified and they shame you into silence."

I often struggled with why I had been unable to stop the abuse. I questioned why I was not more like Gayle, who was braver, stronger, and smarter than I was. In my heart I still felt that everything was my fault. Other questions would surface: Why did I keep silent for so long? How could I have been braver? I started to ride a pendulum between intense anger and depression. This was the backdrop for the entrance of my next would-be predator.

Professor Calhoun was a towering man at six feet, five inches. He was the new supporting adviser to an academic organization to which I belonged. My group was a small, intimate collection of fifteen minority students preparing for careers in academia. We had been together for over a year, and none of us felt comfortable when Professor Calhoun became involved. I felt especially uneasy when he began to focus on me. At every gathering he would sit next to me. In every mixer he found his way to my circle of friends. In every conversation he found some reason to touch me. At first these were harmless touches—a pat on my shoulder, a poke on my arm, or a brief hug.

Over the course of several weeks, his touches began to make me uncomfortable. The pat on the shoulder became more like a caress. The poke on the arm turned into a rub. The brief hug was prolonged. Although uncomfortable, I could not believe that a professor would be coming on to me. I pushed the thought out of my mind, but I could not shake the distress I felt. The fear felt the same as what I had experienced around John and Dad.

My entire body screamed at me that it was not all in my mind. This was confirmed when the dean of my organization went out of town for a couple of weeks, leaving Professor Calhoun in charge. I would soon learn that these "harmless" gestures of affection were rooted in sinister intentions.

One day he telephoned me. "Cheryl, this is Professor Calhoun. I'm calling a meeting for tomorrow. Since we are meeting off campus, why don't you meet me outside my office and I'll drive you and the other students who can't walk there?"

I was suspicious because our group never met off campus but went anyway. When I arrived at his office building, Professor Calhoun was standing alone beside his car. He told me that the other students would meet us at the restaurant. He said he would drive me because it was dark and too dangerous for me to travel alone. (I used an electric scooter to help me navigate the campus.) Professor Calhoun picked up the 250-pound scooter effortlessly and placed it in the trunk of his car. I was terrified at his strength and too afraid to tell him that I did not want to ride in his car. My mind started screaming at me to walk away. Like a robot, I got in the car when he opened the door. As soon as I was inside, I changed my mind. The clicks of the automatic locks sounded like the doors to a prison being slammed shut. I was trapped.

"So, Cheryl, what have you been up to lately?"

"Nothing."

"Nothing? Surely you've been doing something."

"No, I lead a boring life—you know, studying and all." I was trying to keep the conversation boring so that he would get the hint that I did not want to talk to him.

"Do you have a boyfriend?"

Why is he asking me something like this? This is too personal! "No." *Cheryl, why did you answer him? Are you stupid?*

"I find that hard to believe. Someone as beautiful as you are should have a boyfriend." He reached over to squeeze my hand. I snatched my hand away in shock. I leaned toward the car door and kept silent while we drove several blocks to the restaurant. Once there, he unloaded my scooter, and we proceeded inside.

During the meeting Professor Calhoun found a way to sit beside me. I grew more nervous as the meeting concluded because I knew I must not ride back to campus with him. I had a growing conviction that he would try to harm me on the way back, so I rushed to the rest room before the meeting was over and left the building through a back door. I scooted the long way home, making sure I did not take the main roads. Once I made it back to the safety of my dorm, I began to think about how furious Professor Calhoun would be with me.

I had a good plan to avoid being with him. The next day I ignored his calls, purposely waiting until nightfall to call and leave a message on his voice mail to the effect that I was OK. I decided not to address my abrupt departure the other night.

My plan sank when I learned that I needed an emergency letter of recommendation for a Washington, D.C., internship. I had just learned about the program, and the deadline was extended specifically for my application. The dean in charge of my academic group was out of town and could not write the recommendation; I needed Professor Calhoun to write one. I knew nothing good would come of it, but I had to ask.

So I telephoned. "Professor Calhoun, I am applying for this Washington, D.C., internship, and I need a letter of recommendation from a dean in charge of this program. Could you write one for me?"

"Well, Cheryl, I don't know. I don't think I know you well enough to write an informed recommendation. You will have to come to my office. I could squeeze you in right now."

"I think you know me well enough. I have class and can't get over there."

"Well, I disagree. If you want the recommendation, you will have to come over to my office right now."

I was trapped. I needed the recommendation, and Professor Calhoun was the only one who could give it. I told myself that I would insist that the door to his office remain open and I would object to any personal questions. When I arrived at Professor Calhoun's office, he smiled and greeted me at the door. He said that he gave his secretary the rest of the day off so we would not be interrupted.

"I don't have much time," I hedged.

"That's OK, Cheryl. I won't keep you long." He caressed my shoulders as he spoke and stopped when I flinched. "So, Cheryl, tell me a little bit about yourself."

"What do you want to know that's not in my file?"

"There is a lot of information not in your file that I need to get to know you better."

"Like what?" I asked warily.

Professor Calhoun rose and closed the door. When I heard the click of the lock, my heart began to race. Professor Calhoun moved closer to me and began to loosen his tie and unbutton the first two buttons on his shirt. He bent down to whisper in my ear. "I want to know everything about you. Your hobbies. Your dislikes. Your desires."

I pulled my ear away from his mouth and told myself not to cry. My sister always warned me that crying let the person know he had power over me. "Look, Professor Calhoun, I don't know what is going on here, but all I need is a letter of recommendation from you. Are you going to write it or not?"

"Does your disability affect your sex life?"

The question knocked the wind out of me. My eyes began to well up with tears. I was terrified. The flashbacks of John, my great uncle, and Dad started to flood my consciousness. There was no doubt that he meant to harm me. I started to pray, begging God to provide a way for me to escape. "Please God," I prayed, "please don't let this happen to me again. Please don't stand aside and allow this to happen. Please stop this man."

"Can you have sex, or does your disability prevent you from enjoying yourself?"

"I want to leave. Please don't come any closer to me. I . . . I'll scream."

"You don't want to do that. We are just starting our fun, Cheryl."

Professor Calhoun's hands began to caress my back. The moment he touched me, I became fueled with anger. I was sick and tired of people taking advantage of me. I was tired of men abusing me. I was tired of them making me feel dirty. I began to think like those women at the Women's Center. I remember one describing how she took her abuser off guard by bluffing strength. She fought back.

I wanted to punch Professor Calhoun but knew that it would be hopeless trying to hit him. I wanted to run away but knew that no amount of adrenaline would make my scooter go faster. In a split-second decision, I turned my scooter on full power and charged toward the closed door. The impact of my scooter ramming the door echoed through the office and down the hall. I slammed the scooter in reverse and, before Professor Calhoun could react, I rammed the locked door again.

He grabbed my shoulders and told me that he would open the door, but that no one would believe me if I spoke about what had happened. After all, he was a respected professor and I was just a student. I wanted to spit in his face.

When he opened the door, I scooted down the hall and into a female professor's office. I had to compose myself in a safe place. I could not believe what had just happened. Professor Calhoun had not just crossed the line to sexual misconduct; he was threatening my future. After being face-to-face with someone who was out of control, I began to wonder if I was the only person he had treated that way. When I remembered a poster I saw in the Women's Center that said, "Break the Silence," I decided Professor Calhoun needed to be stopped. I did what I wanted to do all my life: I broke the silence. Within one hour I was telling my story to a dean. A couple of months later, Professor Calhoun quietly resigned.

One of my girlfriends told me that I should have exposed Professor Calhoun in the campus newspaper. With such a high-profile case of sexual harassment, everyone would know what he did to me. She said that his career would have been ruined. I would have the ultimate revenge.

A part of me wanted to humiliate him without mercy, but as soon as I entertained thoughts of vengeance, God clearly spoke to my soul: *Vengeance is my job.* Justice and vengeance are two different actions; the difference is within the heart. Once I had tasted the sweetness of vengeance, I began to struggle with my anger. I wanted to see John and Dad punished. I wanted to watch them suffer. My emotions spiraled out of control into the depths of hate.

"Lord, please help me. I don't want to feel like this. I know I'm starting to pull away from you. I know these feelings are wrong. I can't stop myself because I'm so angry. I'm hurting so badly right now and I need you to help me."

I was lashing out in the pain of a wounded soul, but I have always been transparent to God. Whatever I feel, I tell him. Years later I realized that my honesty with him allowed him to heal my wounds and profoundly change my heart.

My dear child, watch your anger. Vengeance only leads to more evil. Do not fret about those who harmed you; I will take care of them in my own way and in my own time. You are becoming distracted by your hatred, and it hurts me to see you like this. You have to trust me more. Spend your time focusing on our relationship. I know the weight of your burdens is causing you to stumble, but you will not fall. I am always here to carry you. I will never abandon you. When you grieve, I will be here to give you my strength. It has never been my will for you to live with a spirit of despair. I know you are mourning. You have to trust me when I promise that I will comfort you.

I feel your hunger for my love. I promise to fill you up and heal your wounds. You have to trust that I will accomplish what I have planned for your life. I promise that you will soon have joy and peace. I know you do not understand my ways. Overcome your doubts and learn to trust in my unfailing and everlasting love for you. I promise to deliver you from this feeling of hopelessness and despair. I have a good purpose for your life. Wait patiently, my child, because I have gone ahead of you to work out all things for good.

Continue to seek me. Continue to ask me questions and to share your pain. I will answer you and erase all your fears. Look at yourself in the mirror. What do you see? I see a beautiful, smiling face that radiates my love and shows no shame. I will continue to remind you that because of me you are victorious over your past. You were not destroyed. I did not let you fail.

I have much more to tell you, but you are not ready to handle it right now. I will help you grow confident in my love for you. And you, my love, need to keep trusting in me. Your hunger for peace, joy, and fullness has driven you into my safe and loving arms. That is where you belong, and that is where you will remain. My promises will never change, and I will continue to remind you until you fully believe me.

PART TWO

Lost in the Shuffle

Why should I feel discouraged, why
should the shadows come,
Why should my heart be lonely, and
long for heaven and home?
When Jesus is my portion, My con-
stant friend is He:
His eye is on the sparrow, and I know
He watches me;
His eye is on the sparrow, and I know
He watches me.
I sing because I'm happy,
I sing because I'm free,
For His eye is on the sparrow,
And I know He watches me.

C. D. MARTIN

CHAPTER FIVE

Yet Holding On

Ain't gonna let nobody turn me around,
turn me around, turn me around.
Ain't gonna let nobody turn me around.
I've gotta keep on a-walkin', keep on a-talkin',
Marching into freedom land

TRADITIONAL SPIRITUAL

I was eight years old when I learned how to fight. Between the surgeries and predators, I had many battle scars. I was an angry little girl inside. No one saw my innermost self; outsiders saw my tough-girl mask. My anger was like a dormant volcano waiting for its moment to explode.

I earned the nickname "Slugger" when I began third grade. I had been through the revolving hospital doors too often to attend public school so was homeschooled with brief stints in day care. Third grade was different. I began going to a magnet school over an hour away from home in an affluent white neighborhood. Dad said that Gayle and I were attending a white school because of desegregation. He explained that since African-American kids had a right to a good education, white schools had to allow us the same access to the keys of success. Gayle complained about having to wake up so early and ride a bus for over an hour. Dad told us that we had better get used to the discomfort because we were African-Americans in a world that would never give us anything. We would have to fight for everything, and even then we would have to be twice as good to be considered equal to whites. Dad warned us to be on our best behavior and make good grades. People died for our right to attend school, so it was our duty to make our parents proud. "Remember that you are representing all African-Americans. What you do can either bring honor or shame to us," he said.

Gayle was a no-nonsense person who always told me the truth as she understood it. "Don't get too happy about being important by going to this school. Nobody, including the African-American kids, cares about the Civil Rights junk. They won't care about you either. You are black and walk funny. Folks won't like people like you."

I was prepared for the worst. My first day at school would be a nightmare. While we waited for the morning bus on the street corner, my heart started to beat faster and my breathing became more rapid. I was scared. I looked down at my legs. There was no way to hide my disability because of the steel leg braces. After having seen so many images from the Civil Rights era, I was pumped into thinking that black people would stick together in the face of the common threat of racism. Furthermore, the kids on the bus were from my neighborhood.

The bus turned the corner and came toward us. When the door opened, I froze at how far from the ground the first step was. There was no way I could get on the bus without unlocking the braces so that my legs could bend. If I allowed my legs to bend, however, I would lose the strength the braces provided. I hesitated while trying to decide what to do.

"Come on, girl, I don't have all day," the bus driver snapped at me. He hadn't noticed my braces yet.

"She's coming. Can't you see she has a problem with her legs?" yelled my sister.

My head quickly turned to Gayle in the horror of the moment. She just told a bus full of twenty kids that I had a disability. When I got on the bus, everyone would be staring at me. My eyes swelled with tears. I wanted to call the whole thing off and go home. I was so angry with Gayle. I unlocked my braces and grabbed the handrails of the bus to pull myself up the steps. My sister pushed me up the stairs from behind. The bus driver just stared, never offering help.

It seemed like an eternity while I climbed those four steps. When I reached the top, I looked up and saw all eyes were on me. My sister told me to ignore the stupid kids staring at me, but their eyes felt like knife stabs. I tried to act normal, hiding my braces from everyone who boarded the bus. My efforts were in vain. Once kids reached the back seats, whispers began.

"Hey, that girl up there is crippled."

"She retarded or something?"

"No, she got this junk on her legs. Go check her out."

It got much worse when we picked up Marvin, a sixth grader. Marvin was a pudgy African-American boy who looked like trouble. He was the bus bully who would harass and curse all the kids who sat in the front. Since I was a new kid, he had to show me who was boss. "So, we got ourselves a cripple on my bus? Where is she?" Marvin yelled.

"Ignore him, Cheryl. Don't even look his way." My sister squeezed my hand for strength as we looked away.

Then Marvin stood over me; I could feel his breath on my neck. It sent shivers down my body. I could feel his hatred. "So, you are the ugly cripple. You are one ugly freak." He looked me over and reached out to touch my braces. I jerked my legs away from him.

"Oh, so you think you can do what you want on my bus. If I want to touch you, I will." Marvin grabbed my legs to touch my braces.

I glared at him. "Get your hands off me!"

"Oh, so the stupid little cripple freak speaks."

He bent to place his face in my face. I could smell him. His breath was hot and musty. His eyes were tight and full of anger. He cursed at me.

I'd had enough, and I pushed him out of my face. The rest of the kids on the bus gasped, and Marvin exploded. He pulled me out of my seat and spat in my face. My sister rose to take up for me, but two other boys held her down. Marvin spat on Gayle too.

I wiped the saliva from my face. Anger and hatred surged through me. I was humiliated in front of all those new kids. I had to protect myself. Marvin turned his head toward me and sneered, "I'm going to teach you a lesson—"

I heard nothing else. I saw him balling his fist, and in a split second, I saw myself punching Marvin in the face, stomach, and chest. I was fighting. The kids rose in their seats, screaming and cheering. The fight ended as quickly as it began. Marvin was on the floor of the bus, and I was still standing. Everyone was quiet. They looked at me, looked down at Marvin, and began to laugh hysterically.

"Marvin got beat up by a third grader!" everyone chanted all the way to school.

Humiliated, Marvin went to his seat and looked out the window.

I went back to my seat. My sister was stunned. "You just beat up a sixth grader."

I smiled.

When our bus arrived at school, I allowed everyone to get off first. I wanted to keep Marvin ahead of me. I looked out the window and saw a sea of white faces. I expected the white kids to yell at us, but they simply ignored us. When I got off the bus, however, all the kids began staring and pointing at me, the crippled girl. I held my head up, looked straight ahead, and walked to my classroom trying to ignore everyone. Dad was wrong. The Civil Rights movement was a long time ago, and the African-American kids did not unite. I did not notice racism in my new white school; I was too busy protecting myself from my own people.

CONSEQUENCES

I hated recess. None of the kids wanted to play with me, and I grew tired of the stares and whispers. I spent most of my time keeping my distance from the ever-growing number of bullies. I soon spotted trouble. Marvin and his posse of eight boys were coming toward me for payback time. I had to escape.

I turned around and briskly walked toward some girls who were playing. The posse paused in confusion. I stayed with the girls until I could slip through an open door leading to the classrooms. A teacher caught me in the halls and tried to force me back outside, so I lied and said I needed to use the rest room. I looked out through the window at the posse. The boys were furious and cursing. There was no way I could avoid them forever. The more I eluded them, the angrier and more vengeful they would probably become. I knew I could not return outside that day. To diffuse the tension, I needed to find another way home.

In the rest room, I paced. I had to come up with a plan. I thought about saying that my stomach hurt, but I knew no one would believe that lame story. I thought about calling Mom and telling her about the bullies and fights but felt that she would cause a big stink and make everyone hate me even more. Furthermore, my summer of hell with my cousin John and Uncle David convinced me that my parents would not protect me.

In a panic, I gripped the top portion of my braces so tightly that my hands began to hurt. I looked down and saw that my hands were bending my steel leg braces. If I could break them, I knew the nurse would send me home. I grabbed my braces and pushed down on them with all my strength. I gritted my teeth and began to shake at the pressure I was applying to my braces. Sweat began streaming down my face. I started to pump down on the braces. With a couple of loud snaps, both braces broke at the knee locks. I looked down at my handiwork and smiled. I wondered if I had done enough to ensure my ticket home.

I started to limp around while I thought about what else I could do. With every step I felt pain in my legs. The ragged steel edges of the broken braces were rubbing my skin. I walked around in circles in the bathroom, silently crying as the steel tore at my skin. Blood soaked my socks.

A teacher came in, found me, and carried me to the nurse's office. I rested on the cot while the nurse cleaned my wounds. I was going home. Marvin and his thugs would not get their hands on me that day. I knew it would take a while to get new braces. Maybe when I returned to school, those boys would have forgotten about me. Still, I knew I could not break my braces all the time. Eventually I would have to face my bullies.

I never wore the metal braces again—they became too expensive to fix. I wore plastic braces for the rest of that school year, but they did not provide enough support to walk properly, so I stopped wearing them. Against accepted protocol for my condition, my doctor took me out of all braces. I walked without braces until I was seventeen. Each year, however, I started walking bent over and began falling a lot. My spine also started to curve during this time. I started using crutches at eighteen, then moved to the scooter/wheelchair at twenty.

When I returned to elementary school that pivotal year, there were many more fights. I won some and lost some. The most striking thing I noticed was the lack of harassment from the white kids. They stared, some even teased, but rarely did they get physical. I came to school expecting to be like the kids from Little Rock who desegregated the schools during the Civil Rights era despite severe racial prejudice. Instead, I ended up fighting my own people while the little white kids watched.

I will never forget the first time I lost a fight. I was in fourth grade and had a string of successful battles under my belt. My father cursed regularly and with skill. I had picked up a few of his colorful phrases to bluff those I figured I could not beat in hand-to-hand battle. I underestimated Pedro.

Pedro was a skinny kid who always harassed me. He was in a funk one day and decided that a cripple could not ride on his bus. Every time I tried to sit down in a seat, he pushed me down to the floor. After being pushed three times, I sized up my odds of whipping him. I scanned the size of his hands, the shape of his arms, and his height. We looked even, so after the third push, I hauled back with my fist and socked Pedro in the face.

My next recollection was lying facedown on the floor of the bus. Pedro had socked me in my right eye. Since I had to protect my reputation as a fighter, I had to get up and get him back. I had to win because if I lost every bully would declare open season on the crippled girl. The moment I got to my feet and tried to raise my hand, Pedro socked me in the right eye again. I was back on the floor. This time I felt blood trickling down my face. My vision blurred, and I stumbled to regain my footing. Before I could make it to my feet, Pedro socked me a third time.

In a foggy distance, I could hear the cheers and screams of the other kids on the bus. I lay on the floor of the bus for what felt like an eternity. I could not muster enough strength to get up. Nevertheless, I knew that I had to. I had to prove to Pedro that, although he won this fight, he did not have the power to keep me down. I slowly pulled my body off the floor. I could hear Pedro screaming and cursing at me, but he did not hit me. The bus driver had intervened and, in effect, called a technical knockout. I was forced to sit in the front of the bus for the rest of the ride home.

When I reached my stop and got off the last step of the bus, I felt a searing pain shooting throughout my body that brought me to my knees. Every time I tried to stand up, I fell. Pedro had whipped me well. I sat on the ground to get my breath and try to figure out how to get home. I began to crawl, oblivious to how strange I looked. After passing several houses, my knees started to hurt, and I pushed up to my feet and began to limp the rest of the way home.

ANCHOR

I quickly grew tired of fighting with my fists. Despite all the times I won, there was always a stronger boy waiting for his shot at me. My sister suggested I win friends by becoming useful to my enemies. I translated that into buying friends. A teacher called my parents when I started giving out presents; I had stolen twenty dollars from Dad's wallet to start converting my enemies to friends. Instead of searching for the cause of my bizarre thievery, Dad beat me for embarrassing him in front of the white teacher. I immediately began looking for other ways to win friends.

My disability affected only my lower limbs, but people automatically assumed that everything about me was impaired. In an effort to protect me, teachers would often prevent me from doing anything outdoors. At first I accepted their protection because I was afraid of all the bullies and hated recess; but when I needed to find ways to become useful to my enemies, the teachers' protection quickly turned to suffocation.

Every year my school hosted Field Day for outdoor competition. Kids would compete against each other in individual and group games such as dodge ball, sack races, tug-of-war, and volleyball. I had good upper body strength and knew I could play tug-of-war and tetherball. My teachers thought the games were too dangerous and told me, "Cheryl, we don't want you to get hurt."

Watching my classmates at tug-of-war, I saw when they started to lose. The anchor was one of the bullies. When my teachers momentarily left me alone, I bolted toward the tug-of-war team to tell the anchor, "Dan, you are going to lose it for the team. You aren't strong enough."

"Shut up, Cheryl! I'm strong enough. I just hurt my hand."

"Yeah. Whatever. Let me take your place."

"Are you crazy? You are crippled. You can't play tug-of-war!"

"There is nothing wrong with my arms, stupid," I insisted.

"But you still need your legs to play this game."

"My arms are strong enough to make up for the weakness in my legs. Come on! We are losing."

Everyone began yelling for Dan to pull harder. Dan was stuck. He was hurt and knew that if the class lost, everyone would blame him. So he quickly stepped aside and let me take over as anchor. The other team members laughed when they saw me.

I sat down on the ground and began to pull on the rope. When my team began backing up, I got to my feet, unlocked my braces, and pulled from my knees. To everyone's surprise, my team won. Everyone piled on top of me in excitement. For the first time, I felt that everyone overlooked my disability. After winning four more matches, my class won first place. All the kids began chanting my name. I found acceptance and success intoxicating.

However, my teachers were mortified that I had disobeyed them, and I received a paddling. I was fighting a losing battle. The school had labeled me "disabled," which meant I could not do anything normal. I was a "special" student, allowed to do only the things that other special kids did. My teachers could not understand that my disability was not synonymous with total incapacitation or helplessness. Instead of seeing me as an individual, they saw me as a stereotype; it was my job to conform to that helpless stereotype.

ISN'T THAT SPECIAL?

Trying to buy friends or win them by excelling at sports was futile. I did not have enough money to keep everyone happy. It was too stressful always trying to be perfect. I felt responsible for the team's success. If we failed, I knew I would be the obvious person to blame. I decided to focus on being smarter than my enemies. I told myself that someday everyone would work for me, and the power I had over them would protect me. So I had to earn a reputation as a smart kid.

"Because you are African-American and walk differently, you have to always work harder than the other kids. People will always tell you what you can't do. They will always focus on your limitations. You have to be strong and prove them wrong," Mom would say.

It was hard to prove myself educationally. The doctors first raised the possibility that I would have mental impairments in addition to my lower limb deformities. My parents felt that having mental impairments was a death sentence for an African-American child; it would be hopeless for me to rise above so many invitations to discrimination. In their minds, the stigma of not being intelligent was worse than walking differently. As long as I was smart, there was hope that I could be something in life. With mental retardation, they did not see much hope. We distanced ourselves from anything that implied mental impairment.

We were running from stereotypes. When my parents and I would go places together, sometimes people would engage me and automatically raise the volume of their voices and talk slower, as if I could not understand them otherwise. Mom would ferociously protect my image as a normal person. She would yell at condescending people, "She simply has a problem with her legs. You don't have to talk to her like she is stupid."

My first class in third grade was a special class in which many of the kids, mostly African-American, could barely read. The kids at school called them stupid classes. When I looked at my class schedule, I noticed that all my classes were special classes. In tears, I called my parents and told them I wanted to come home because everyone was calling me stupid.

So Mom began her crusade against the school system. No child of hers was going to be kicked out of the mainstream to languish in a place for neglected and stigmatized kids. My parents saw nothing redeeming about special education. They were insulted that anyone would assume that a child of theirs needed special classes. The principal unsuccessfully tried to convince Mom that my classes were simply a way for the school to offer special-needs children the services they required.

Mom was not convinced. She insisted the school move me back to regular classes with the normal kids. Her child did not have a mental problem, and she would not allow the system to push me into educational suicide that would ruin my future. It was to be a continual battle. Each time I moved to another school, my default placement was in special education. Although I made good grades in elementary school, when I started junior high, all my classes were in special education. I had a new foe: the aptitude test.

I choked each time I took the tests. When I choked in junior high, I was automatically placed in remedial classes. I knew the other kids would be ruthless about these, the official stupid classes. I still hear them in my head calling me the stupid crippled girl. I refused to go to class and called my parents instead.

Mom and Dad hated aptitude tests because the results were used as scientific proof that I was not intelligent. My scores reflected my need for remedial classes. My grades, however, indicated that I was above average. My parents discounted the tests and considered it abusive to place me in special or remedial classes; they wanted me in gifted and talented classes. My principal resisted, saying that my test scores did not support such radical action.

Mom raised her voice in anger. "You will not let one test nullify all that Cheryl has accomplished in school. You will not destroy her future. This is discrimination. Why aren't there more African-Americans and kids with physical problems in your precious gifted and talented classes? I'm not going to sit here and let you hold my daughter back because of one stupid test. Maybe I should just get a lawyer. . . ."

My mother had pulled out the trump card with the accusation of racial discrimination. She knew the principal would flee from being labeled a racist. "OK, Mrs. Green, I give up. I will allow Cheryl in gifted and talented classes for a probationary period of one semester."

I had to prove everyone wrong about my intellect and prove I belonged with the smart kids. The battle to prove my worth moved to the classroom. I wanted to be with the smart kids. As the pride of the school, gifted and talented kids were protected from thugs.

So I worked hard to remain among the elite. I made the honor roll that semester, but no one said a word to me. I made the honor roll every semester. Although no one commended me, I was proud of myself because I proved that a person could be African-American, disabled, and smart, despite what the aptitude tests said. Many of my teachers called me an "overachiever." I never took that as a compliment. I always felt they were telling me that although they believed I was not intelligent, I relied on hard work to overcome my limitations. I could not understand why everyone at school thought the test was infallible. Why did they have to accept the results of one test over the proof offered by years of accomplishment?

By junior high, circumstances set me up to believe a lie. I thought my future depended solely on my own abilities. Self-reliance would erode my faith in the God of hope. Making it required me to believe mostly in myself and fight hard. I began to lose sight of the God of hope, who was silent and distant. Everything rested on me, and I trusted no one.

Self-reliance has a dark side. If I failed, it meant that I was not strong or smart enough to overcome the obstacles. If I earned anything below an A minus, I would panic and become depressed. Constructive criticism from teachers felt like abuse. I wanted to please them so they would not kick me out of gifted and talented classes.

My parents had been successful in transferring to me their source of hope. To make it to the promised land, I thought I had to put my faith in education and myself. That foundation would not be enough to nurture lasting, soul-satisfying hope. My family built its spiritual foundation on what was powerless to withstand the raging storms that would sink us into poverty.

My child, the storms are coming. You will fear that all hope is lost, but when you come to me weeping, I will let you know that I am able to save you. It is time for you to hear my voice and know that I have been by your side from the very beginning. I will bring calm into your life and help you see me face to face. I have so much to tell you, but it is still too soon. You are not ready. I know you doubt me, but I will show you the power of faith as small as a mustard seed. I promise that your small, fragile faith is powerful enough to bring you close to me. You will rest forever in your Daddy's arms.

CHAPTER SIX

Not My Home

This world is not my home,
I'm just a-passing through.
My treasures are laid up
Somewhere beyond the blue;
The angels beckon me
From heaven's open door.
And I can't feel at home in the world anymore.

TRADITIONAL SPIRITUAL

The storms started slowly with Dad losing his job when I was twelve. Our response was to root out fluff in our budget. Gone were vacations, movies, and gifts. The pantry dwindled to merely the staple foods. I remember whining about how poor we were when Mom stopped buying soft drinks. Soon I would know what *poor* really meant.

I resisted the fluff-free life. At Christmas I would search the house for lost trinkets and pack them under the tree. I made sure that each person had three presents. When I ran out of trinkets, I started wrapping clothes I found in the back of the closet. I abandoned the ritual when I could find only underwear and socks to wrap. Opening a present of underwear was more depressing than having nothing under the tree.

As Mom and Dad started to argue more about our dwindling resources, Gayle and I collected pennies for two season passes to the amusement park. Armed with our season passes and sandwiches, she and I would escape reality by riding roller coasters for eight hours. We never told Mom and Dad that we found a small treasure in pennies because they would have taken it. Gayle and I lied, telling our parents that we won our season passes by earning good grades.

To supplement our income, my family began collecting aluminum cans. Since recycling was not a priority in my neighborhood, a small fortune in cans littered the highways. Mom would pull out her wide-brimmed straw hat and leather work gloves. Dad would clean out the car and load up on ice water. We lathered our bodies with insect repellent and spent hours in the new "cotton fields."

Mom and Dad did not tell us how bad our financial situation had become. Gayle and I discovered the gravity of it when a ladies ministry from a local church came to our house with boxes of food. The leader of the church group, Ms. Jerome, was one of Mom's archenemies in the homeowners association. She and Mom had clashing personalities and fought bitterly. After word had quickly spread in our neighborhood that we were hard on our luck, Mom complained that everyone was laughing at us. Dad dismissed her perceptions as evidence of her paranoia, but Ms. Jerome's box of food seemed to prove Mom's theory.

The ministry group of fifteen women arrived with great fanfare. They prayed for our finances and hugged each one of us, saying, "God promises to take care of his children. He will provide." When they left, we opened the boxes of food and found only bottles of Magic Shell ice cream topping and corned beef hash. Mom started cursing, and Dad had to hold her back from throwing the boxes of food in the trash. We applied for food stamps the next day.

Mom and Dad loathed the thought of public assistance. They felt it was beneath them to beg. I hated public assistance. I was embarrassed about looking poor and giving others yet another reason to reject and ridicule me. I was also irritated at wasting my life away in the government bureaucracy. There were lines for everything—to get a number, to get an application, to be placed on a call-back list, to go inside to talk to someone, to get pictures taken, and on, and on. Waiting seemed to eat away our entire lives.

I also recoiled at the way the workers treated people who were applying. They were typically condescending and rude. My parents went to the welfare office together and stormed out when the intake counselor looked at Dad and asked him why he could not support his family. The next time they tried, Mom went in alone. She felt the system was suspicious of her, too, because she held a master's degree. She would complain that everyone in the office was wondering why, with all her education, she could not be the wage earner of her household. Mom left the office in a fury when yet another counselor asked her why she could not find a job with all her education.

"You know, I am a person. I have feelings and a brain. You will talk to me like a person," Mom said.

"Look, do you want help or not? You people ought to quit being lazy and just get jobs like everyone else," the counselor replied.

"You don't know anything about me. How dare you talk to me like that? The only reason you even have a job is because of people like me. You are over there sitting on your high horse looking down on me, and I just won't have it. You will talk to me with respect because I am somebody."

It is a losing battle, however, to demand respect from the workers in the welfare offices. Wasting time standing in long lines and putting up with condescension are the price each applicant pays for receiving help in time of need. Everyone always said that the system was designed to strip a person of all dignity. Well, Mom and Dad decided to play the game. They knew they would not qualify for assistance without a more compelling reason for their unemployment. I became the compelling reason. I doubt my parents thought about what it would do to my self-esteem to exploit my disability for welfare. They knew we would receive assistance and they could preserve their pride if they could convince themselves and others that my health needs consumed the family's resources.

I became the family antipoverty mascot. I had to accompany them each time they applied or reapplied for assistance. When we arrived, I had to exaggerate my limp and look solemn. Our survival depended on my looking and acting like a poor, helpless, disabled child, which confused me deeply. I was glad that we had food, but getting it cost me my dignity and self-worth. My parents, however, appeared energized; they quickly convinced themselves that they had sacrificed their lives to ensure their disabled child would have a future. Instead of the counselors seeing them as deadbeats, my parents were admired for their sacrifice and perseverance.

Dad later found a job as a manager of a fast food restaurant. Then we were denied further public assistance because we made too much money. The mortgage, utilities, and transportation costs consumed all of Dad's check. Mom began going from one church pantry to another for food. Dad would bring home discarded food from the restaurant. The fast food industry was tumultuous; managers were fired as quickly as they were hired. Dad would stay at a restaurant only several months before he was fired. During that cycle of employment and unemployment, we could no longer afford our home.

GET OUT

I was sixteen when the Book of Job started to come alive. Gayle was a thousand miles away at college, so she escaped the worst of our nightmare.

There was a knock on the door. We opened it to the uniforms standing outside. One said, "I'm Constable Johnson. You have two weeks to vacate these premises. When we return, we will throw all personal property out on the street. If that property is left there by the next morning, we will impound it for thirty days. After that time, if you do not pay the storage fees, you will forfeit your rights to the property, and we will sell it. Do you understand what I have explained to you?"

My parents nodded and looked away.

"When you vacate, you will need to remove all the curtains and blinds on the windows. An officer will come by periodically to look in these windows to make sure you have vacated the premises. If we find you here, you will be arrested for trespassing."

Dad pulled the constable aside and started talking to him. Mom just looked out the window blankly. When the constables left, they posted a neon-pink foreclosure poster on our front door and garage. Mom tore the posters down and threw them away. When she passed by my father, she stared at him angrily. They started to argue about who was at fault.

Later, while I was in my room, the lights suddenly went out. I heard a van pull away. I looked out the window and saw the van from the power company. We were now without electricity because Dad could not pay the four-hundred-dollar bill. Houston was miserably hot. The heat wave made it feel like one hundred degrees in the house. Mom began pulling food out of the refrigerators to place in coolers. Dad stormed out the house and drove off in a car he borrowed from a friend.

"You want to know what's going on?" Mom asked.

I nodded.

"Your Dad screwed up big this time. He walked right in the trap those racist men at work set for him. He gave them a perfect excuse for firing him. He also used all our savings to go into business with the father of your friend Tabitha. That crook stole all our money. Now we are being kicked out and we don't have anywhere to go. He's trying to blame me! It's not my fault. I am not taking the blame for this. This is his fault."

"Why can't you find a job either?" I asked.

"I can't make anyone give me anything. So are you trying to blame me for this too?"

I decided to walk away because Mom felt threatened and wanted to fight. I did not want to join their dance of shifting accountability. They were both at fault. When Dad returned home, he went to our neighbor to "borrow" electricity. He ran several extension cords across the fence. We also borrowed a television, fan, hot plate, and a lamp. One of Dad's friends rented a storage space for our property and a moving van.

Within a week, every room in our house was empty. I walked through the house and stopped at the door leading to the kitchen. I noticed the dents in the door frame where I had repeatedly crashed my Big Wheels toy scooter when I was little. I turned around, staring at the hardwood floor, and remembered the times my sister and I would wear socks and pretend to ice skate.

In the kitchen, I remembered the times Gayle and I would pull the food from the pantry and play grocery store. In the living room, I remembered the houses we made out of sheets, boxes, and couches. I could almost hear all the times I practiced my piano and violin in the room. I walked to the back of the house and looked at the swing set in the backyard. Gayle and I used to compete to see who could swing the highest. I could almost hear our laughter from the times we played in the water sprinklers. Despite the pain of living in this house, it was my home.

When the constables returned, they took the house keys from my parents. Constable Johnson had a smirk on his face. "Maybe next time you people will pay your bills." He closed the door and left us outside, looking lost.

We piled into our borrowed car and started to drive. No one spoke. Dad pulled into a used car lot. He needed to buy a car because he had to return the car we were borrowing. When he returned, he held the keys to a four-hundred-dollar, 1977 Plymouth Volare. The dealer practically gave Dad the car by waiving a down payment and requiring only twenty dollars a month. The car was in good running shape but looked like something in a low-budget comedy movie. I was embarrassed by the car's appearance; our Volare screamed to the world that we were poor. It was an ugly boat covered with dings and rust. The ignition system was broken, so Dad rewired the starter to run by a push of a button rather than by a key. Dad tried to make light of his invention by saying that we were going back in history when cars were started with a button.

We drove around Houston aimlessly. We had no one to go to for help. By this time Mom and Dad were estranged from their families. My relatives thought we were Uncle Toms or "Oreos"—white on the inside, black on the outside. One of my mother's siblings told her that the family was waiting for the time when the world showed us that despite having fancy degrees, we were still "niggers." Mom and Dad never used the N word and never allowed it to be used in our house. Mom was livid at the taunt, and the fight that followed caused a permanent rift in her family. Mom and Dad told me that once the word of our eviction reached rural Texas, our relatives would be smugly satisfied that we had been put in our place.

It had been four years since Mom's commitment to the psychiatric hospital in 1982. Although she was less paranoid, she still thought people were plotting against her. She mistrusted anyone who tried to get close to her. Therefore, she had no friends for us to call on. Dad had spent over four years borrowing money from many of his friends; he was trying to keep the house going while investing in his start-up misadventure in the insurance industry. He could not approach any of them without repaying the loans. He had several friends who had never loaned him money, so we drove to their houses for a visit. Each one of them told us, "I'm so sorry to hear about what's happening. I'll pray for you, but—"

Dad would never let them finish the sentence. He would say, "That's OK. I thought you were my friends and cared about my family, but I see that is just not the case." He would curse under his breath as he herded Mom and me back to the car.

"Cheryl, you just remember this. You never know who your real friends are until you get hard on your luck. When you have money, you have many friends. When the money runs out, they abandon you."

That night we slept in our "new" car in a park near our home. Although I had the entire back seat to myself, I could not sleep. Dad's thunderous snores shook the car all night. I was also scared. Visions of thieves and murderers sneaking up and killing us streamed in my mind. When school started in a few days, I knew I would not be able to put a happy face on this.

For the next several weeks, we replayed the same scene. We would call upon remote family friends, tell them our story, but end up sleeping in the car. The temperature during the night was more than ninety degrees, making us miserable. I used a spray bottle to mist cool water over my body. In the mornings we would freshen up in the rest rooms of fast food restaurants or at friends' houses. Mom would wash clothes at the local laundromat. She used a hot plate at the facility where our furniture was stored to scramble or boil eggs for our meals. Egg sandwiches and water became our daily meal. Although I began to hate eggs, I was thankful that they quieted my rumbling stomach and hunger headaches.

We would drive by our house each day to see if the constables were there. Every time we went home, we had to pass Tabitha's house. Mom would curse at their house and call Tabitha's father a con artist. One day Tabitha's family had a new Cadillac in the driveway. They were doing better than my family because they stole our money.

"That is just messed up!" Mom yelled. "He steals from folks and leaves us penniless, yet he can afford to buy a new car? That's not right."

Dad opened his mouth to say something but looked away instead. I knew he dropped the issue because he did not feel like fighting.

When school started I was still living in the car. I told Dad that I could not take living in a car and going to school. Dad drove us to the storage facility. When we reached our spot, he began pulling out the boxes to create a living space for us. He positioned all the boxes to one side and set up the bed for Mom and me. It had to be more than 100 degrees inside, with an overpowering stench of decomposing rats. The access gates closed at 10:00 P.M., and there was no security. Dad replaced the bulb in the storage space with an adapter that allowed us to plug in a lamp and fan. By ten o'clock Mom and I were inside the storage space; Dad closed us in and drove the car away. The living conditions were miserable, bearable only because I did not have to listen to Dad's snoring. Within several weeks, however, the mosquitoes drove us back to living in the car.

One day we drove back to our repossessed house. Everyone had reached the breaking point, and Dad jumped angrily out of the car. He went around to the back of the house, broke a window, and unlocked the door. "Let's go back inside. We'll just stay here until I figure out what to do."

It was dead inside the house. The darkness that engulfed us scared me. We were breaking the law and trespassing. I could see the constables arresting us and taking me away to foster care. Gayle and I were always terrified of being placed with foster parents worse than our own parents. Dad went to our neighbor to borrow electricity. With several extension cords running across the backyard fence, we had electricity in one room of the house.

We sat quietly. The silence was protective since no one had the energy to argue or to remind one another that we might be caught. Mom began to prepare the nightly meal of scrambled egg sandwiches and water.

Camping out in the house was much better than living in the car or the storage facility. Although it was as hot as the other places, I felt safer within the protective walls. I would close my eyes and pretend that everything we were going through was a nightmare, and I would wake up to a normal life. I began to long for the days when we were simply dysfunctional.

The feelings of safety and security were fleeting. The neighborhood dogs would routinely chew on the extension cords and pull them apart in the middle of the night. Since we were the ones in need, we never bothered our neighbor after 8 P.M. Whenever we were suddenly without lights, Dad would pull out the kerosene hurricane lamp. By the light of that lamp, I immersed myself in my homework or reading. I wanted to keep my grades up so that I could get a college scholarship and be free like my sister.

When it was time for bed, we moved everything to the only room in the house without windows. If the constables patrolled that night, they would not see us there. Dad had contacts in the constable's office who told us when they were about to check the house. On those nights we slept in the car or in the storage facility. Dad knew that with Houston's stagnant economy, the housing market was dismal, so no one would purchase our home anytime soon. We would be safe for months.

One day when we passed by Tabitha's house, I noticed that her family was enlarging it and had purchased another new car. I liked Tabitha, but my increasing anger toward her father was eroding our friendship. Everything was making me angrier. I chanced to pray for the first time, never consciously expecting God to answer me.

"God, I know you don't hear me, but just in case you do, I don't know how long I can stand living like this. God, I've never asked you for anything before. I don't understand why you hate us so much— why you hate *me* so much. What did I ever do to deserve living like this? Will you stop this from happening to us? Will you do something? I don't know if you are even listening to me. Why would you? I'm nobody, and I'm sure you have more important things to do. Why should you care about my problems? I thought you and Dad had a special relationship. Could you at least help him so that he can help us? I hope you are real. If you are real, will you please help us?"

I would not pray again for two years.

HAIL MARY

I loved school because it was my escape from the reality of my home life. School had lights, air conditioning, running water, and food. After months of living like a fugitive in our house, I grew more irritable and tired of wearing a mask in public. I was tired of pretending that everything was fine. Life was far from fine. We were homeless, and I was sick of hearing my father's snoring every night. I was angry with Gayle for leaving me behind when she went to college. I was tired of being afraid of the constables catching us. I was tired of going to bed hungry. I struggled to control my escalating anger, but I was ready to explode.

When the school bus arrived one morning, I was seething with anger. Tabitha saw me get on the bus and motioned me to sit with her. "What's wrong with you?" she asked.

"I don't want to talk about it."

As I sat down, I noticed that Tabitha had on a new outfit. She had new jeans, a new shirt, and new shoes. I could see that she had been to the beauty shop. As we drove away, she waved at her father. He was smiling, standing next to their new car. I could feel myself losing control. My conscience was telling me that Tabitha had no control over her parents and I should not punish her for what her father did to my family. She was my friend, but I was about to unleash my venom on her. I felt guilty about my anger. I started to beat myself up for being angry with an innocent person, but I could not keep my eyes off her shoes—her pretty, expensive shoes. Her family was using money that my family should have had.

"Are you listening to me, Cheryl?"

"W . . . what? Sorry. I was thinking about something. What did you say?"

"I'm just so upset today. I don't think Mary is my friend anymore. She said that I'm not popular enough to hang out with her. She's trying to become homecoming queen."

I could not believe what I was hearing. My family was homeless and suffering because of her family, and she was whining about her popularity! I wanted to slap her and spit in her face. I wanted to punish her for what her father did to us. I wanted to make her feel some of the pain I was feeling.

"What are you talking about, Tabitha? I could care less about your popularity. What are you? Stupid? Who cares about your popularity? Who cares about your lack of friends? Who cares about the stupid things you are talking about? You are talking about stuff that has no importance in the real world. I don't care about your friends, about what you are wearing, or about the petty things you are talking about. In fact, I don't want to hear anymore of your stupid whining!"

I moved to another seat. I knew Tabitha was stunned, probably crying. I didn't care anymore. I had released my anger, but I felt awful. I began to quietly sob. Once I started to cry, I knew I would not be able to stop. Gayle always told me that only weak people cry, but the emotions were too strong. I began to yell at myself to stop crying. The more I yelled, the harder I cried. By the time I got to my first class, I was out of control.

The next thing I knew I was in the counselor's office with my head buried in my hands, wailing. After trying unsuccessfully to console me for several solid hours, my counselor called in the school psychologist. When the psychologist arrived, I spent the next four hours telling her my story.

The social work team went into action. My counselors visited my house and talked with my parents. One of the members of the intervention team knew Warren Moon, quarterback of the Houston Oilers at the time. Warren Moon offered to pay for an apartment for us while Dad looked for work.

Shortly after a year of moving into our new apartment, Dad lost his job and Mom had another breakdown. One day, my father opened the door to find two constables pushing their way inside, waving a piece of paper. We were being evicted again.

CRACK HOUSE

It took Dad a week and a half to find us a place to live. When the deadline for forcible eviction loomed, my stomach churned in nervous anxiety. I did not want to live in the car or hide out anymore.

Dad came home to tell us, "I found us a place to live. It's not a nice place, but it is all I can afford."

"Where is it?" Mom asked.

"It's right down the street. Let's start loading up the car and moving things. We don't have much time. I don't want to hear complaining when we get there. It's the best I could do."

Driving to the new apartment, I grew nervous because we were heading for a rough part of town. All the apartments in this area were in old, dilapidated buildings that probably were not up to building codes. When we drove by, I saw prostitutes and people pushing their belongings in shopping carts. Groups of menacing-looking men stood on the street corners watching and cursing people who passed by.

Dad drove into the parking lot of a large apartment building. The paint was peeling badly. Potholes riddled the parking lot and made the area look like a minefield. The building was shaped like a U with all the apartments facing the inner courtyard. To enter the courtyard, we went through one of two entrances that were long, enclosed walkways. Used drug paraphernalia and condoms littered the ground. The swimming pool in the middle of the courtyard was full of sludge and trash. People openly smoked marijuana; some crouched in the corners of their patios to smoke crack.

"Don't ever walk around here by yourself," Dad said to me.

"Don't worry," I said.

When we opened the door to our apartment, it smelled of mold. The brown carpet was matted with dirt. Brown sludge stood in the toilets, bathtubs, and sinks. Hundreds of roaches scurried along the floor as we walked inside. The walls were dingy with grime and mold. Mom let out a groan as she walked through the apartment. I could not believe that we had to live in a crack house, but it was better than living in the car or the storage facility.

No one said a word. Mom and Dad started unpacking the car. Mom pulled out her disinfectant and started sanitizing the apartment. For hours she cleaned the toilets, sinks, walls, and carpet. She fumigated the apartment to drive out the roaches. I helped her clean. It was the first time in a long time that I felt close to her.

Over the next several months, we made our apartment into a haven within the drug-infested complex. Every day, however, I needed my father's escort through the walkway to catch the school bus. I needed protection from the men who lined the courtyard and saw me as nothing more than fresh meat. Whenever I was home, I never looked outside the windows. I pretended we lived in a better place.

It was hard, however, because police sirens wailed constantly. There were always disturbances in the complex from drug busts, gunshots, yelling, and fighting. Domestic violence was rampant. Many times I would awaken to the sounds of a screaming woman being abused. While freebasing, crack addicts set the complex on fire twice.

I hated living in this apartment, but I had hope that my time in hell was ending. I was going to graduate soon and leave my parents behind. If I could hold out and not blow it, I would be free like Gayle. Even with this hope, I was terrified of the future. I believed my success depended solely upon me. If I failed in life, it would be my fault. If I could not break free of my parents, it would be my fault. If I did not learn how to control every aspect of my life, I would fail. Deep within my soul, I was a frightened little girl who felt alone in a mean world. I felt abandoned by God, who had yet to offer tangible hope that I could understand.

I began to panic when I realized that I was basing my hope on something my parents thought was capable of providing happiness, belonging, and security. If education and sheer will were my tickets to the promised land, why did they fail my parents? How could it be possible to believe in a future when everything in life told me that I would only fail? How could I believe that I would ever be something other than the messed-up, miserable, crippled black girl I saw in the mirror? I feared a person like me could never make it. Furthermore, I could not understand why my God of hope was still silent and distant. When would he deliver me?

My dear child, I know you do not know me, but I know everything about you. I have been with you since before you were born. I will never hide from you; you just cannot see clearly yet. I know how much you are struggling with the sorrow. It breaks my heart to see my dear, sweet child in so much pain. I feel you grasping for me, and I hear your groans. I have not abandoned you. While you were still in your mother's arms, I was teaching you to trust me. I have been helping you grow all your life. The time has come for you to see your Daddy's face and hear my voice.

I have searched your heart, and I know what is on your mind. I know you are feeling the pressure of trying to save yourself by your own strength. I will teach you to depend on me for your strength because nothing is too hard for me. I will teach you how to find everlasting confidence and peace about your past, present, and future. I promise to turn your mourning into gladness and comfort you when you are depressed. There is hope for your future, my child. There is hope because I hold your future in my hands.

I have sent someone who will help you come to know me. A time is coming when you will know me and trust me as your Daddy. I have never stopped loving you. I know you think that I am punishing you by withholding my love. When you fall in love with me, I promise to wash away that spirit of fear and fill you with a peace that passes all understanding. It is time for you to come home to me. Listen, I am calling your name. I am showing you the way.

CHAPTER SEVEN

Somebody's Calling My Name

Hush, hush, somebody's calling my name.
Hush, hush, somebody's calling my name.
Oh my Lord, oh my Lord, what will I do?

NEGRO SPIRITUAL

I was seventeen when I felt the full weight of the fear that God had abandoned me. I was tired of believing that the God of hope would deliver me. He was ignoring me. As soon as my fingers loosened on this sustaining hope, I began sinking into the quicksand of despair. I always heard that thrashing about was the surest way to suffocate in quicksand. So I was numb and still, yet dying inside as hopelessness engulfed me. My thoughts were like bricks hastening my drowning. I could not shake my new best friend: loneliness. I was having night-mares about permanent loneliness and abandonment from a month of living alone while Mom was recovering in the hospital from another mental breakdown and Dad was hospitalized after a mild heart attack.

I will never forget the sinking feeling in my heart when Dad's coworker told me that Dad had collapsed and been rushed to the hospital. My first reaction was not concern for his health; it was panic for my own welfare. If Dad died, no one would be there to take care of me. I realized that Dad had not done the best job of providing for me, but at least I had not been alone. Even though I could not trust Dad anymore, I realized that if he died, I would be alone forever.

The brick that did me in was anticlimactic. I received my first D. I almost flunked a test and felt as if I had been diagnosed with terminal cancer. I started to panic and my mind began racing. I thought of all the ways I would fail in life and die alone. I remember saying to myself, "I give up." Life was too hard, and I'd had enough. If I were stronger emotionally, I could have placed the grade in perspective. After years of struggling, however, I asked a question for which I did not have an answer: "Does my life matter?" When I could not answer, I felt as if my fingers let go of my hold on hope one by one. As I began to suffocate in despair, I would stop at nothing to end the excruciating pain of my empty soul. The agony drove me to a horrible choice.

SOFTLY AND TENDERLY

Most people think the face of suicide is grim and dark, but it is not. It is more like a lying mask of contentment. Once I finished my suicide plan, my face suddenly showed happiness and relief. I thought I was going to buy my own freedom. I could identify with the slaves when they sang about the ultimate act to obtain their freedom. I could hear their singing, "Before I'd be a slave, they'd bury me in my grave." I could never remember the entire song, but that phrase always haunted me. I was fed up with life's misery enslaving me.

I had the same simple plan. I would hasten my freedom. When I returned home from school that day, the house would be empty. Mom would be away at a funeral, and Dad would be at work. I had five hours to complete the job. Mom never threw away her old antipsychotic medication, for which I now found a use. I had already counted 100 pills, crushed them, and placed the powder in an envelope in my drawer. I would pour a glass of milk, stir in the powder, and lie on my bed for my final sleep. My plan was perfect. For the first time in years, I felt a somber, yet empty, peace.

My day at school was uneventful. By the final class, I began rehearsing my suicide plan in my head. Monica, the class clown, sat next to me and smiled. I liked her, but she had never spoken to me before. Monica was a popular girl who hung around another popular girl named Denise. They were inseparable, and I always envied the closeness of their relationship. They looked like sisters. I would find myself staring at them in the halls, during class, or on field trips. Gayle and I used to be that close.

"I just noticed that you look so sad and was wondering why," Monica said.

"Nothing is wrong with me."

"Doesn't look like nothing is wrong."

"Leave me alone. OK?" I said.

Monica looked in my eyes. It was as though she knew that I was planning to check out. "It looks like you need a friend to talk to right now."

I looked at her suspiciously. I wondered why she was pushing so hard to be my friend. "Why do you care?"

"Because I like you, and I miss seeing your smile."

I stared at Monica, looking for a hint of insincerity in her face and body language. Like a rushing wind, I felt something inside tell me to open my heart to her. Nevertheless, I did not want to trust anyone, so I decided to test her by dumping my life's story on her. If she walked away and began avoiding me, I would know that she was a fake. I described to her why my life was hell and then waited for her response.

"Hmmm, so you feel like no one cares about you?"

"I know that no one cares about me."

"What about God? Do you feel like he doesn't care about you?"

I groaned and rolled my eyes. I was tired of religious people claiming to be in good with God. I vowed that if she started to preach to me, I would leave.

"God cares about you. He loves you."

I bristled at the cliché Christian. I told Monica that I did not need a stranger telling me how loving God was because if he loved me, then I would not be living in a crack house with a messed-up life.

"I can see that you are angry with him. I also sense that deep down inside you want a personal relationship with him so that you can hear him talk to you. I have some friends who can help you," Monica said.

"No one can help me."

"Then you have nothing to lose by meeting them."

Monica was right. Although I was angry and frustrated with God, I wanted him to help me. Instead of going home that day, I went with Monica to Denise's house for dinner. I still could not discern God's whispers, but I felt compelled to find out if Monica's friends could help me talk to God. My body was responding as if it could sense that someone was calling my name.

Cheryl, this moment did not happen by accident. I knew you would be making this horrible choice, and I am calling you away from it. I know you have been seeking me and reaching out for my hand. Now you will know that I have never been far away.

WE ARE FAMILY

I learned about God over family meals and bowling. Denise's family adopted me and began teaching me about God indirectly. I was mesmerized by the love displayed in the family. Mr. Hall was a quiet yet strong man who cracked dry jokes that were so bad, they made me laugh. Mrs. Hall was a spitfire. She was a vocal, no-nonsense person who was slow to speak but sharp and funny. Her jokes always hit the mark, and everyone would squirm in their chairs in laughter. Karen, Denise's younger sister, was the family clown and actress. She lived for laughs. I had never laughed so much in my life.

I spent most afternoons and every Sunday at the Halls' house. Although they knew I was searching for answers in life, they never made a hard religious sell. God became the subject of conversations naturally over family meals. They always discussed the Sunday sermon, inviting me to speak and ask questions. I mostly listened to their passionate debates over the meaning of the lesson and its implication for their lives. Sometimes family members would disagree about something the minister said. Although they debated their opinions, they never yelled or grew angry with each other. Once Denise disagreed with Mrs. Hall in a tone that she thought was disrespectful. Even when they disciplined Denise or Karen, Mr. and Mrs. Hall exuded love and respect. I wanted them to legally adopt me.

Denise introduced me to her youth group's bowling and Bible study night. I stank at bowling; I was queen of the gutter ball. No one cared. The youth group bowled strictly for fun and cared more about bonding between the members. Fifteen teens gathered every week to share pizza, bowling, and life. The first night I went bowling with them, one of the teens told the group that her boyfriend had assaulted her. When she started crying, the group quickly rose and circled her. Each person hugged her, and the youth minister started to pray as she cried. I was uncomfortable and intrigued at the same time; the praying made me uncomfortable, but the hugs and acceptance from the group touched me. The youth minister started talking about the Bible, but I tuned out. I started to wonder how I could become one of them. I wanted to be a part of something built on love and acceptance.

After weeks of bowling and Sunday meals, I mustered enough courage to ask my first question: "Mrs. Hall, how can I find out if God loves me?"

Mrs. Hall stopped preparing the meal to sit at the table next to me. "Why do you feel like God doesn't love you?"

"My life is miserable, and I want to find out what I did wrong to make God hate me so much."

"God does not hate you."

"It feels like he does. Why else would he allow the disability, abuse, and all the other misery? My parents used to say that I'm special to God, but I don't feel special."

"Being special does not mean that God will make your life easier or even stop all the pain. God made you for a reason. Here, I want you to read this passage in the Bible. People tend to blame everything bad in life on sin. The people back in the Bible did the same thing to this man born blind. The leaders asked Jesus who sinned so that the man was born blind. Was it the parents or the man himself? What did Jesus say?"

"He said that neither the man nor his parents sinned."

"Yes, Cheryl, Jesus said that his blindness happened so that the power and glory of God would be displayed in this man's life. Now, mind you that Jesus is using this as a metaphor for another spiritual lesson, but there is some application here for you. God will work in everything that has happened to you to reveal his power."

"How? I don't understand how he can make this hell into something good."

"That is why he is God—nothing is impossible for him. You just need to believe and have faith," she said.

"I want to believe, but how can I believe when nothing in my life says that God would do anything special for me?"

"He will, sweetie. Having a personal relationship with him will help you see his mighty hand at work in your life. Don't get bogged down trying to understand everything. You need to step out on faith, and God will help you develop more faith in him."

"It's scary to trust in something you can't see," I said.

"That's why it's called faith. But God will help you know that everything he promised is true. Keep searching and start praying to God." At that moment Mrs. Hall asked me to pray to God. I was scared. I wanted to believe that my God of hope would finally speak to me, but he had been silent for my entire life. Why would he talk to me now?

"Dear God, I don't know if you are listening to me, but I'm asking for you to help me. I want to hear you and feel you in my life. I want to know that you love me. I don't feel that you care. What do I need to do to make you love me? What did I do to make you so mad at me? I think I could stand being yelled at—at least you would be talking to me. But I'm having trouble with you ignoring me. Please talk to me and tell me what I did so wrong that you hate me so much—"

My voice cracked, and I started to cry. It was the first time I told anyone that I thought God was punishing me. Could it have been my fault that bad things always happened to me?

Mrs. Hall took my hand and squeezed it. She whispered, "Don't try to talk, sweetie. God knows your heart, and your cries go up to his ears as prayers. He will wipe away your tears and heal your wounds. He is so proud of you. Praying to him—although you do not understand him—sweetie, that is a powerful act of faith. Keep reaching out for him. God is near."

Although I did not understand everything Mrs. Hall told me, I felt a rush of security and love when she placed her arms around me. I never wanted to let go.

My child, the peace and security you feel comes from me. I am gathering you in my arms, holding you close to my heart, and leading you to me. I promise to show you the way to peace and security in your life. I will teach you to hope in me so that you will run and not get weary, that you will walk and not faint. Keep listening for my voice. Soon you will hear me clearly. I'm calling you home.

SINNER MAN

It was tough convincing me, a lifelong victim, that I was a sinner. Sin was something that people did to me. Sinners were murderers, child abusers, and sociopaths. I was the victim. I was too young to do anything bad enough to be considered sin. I was a good person. My adopted family was trying to convince me that it was my fault God was distant from me. I kept telling them that I had not done anything wrong.

It was easy to convince me that I did not deserve God's love because my self-esteem had been shattered early. I believed that I was worthless. But I resisted my new family members' efforts to explain sin to me because I had always held to one fact: I was a good person and everyone else was bad. I remember raising my voice to them, saying, "I never did anything wrong to hurt God. He's hurting me!" My statement reflected the self-centeredness my legacy of abuse and family dysfunction had given me. My life consisted of protecting myself, thinking about myself, moaning about myself, and licking my wounds. I viewed life with me as the center of attention, and I was angry that my new family was trying to shake my comfortable foundation.

Everyone backed off when I became defensive. Mr. Hall drove me home without saying anything. As I walked to my front door, he gave me some books about sin that he asked me to read. I promised I would try to read them. I lied because I knew I could not read anything that would try to tell me I was a bad person.

Instead, I picked up a book exploring the nature of God. I opened my Bible and read about his holiness. Seeing all the standards and laws God had for his children, I decided to list all the ones I upheld. I wanted to prove to the Hall family that I was a good person. Although I was not a murderer, abuser, or degenerate, I saw other ways I failed to meet God's perfect standards for my life. For instance, my list revealed that I was a liar. I lied all the time to protect myself or for my benefit. I cursed routinely. The hatred toward my parents was festering in my soul. I gossiped. And the list continued.

When I finished my list, I started crying. I held proof in my hand that I was a sinner; I had failed to live my life at the level God expected. I knew that God, being holy and perfect, could not be close to anything unholy and imperfect. I felt it was my fault that God was distant from me. I decided to clean up my act. I had to make myself presentable to God.

So I tried to stop cursing; I failed in three hours. I tried to force the hateful thoughts about my father out of my mind; that night Dad had one of his special talks with me, and I felt dirty and wished him to hell. After two days of trying to be holy, I gave up in frustration. The more I tried to be holy, the worse I became. "Dear God," I prayed, "this seems so unfair to me. How am I supposed to be clean enough to be with you? I'm getting frustrated. This seems impossible."

I called Mr. Hall the next day in frustration. "OK, I give up. I am a sinner and separated from God. Now what? What can I do to be with God? I don't want to live forever like this. I can't take the pain and emptiness anymore."

Mr. Hall told me that it was time to meet the One who could save me from eternal separation from God, the One who gave me the privilege to stand confidently before God, my heavenly Father. I already knew about Jesus, but I did not know him or why he was significant. I sang songs about him when I played my slave songs and gospel music; I read about him in many of the Civil Rights era biographies. I could not explain why or how I believed that Jesus was God's Son who died and rose again, but I believed it. I did not know anything about why his birth, life, death, and resurrection were important. Over the next several days, the Hall family and I studied the Bible, prayed, and talked about Jesus and God. I had found the missing piece I was searching for all my life. I found the way to God.

My child, I would like to introduce you to my Son, Jesus, whom I love dearly—just as I love you. I know that you struggle with living up to my will for your life. It grieves my heart that you and I cannot be together as I have always desired. I am proud of you for realizing that without me you are powerless to bring about the perfection and purity I desire in your life. I am now calling you to depend on me to mold you into the person I designed you to be. Look at my Son and you will see me. Examine and follow his life and you will understand that he is proof of my love for you. I know that by yourself you could never stop sinning against me, that you could never be able to rest in my arms. I am not counting all the times you fail to measure up because I love you. I have provided a way for you to see my face and be with me forever. I sacrificed my own Son's life to insure that if you believe in him, there will be nothing to stop your coming home to me. I did not hold back anything to provide you with the way home. There is nothing else I could do to show you more how much I love you.

My child, you have a choice. I offer you a gift in my son, Jesus. If you accept this gift, nothing will ever separate us again. It is time for you to come home to me. After the party I will throw for you among the angels, I will rock you in my arms and guide you in your life. As your Father, I have carried you through hell to bring you to myself. Nothing will ever change the fact that I am your Father for all eternity, but you now have to choose whether to you want to be my precious and treasured child.

Life with God for eternity or life without him. The better choice was obvious. I wanted to be God's child. I wanted a family, peace, and hope.

BATTLE LINES

I hoped that salvation would include a physical component. I wanted eternal life with God, but I also wanted a calm, peaceful life on earth. Looking back, I wish I had told someone about that misguided hope. Becoming a child of God did not mean my life would be free of suffering, but that God would bring peace in the midst of suffering. I would struggle for many years over why I could not live a spiritually and physically peaceful life. I should have known that my new life as God's child would be more like a battle when I broke ranks with my Dad's cultlike authority.

When it was time for my baptism, I was scared to tell Dad. I grew up being Dad's most trusted disciple. He pinned his worth as God's chosen one on my belief in him. I was about to forsake him. I was about to publicly announce that I had my own relationship with God and no longer believed that Dad's visions and teachings were my way to God. I did not know what Dad would do if he felt I betrayed him. The first thing I learned was that committing my life to God would cost me comfort as I began to fear possible retribution from Dad.

"Dad, I want to tell you something before I go to school."

"What is it?"

"Well, over the course of several months, I've been studying the Bible on my own."

Dad, puzzled, looked up from reading the newspaper. "What are you talking about, Cheryl?"

"I'm going to be baptized on Sunday."

"What?" Dad jumped off the couch and rushed toward me.

"I want my own relationship with him. I've been studying and praying on my own. I've learned that I don't need to go through another person to talk to God. I have my own relationship with God, and I just want you to be happy for me—"

"I forbid it! Is that what that Denise girl has been doing to you all the times you've been over at her house? Is she trying to get you in a cult? I forbid it!" Dad said I had to honor and obey him because he was my father. He said the Bible gave him that authority over me.

"In this case, I don't think you are right, Dad."

"Don't you take that tone with me! I forbid it and that's that. Go to school. I'm not walking you to the bus stop. Go by yourself and see how far you get without me."

I left the house confused. I could not understand how my own father could forbid me from being baptized. I could not understand why Dad, a supposed follower of God, would be angry with me. I was hurt that Dad's anger left me vulnerable to the drug addicts who lived in my apartment complex.

Do not be afraid, Cheryl. I am with you. Just have faith in me.

I walked down the enclosed courtyard, past the men standing around smoking and drinking beer. I was so absorbed with my thoughts that I barely noticed the lewd gestures they made as I walked by. When I arrived at school, I immediately searched out Denise. I needed answers. Denise called her parents and told them what happened. Both of them met us at school for lunch.

"Well, Cheryl, the Bible is explicit about honoring your mother and father. But it is equally explicit about obeying Christ even if it means going against the commands of your parents. Your father is in error in light of what God says in the Bible," Mr. Hall said.

"That's what I felt too."

"Jesus said, 'He who honors father and mother more than me is not worthy of me.' There is the biblical authority for what you know you must do. This is the most important thing you will do in your life. This decision has eternal consequences. You must stand against your father on this issue."

When I returned home, I did not bring up the issue until Saturday night. "Dad, I'm going to be baptized tomorrow at church. I'm sorry that you don't agree with my decision, but I have to obey God over anyone else, including my parents."

"I'm not driving you there."

"I'm sorry you feel so strongly against it. I have a way there."

"I forbid anybody from that church in this house!" Dad said.

"I'll meet them at the car."

"I won't walk you outside."

"I'll be OK. God will protect me."

My journey to find God was remarkable. I wanted to know him and ask why he created me. I needed to know why I was born and where my life was going. I needed to know my purpose and future.

When I was younger, I wanted to tell him that I was not a bad person—that I never did anything to him. I was preoccupied with God's delivering me from earthly sorrow. Although God had finally broken my father's spiritual hold on me, I needed to unlearn much of his teachings. I had a future and a purpose, but God would test my faith, build it up, and refine it through more trials. God would help me grow in my faith, and I would come to learn the meaning of bearing my cross.

Come, Cheryl, follow me. You now have to learn how to trust me. Tough times are coming, but I am telling you now that you do not have to worry about your life, what you will eat or drink, or about your body, what you will wear. I know what you need. I want you to keep trusting me and following my guidance—I will take care of everything you need. You will come to understand that following me is not going to mean you will not suffer or have conflicts. It will take time for you to understand what I am teaching you, but I know you will remain in my arms. Sweetheart, I want you to tell others about me and show them the way home to me. I will guide you, helping you know what to say. Do not be afraid. I am with you. I am your Daddy and you are my child.

PART THREE

Godspot

A brother will let go of your hand. A
* sister will seldom understand.*
A mother can't always dry your tears.
* A father at times can't be there.*
And even your best friend, it seems
* can't be found.*
There's Jesus, He'll never let you
* down.*
When your house just don't seem like
* a home. Family is all around you,*
* yet you're alone.*
The phone rings, but there's no good
* news. Everything is wrong no*
* matter what you do.*
And even the happiest people are
* wearing a frown.*

Hold on. There's Jesus and he'll never
    let you down.
He'll go with you through the storm,
Through the rain,
Through sickness,
Through pain.
The Lord will never let you down.
He'll never let you down.
I know you been hurt.
You might have been abused.
You may have been mistreated.
Sometimes we get misused.
But the Lord won't ever let you down.

S. ROBERTS, S.R. MUSIC (SESAC)

CHAPTER EIGHT

Family

> Swing low, sweet chariot,
> Comin' for to carry me home.
> Swing low, sweet chariot,
> Comin' for to carry me home.
> I looked over Jordan and what did I see,
> Comin' for to carry me home;
> A band of angels comin' after me,
> Comin' for to carry me home.
>
> NEGRO SPIRITUAL

When my sister was in high school, I went to her choir's production of the African-American version of *The Wizard of Oz* called *The Wiz*. At the end of the musical, instead of Dorothy singing "Somewhere over the Rainbow," she sang "Home." I do not think there is an African-American around who is not moved by this gospel-influenced song longing for home. The Dorothy in my sister's musical had a powerful voice; she brought the audience to tears. The song hooked me at the beginning: "When I think of home, I think of a place where there is love overflowing. . . ." I stopped caring about controlling my emotions when Dorothy reached the climax of the song and sang, "If you're listening, God, please don't make it hard for me to believe in the things that I see." My sister and I had spent many years dreaming about what made a real home. I also wondered why God made home so elusive.

Gayle and I had definite ideas about what we wanted in a home. I used to say that I would be happy just to fuss with my parents about curfew or the purchase of a new outfit. Gayle simply wanted parents who did not hit her and would listen to her. Mom and Dad told me that when I was seven, I asked them, "Why is there no love in this house?" They used to bring it up to prove that I was too emotionally sensitive. I *was* sensitive—I knew something was missing in our house. I knew that we did not have a home, and I was longing for one.

The closest I came to home was my relationship with my sister. We started out rocky. Gayle never liked me because she felt Mom and Dad loved me more. I did not like her either because I thought her life was better. After all, she was not disabled and had Mom and Dad all the time while I was in the hospital. The only time we joined forces was when Mom started abusing Gayle. I could always distract Mom by falling down and crying. By the time I was nine, Gayle and I had developed an unusual relationship. In public, she was more like my surrogate mother. She always protected me and stood up for me whenever someone started harassing me. At home, she and I were aggressive toward each other.

One of our most violent fights happened after Mom and Gayle returned home from shopping for clothes. I always made an excuse to stay home when they went shopping because Mom used to humiliate Gayle about her weight and size in public. Instead of buying Gayle clothes in the juniors section, Mom would force her to try on clothes that were too small. She would loudly tell Gayle, "I'm not the one forcing food down your throat. It's not my fault we can't find clothes to fit your fat behind." Despite the fact that I did not like Gayle, when Mom berated her in public, I felt humiliated and embarrassed too.

My sister began to resent me because she felt that my disability allowed me to escape the abuse she received. I told her we could switch places if she thought being me was such a picnic. Gayle called me a spoiled brat and said that I needed to be spanked more. Before I could respond, she grabbed me, pulled me across her knees, and began to hit me. When I broke free from her, I was enraged.

I turned toward her and punched her in the stomach. Gayle vomited. When she rose to her feet, she slapped me. We started exchanging punches as we backed toward the bathroom. Once I had her cornered in the bathroom, I pushed her and she fell backward. The sharp edge of a broken bathroom trash can stuck in her leg. She started screaming and pulled herself off the trash can.

"When I get my hands on you—!" Gayle screamed.

I ran into my bedroom and locked the door. That was the last major fight my sister and I had. Shortly thereafter, Dad lost his job and Mom suffered from full-blown mental illness. Gayle and I began to realize that we were all we had in the world.

In retrospect, I can understand the relationship my sister and I shared. Gayle felt our family had a double standard. From her perspective, Mom and Dad required her to do all the chores, take all Mom's abuse, and take care of me. She felt that Mom and Dad treated me gingerly because I was disabled. Whenever we fought, she always screamed that she was tired of their loving me more. She constantly recounted the times she sat alone in hospital waiting rooms while Mom and Dad visited me. Looking back, I am sure that when Gayle was little, an hour waiting alone in a big scary hospital must have seemed like an eternity.

Another problem for Gayle was stigma by association. Simply because she was my sister, Gayle shared the effects of my disability. Kids at school and in the neighborhood avoided her just as they avoided me. She was teased and harassed simply because she was my sister. My parents did not have a clue that Gayle was being ridiculed and shunned because of my disability. I know they talked to her about racism, but they never prepared her for people rejecting her because of my disability. So it was natural that Gayle began to resent me. Nevertheless, she still protected me in public. Our relationship was full of mixed emotions. We teetered between love and hate, competition and devotion.

I remember watching Alex Haley's *Roots* on television when I was about seven or eight. Many scenes in the movie struck me, but one of them left a lasting impression. Kizzy, a female slave, had been raped repeatedly by her master. When she and her fiancé were talking about the rapes, Kizzy said, "Massa may have power over my body, but he can't steal my spirit." I immediately thought of Gayle's first lesson to me.

Gayle could take a beating from my parents like a slave. With every lash, she would grit her teeth and will herself to show no emotion. If a moan escaped her mouth, she would quickly stifle it. My sister never cried. In the face of verbal or physical assaults, she wore a face of stone. Often my parents made me watch them discipline Gayle so that I could learn from her mistakes. Although it was a humiliating experience for both of us, I was fascinated by Gayle's strength. I was intrigued by her eyes. No matter how hard the blow, her eyes never closed and never welled with tears. All I saw were eyes of fury.

"Are you through?" my sister often asked during pauses in the blows.

Her act of defiance and resolve only enraged my parents more. They would change to a switch or extension cord or increase the intensity of the blows. I marveled at my sister's stupidity and strength. I could not understand how she could knowingly say something that would provoke my parents into stepping up the beating. I also could not understand how she could control her emotions. My sister was my hero. I wanted to be strong like her.

"I don't understand you, Gayle. Why do you refuse to cry?"

"You can't cry in front of people. If you do, then you let them have power over you."

"How can you stop from crying when things hurt?"

"Bite your lip, clench your fist, or think of beating up whoever is hurting you. The bottom line is that you have to draw power from the pain and use that power to show how strong you are," she told me.

"Why do you say such stupid stuff that gets you in more trouble when they start hitting you?" I asked.

"I just want them to know that no matter what they do to me, they will never break me down. I will never let them have power over me."

Another key to Gayle's ability to control her emotions was her intense desire to be free. She began counting down the days to her eighteenth birthday. She always said that when she graduated from high school, she would leave and never return. I asked her if she thought our parents loved us. Gayle told me to never worry about whether or not someone loves you. "It will eat you up. People only care about themselves, so don't expect anybody to love you. The more you want people to love you, the more power you give them to hurt you."

My love for Gayle and dependence on her strength intensified after Mom tried to kill me. I remember thinking I would have been dead if Gayle had not been there to rescue me. I wanted to be with her forever. Gayle's desire to be free, however, took precedence over her feelings of responsibility for my welfare. Gayle knew that education would be her ticket to freedom. She was looking for the promised land too. Her sense of freedom had less to do with racial equality or financial security than the desire to escape the assaults. The anger and hatred she felt toward our parents could have destroyed her, but she channeled the energy into school.

A guidance counselor told her that as a poor African-American with good grades, she would not have to worry about obtaining a college scholarship. My sister made me proud when she became senior class president and graduated at the top of her class with honors. She was also the first person in our predominately low-income, African-American school to be accepted to Yale University. When I looked in her eyes as she read her college acceptance letters, spoke before her graduating class, and packed her clothes for college, I saw a slave proudly holding her papers attesting to her new status as a free person. But that freedom came with a price: my sister had to leave me behind.

"But what about me? What will happen to me when you leave?" I remember asking her.

Gayle would not look at me to reply. "Cheryl, I have to go to college."

"You can go to a college nearby, and we could live together. I don't want you to leave me here by myself. Who's going to protect me?"

"You are strong enough to protect yourself. I can't be with you forever. You just have to learn how to rely on yourself. Mom and Dad can barely take care of themselves, so just depend on yourself. I have to get away from here. If I stay, I'm never going to be anything. I'll be just like them and I'll die. I'm sorry, but I have to go away. I need to live my own life."

I began to distance myself from Gayle emotionally. I had to learn how to live on my own, so I stopped asking her questions and looking to her for advice. Since she had a boyfriend, they spent most of their free time together doing activities away from the house. I spent most of my time studying and daydreaming about where I would go to college—to freedom. Instead of crying about her leaving and begging her to take me with her, it was easier to be angry and tell myself that I did not care about her.

We drove Gayle to Connecticut for the start of her freshman year at Yale. When it was time for us to return home, I could tell she was having mixed emotions. She was happy to be free but sad that she was leaving me behind. I could see the regret in her eyes. We hugged, and I got in the car to leave. I did not cry. I learned my lesson from Gayle—I wore my stone face. I did not know when I would see her again.

When my parents and I returned to Houston, we quickly plunged into homelessness and poverty. Gayle and I could not contact each other. My sister had been my sense of home, and when she left, the void I felt was transformed into a bottomless pit of need. I needed a home—a place overflowing with love.

ADOPTION

I understand how it feels to be an older child waiting for adoption. By the time I reached seventeen, it had been almost three years since I had seen my sister. I would dream about how perfect her life must be at college. Gayle and I differed in our longings. She wanted to be free from our parents' tyranny; I wanted freedom and a sense of belonging—a home.

The longer I waited for a home, the more cynical I became. It was evident that no one wanted me. The Hall family and the South Street Church felt like a family for a short time after I became a child of God. Everyone hugged and kissed me, telling me that I was now an adopted member of God's family—a family that included millions of people all over the world. God, as my Father, told all his children to love one another and be there for each other. I was excited. There was hope that this new family could fill that awful void in my life.

It was difficult for me, an older "adopted" child blending into the family. I was preconditioned to believe that if I allowed myself to get too close to people, they would either hurt or leave me. My fear of rejection was the greatest burden I had. I was hypervigilant of any sign that someone was pulling away. Whenever I saw a sign of impending rejection, I bolted first.

After becoming a Christian, I thought that Monica and Denise would allow me into their tightly woven circle of friendship. They looked and acted like sisters; now that I was a new member of the family, I felt that I could substitute them for Gayle. I do not know if it was my paranoia or reality, but after I was baptized, I felt Denise stopped paying attention to me. Before baptism, I was always at her house. After baptism, the invitations slowed. Whenever Monica was present, the two of them shared inside jokes, laughing raucously. They had nicknames for each other and always talked about things they had done together. I am sure they did not change all of a sudden, but my expectations had changed.

Before my spiritual adoption, I merely hoped to become a member of their intimate friendship. Now that I was adopted, I expected my insider's card and was hurt that it never came. Each time Monica and Denise excluded me from their inside jokes, it hurt. They did not realize the emotional bond I felt with them. Since they had helped me find God, I was grateful and hopeful that we would be closer as a result.

One day they started talking to a new girl at our school. The following Sunday I overheard them asking her over to the Hall house for dinner. I suddenly felt like old news. Monica and the Hall family were moving on to find another child. I felt like I was a notch on their Christian-making belt. Once I became a Christian, I felt they abandoned me. I cannot determine whether my feelings were justified or not, but to protect myself, I pulled away from Monica, Denise, and the others in the Hall family. I had trained myself to allow only one hurt per person.

Being a member of a new family centered on learning how to trust again. One of the biggest problems of adopted children is the fear of being rejected by the new family. I was afraid God would do the same to me. Although I read the Bible and heard him say many times that he would never leave, it was too scary to believe. If he failed me only once, I could no longer believe in him—and if I did not believe in him, I would have no hope left. Without hope, I would be back to the pills and plotting a way to kill myself. Trust, however, could not be developed until my faith was tested and refined.

I wanted to trust God, but I was more afraid that he would do something to hurt me. I started to play an approach-avoidance dance with God; each time I ran toward him for intimacy, my fears would trigger me to push away. Trust in God would not develop instantaneously. I had more to learn about my new Father.

LOST AND FOUND

Despite being a member of God's family, I missed Gayle. When I could not develop a sister relationship with Monica or Denise, I focused more attention on finding a way to be with Gayle again. Following her example, I believed education would be my ticket to freedom. I, too, would graduate at the top of my class with honors. The acceptance letters to colleges began streaming in, but I was waiting on only one: Yale. When I was accepted to Yale and made plans to reunite with my sister, I felt my sense of home had returned. Gayle and I would be together again, both of us free.

Three years had changed us. I was no longer the overtly emotional girl who looked to Gayle as protector. I had survived homelessness, poverty, and living in a crack house. Although I was still young in my faith, I had a radiant hope that he was changing me and making my life into something better than I could imagine. Gayle, however, was the same. Freedom did not bring her happiness. She was still the stony-faced stoic who kept everyone at bay. She did not know that freedom meant more than living apart from our parents. Freedom meant coming home to God.

Within a month of my arriving on campus, my sister began noticing my love and confidence in God. She noticed that I went to church on Sundays and studied my Bible regularly. I was not a "holier than thou" Christian; a curse word would slip in periodically, and I would struggle with anger at inconsiderate and offensive people on campus. Whenever I slipped, I was honest with Gayle and apologized to her. I never made a big deal about her needing a personal relationship with God. I never made a hard sell. If Gayle came home to God, it would happen because I loved her enough not to push.

I knew she was looking at me to see if God had made any difference in my life. In the eight months since my conversion, I would often wonder if I looked any different on the outside. Internally, I hoped my life would turn out to be something. I could feel God listening and talking to me; that feeling made the strongest impact in my life. I could not take being ignored. It didn't matter so much what a person said, as long as what I said was acknowledged. Love, to me, meant listening and responding. When I looked at my sister, I saw a big tough girl who was scared to admit that she needed to be loved. To her, needing anything was an admission of weakness.

"Why did you become a Christian?" Gayle asked.

"Because I wanted my own relationship with God. I was tired of Dad telling me what God's plans for us were. I wanted to talk to him myself. I wanted to feel him in my life and know that he loves me."

"Dad used to make me sick with all that God stuff. He talked so holy, yet he did so much bad stuff." Gayle said.

"Well, that was Dad. It has nothing to do with God and you."

"What about God and me?" Gayle asked. She knew about God and Jesus. She also believed in the Bible. I did not have to start proving God, Jesus, or the Bible to her.

I pulled out some of the booklets I used to gain a clearer understanding of God. I tried to appeal to Gayle's need for love, but she was not interested. She rolled her eyes each time I talked about love. I quickly realized that I needed to tailor my discussions with her according to her needs, not mine. I spent time listening to her. Gayle had the same stumbling block I did: how can lifelong victims do anything bad enough to be separated from God? She also thought that she was a good person because she was not an abuser; therefore, she was good enough to be with God.

I asked her to study the holiness of God, then see how she compared, as I had done. Gayle's list of sins astounded her. Some of them made her feel ashamed. She came back to me asking, "I guess I'm not so good, after all. So I'm going to hell?"

I wanted my sister to run to God's loving arms, not merely run away from hell. Gayle, however, was more motivated by the fear of punishment. She decided to become a child of God to escape the threat of hell, that fiery pit of wailing and pain. Regardless of her reason, I was happy that she wanted to be a part of my spiritual family. I thought that she and I could build the home we had always dreamed of.

After Gayle became a Christian, I was protective of her. I knew her starting point in faith and I wanted us to explore God's love together, rather than focusing so much on his judgment. She and I would spend most of our free time together, either focused on spiritual matters or catching up on our three years apart. She and I grew closer than we had ever been before. My sense of family was restored, and for a brief time, I thought my void was filled.

I did not realize that my search for an earthly home had superseded my search for the promised land. I thought I would fill the void by becoming a child of God, but I was acting as if that were not enough to satisfy my soul. I was searching for a tangible manifestation of my lifelong dreams. I wanted a human mother, father, and sibling; I also wanted my own husband and children. I was searching for all of these people within the churches I attended. I could not make Monica and Denise my siblings, but now I had my own sister. I would spend years trying to fill the other roles in my patchwork family. I was clueless that I was searching to fill my void with something that could never last or fill me completely. I was on a path toward the wrong promised land.

NOT IN MY HOUSE

I remember when I discovered that God's family was not perfect. It was a week after Gayle was baptized at the African-American church we attended near campus. Yale was located in a predominately poor, African-American urban center. There were tensions between the Yale community and city residents; most problems centered on economic disparities between the two camps.

When around African-American residents, my sister and I purposely avoided many conversations that steered toward Yale or anything remotely considered "white-folk" topics. There was always a presumption that because we attended Yale, we were from privileged backgrounds far removed from the "real" African-American community. To gain acceptance among many of the residents, my sister and I had to emphasize our disadvantaged upbringing. We had to wear our poverty like a badge of honor when we were around them. If we did not, they avoided us.

I never expected the tensions of prejudice to spill over in my church family. Although I had been attending my congregation since arriving at Yale, I had not interacted much with the members. I must have feared the congregation would reject me because I never told anyone I went to Yale. After Gayle's baptism, she told everyone we were students at Yale. The older members expressed their pride in us and commented how proud Martin Luther King Jr. would be. The younger members—most of the church—however, distanced themselves from us. No one invited us to lunch. No one called. No one hugged us. No one conversed with us after church. People avoided us as if we had a scarlet letter *Y* stamped on our foreheads.

"Cheryl, why won't folks talk to us?"

"I don't know. I think that the avoidance of Yale people has crept into the church, and we are outcasts."

"That's not very loving," Gayle muttered.

"I know. Don't worry about it, and don't let it weaken your faith in God. People have a way of messing up everything God intends to be perfect."

Gayle and I thought about leaving the congregation after members began telling us that because we went to Yale, we did not know what it was like to be African-American. "The stuff you share in Bible class just doesn't hit home with many folks," said Brother Gray in front of class.

"What are you talking about? I'm not saying anything fancy," I replied.

"Well, everyone can't go to Yale and live a life like you. Folks here come from bad homes and live from paycheck to paycheck."

"Are you insinuating that to be African-American I have to prove it by detailing my disadvantaged background?" I asked.

"I'm just saying that no one can relate to you and Gayle."

"You folks are just as bad as white people who stereotype us. How dare you assume that you know us just by where we go to school? I would think that you should be proud of a sister going to a predominately white campus, proving to the world that African-Americans aren't inferior to whites. No, all I have gotten since the first day in this town is an attitude that only poor African-Americans are true African-Americans."

Brother Gray had the gall to tell us that since he believed we grew up with money and lived in luxury, we did not know what it meant to be one of them. He thought the things we commented on in church revealed how out of touch we were with the issues of the African-American community. Upon hearing that, my protective instinct kicked in, and I told Gayle that we would leave the congregation. I refused to argue about what made a person African-American. I refused to prove that I was one of them by airing the poverty of my family. I stopped talking because I was growing more angry and frustrated by the minute.

When class was over and worship was about to start, I decided to calm down and stay, just in case I was overreacting. Although Gayle and I sat in the middle of the church and the auditorium was full, no one sat next to us. I looked around and noticed that every pew in the church building was filled except our pew.

With that, I knew it was time to leave. My sister was a baby in her faith, and I felt a strong need to protect her. I would not pull away from God because of the behavior of some of his children, but I was not so certain about Gayle's response. We walked out of the congregation facing straight ahead and avoiding the eyes of everyone along our path. We never returned. No one from the congregation ever called.

I never expected rejection from the church. I did not expect the prejudices of the world to creep into the church and divide people who were supposed to have unshakable bonds through their relationship with God. I know that I was frustrated mostly because I thought I could find a mother or father figure from among the people in the congregation. I had high expectations for God's family, but twice already I had felt the sting of rejection.

Gone Again

Gayle married her high school sweetheart in December 1988 and graduated from college in the spring. She would be returning to Texas to build her family. Although I knew we had only a year together when I arrived at Yale, I felt a similar emptiness as when she left for college the first time. I would spend the next four years trying in vain to find someone else to replace that sense of family. I made friends, but at the first sign of trouble in the relationship, I bolted. I could not allow myself to be hurt again, despite how badly I wanted a surrogate mother or father within God's family.

I often wondered how many other people hopped from church to church in search of that elusive sense of a perfect family. I remember praying repeatedly, "Dear God, why is it so hard to find a family? Why can't I find a place to belong?" I was looking for perfect love and did not yet understand that such a love could only come from God.

My dear child, your home is in me, and the love you long for can only be found in me. I see the lack of confidence you feel in your standing as my child. Your desire to love and to be loved is your sign that you are my child, because I am love. But don't be consumed with attempting to find a perfect love apart from me. You must learn to love me more. I am going to help you know and rely on my love.

Fear is driving you now. You still fear that no one loves you, including me. Fear has to do with punishment, but the love I am filling you with is a perfect love that will drive out fear. Be patient, my child. I long to fill you with so much joy and peace that your heart overflows with hope. But you must trust me. You must trust that I am enough to fill all your needs.

CHAPTER NINE

Making It

When Israel was in Egypt land, let my people go;
Oppressed so hard they could not stand, let my people go.
Go down, Moses, way down to Egypt land,
Tell ole Pharaoh: Let my people go!

NEGRO SPIRITUAL

Moses and the Israelites have always fascinated me. I held out hope
that God would also send someone to deliver me. I did not know what
my promised land was, but I knew I wanted to go there and be free
from the shackles of my past. I never felt comfortable criticizing the
moaning and doubting of the Israelites. I identified too much with
them.

I could relate to their complaints of dying a miserable death in the
desert after they watched Moses part the Red Sea. With so many years
of slavery behind them, even the Red Sea experience probably felt like
a fluke. Freedom seemed unreal. It was hard to feel free while suffering in a desert. Maybe they even felt that God changed his mind about

taking them to the Promised Land, and now they would die in the desert.

I understood the Israelites. They had spent their entire lives dreaming of freedom. Their dreams probably consisted of a grandiose plan in which God would swoop down, gather them in his arms, and quickly place them in a perfect place of rest and happiness. As they wandered in the desert, their dreams of freedom most likely did not consist of hunger, thirst, and pain. The years they spent moaning probably made them feel as if God had abandoned them. He did not rescue them the way they envisioned he would.

The story of the Israelites taught me about the power of unfulfilled expectations to erode faith. Parting the Red Sea told me that God had the power to deliver me with a mighty and swift miracle. My developing trust in him, however, could not be based on his fulfilling my simplistic expectations. Brother Jones, an African-American scholar and friend, once told me that the Israelites and the slaves in America shared similar illusions of deliverance and freedom. American slaves spent their lives dreaming of a better life up North as a free people. They prayed and dreamed of freedom day and night.

When many of them finally arrived in the North, they found joblessness, poverty, and laws restricting their rights as human beings. They were off the plantations, but most of them still suffered great hardship. Instead of slave masters breaking up the family, finances did; men would have to leave their families in search of work. Brother Jones told me the biggest problem with the Israelites and the slaves in America was reconciling long-held expectations with the realities of God's methods of deliverance. He told me, "That will be your greatest challenge as well."

I grew up with extensive dreams. In my dreams I would be free from my parents, find a new family in the church, get married, have children, have a wonderful career, and live happily ever after. The key to making my dreams come true was leaving my parents and completing my education. The dreams of my better life drove me to pour myself into my studies.

As did my parents, I wanted a better life. They wanted an idyllic life away from the harsh rural living on the farm. Gayle and I mainly wanted a life away from them. In my fairy-tale dreams, the promised land was a place of constant peace, love, and acceptance. The land flowing with milk and honey became the perfect earthly home I pursued. I still did not realize the fullness of being a child of God in light of continuing sorrow and problems. I always believed that when I found God, I would also find my earthly sense of home. The same determination, self-reliance, and dreams that I relied on growing up had become a barrier in my developing trust and faith in God. On the course toward my dream God used various circumstances to strip me of my illusions.

WAKE UP

I thought I was free when I graduated from high school and began my first year as an undergraduate at Yale, but the illusion of freedom was shattered that summer. Unlike most of my Yale friends, I did not have anything exciting to do over the summer. I knew I did not want to go back to Houston and live in the crack house with my parents again. I had never held a job before—didn't even know if I was employable. So I moved to Dallas to live with my sister and her new husband. They were newlyweds, and it wasn't long before I felt I was an imposition. I thought that if I could find a job I would move to a short-term apartment and not be a burden on them.

I had a brilliant plan. I would enroll in a program that helped minorities gain business experience through internships; with an internship, I could afford my own apartment. After excelling at all the job preparation classes, I was amazed that after a dozen interviews I was the only one in the program not offered a job.

I approached the program director, Ms. Downs, and asked her if I was blowing my interviews. She told me that all the prospective employers liked me but decided to hire another student. One skill I had developed over the years was the ability to detect insincerity.

Ms. Downs's body language showed signs of nervousness. Because she would not look me in the eye, I knew she was hiding something.

"Well, the problem can't be because I'm African-American. We are all minorities. It's not because I'm a woman. Over ninety percent of us are women. I guess the only thing left is my disability. Is that the real issue here?" I asked.

Ms. Downs shifted in discomfort. "Well, Cheryl, the employers did express concern about your ability to handle the physical demands of the job."

"What physical demands? It's a desk job. I'm not trying to be a construction worker."

"I know. I told them that too," she said anxiously.

"You realize that this is discrimination? They can't see past my disability to the fact that I'm a sharp woman with a promising future. I attend Yale University, for goodness' sake."

"Well, discrimination would be hard to prove."

I knew that African-Americans reported employers who demonstrated less obvious acts of discrimination. I knew that activists took on more difficult cases. I thought it was a clear act of discrimination. The employers were "concerned" about my disability, so they decided to choose a safer person. They did not even give me a chance to prove my abilities. Looking at Ms. Downs, I knew that she did not plead my case with the employers. I knew that all she saw were the things that I could not do.

"Did you fight for me?" I asked.

"I did tell them about your strengths."

"Did you fight for me?"

"I—I don't know what you mean."

"I guess I have my answer. Nobody is going to give me a chance. I don't even know why I even bothered going to Yale. All folks see is my disability and not any of my abilities. This has happened all my life. Why did I expect things would change for me because I'm older? The bullies now have *more* power over me."

"Sweetie, I—I don't know what to say. We will find you a position. We just have to hang in there."

"I'm tired. Nobody is on my side, and nobody will let me prove myself. I need someone to be my advocate. I get this feeling that you don't believe in me either," I said.

"That is not true. I believe in you one hundred percent," she protested.

"Then why didn't you fight for me?"

"Cheryl, I did the best I could. People just don't know how to deal with disability. It's not that they are out to get you."

"People said the same thing about race and gender in the workplace, but that did not stop folks from protesting. My only problem is that I walk differently from everyone else. That does not mean that I can't think or I can't do the job. It's discrimination, and if you don't fight for me in this position, then you are part of the problem."

"Cheryl, I don't think that is fair."

"Fair? Let's not talk about fairness right now. It's the truth and the truth hurts. My intention here is not to make you feel good about yourself. My intention is to show you that I've been wronged, and you stood by and did nothing about it. I'm tired of people letting me down."

As I rose to leave, I was not surprised that Ms. Downs did not follow me or try to stop me. On my way home, I thought I was wasting my time at Yale. If one of the best schools in the country could not ensure my future, then what hope did I have? Feeling like a failure, I could not hear God's reassurance that he was taking care of me. I was in a panic.

Without a job, I knew that Gayle and her husband would tolerate my living with them for only a short time. The apartment was small, and Gayle had student loans to repay. She did not have the money to support me. My sister, running from poverty as I was, would grow angry if I became dead weight to her as my parents had been to me. When I asked her to help me pay one of my credit cards, she snapped,

"I can't pay your bills and mine too." It was time for me to leave. My hypervigilance for rejection started sounding the alarm bells—Gayle was growing frustrated with me. I was pulling her down.

Needing to preserve my fragile sense of family with her, I made the hardest call of my life. I called Dad. Six hours later, I was on my way to Houston, going back to live with people from whom I was so desperate to escape. My dreams of a complete break from my parents were shattered. I had thought I would never see them again. I had thought I would never see the crack house again. I felt my life was in backward motion. I knew this could not be how God would deliver me—not by returning to slavery and hell.

Despite the disappointment and self-pity, I knew I could live with Mom and Dad because there was nothing left to lose in our relationship. I had everything to lose in my relationship with my sister. We had just found each other after three years, and I wanted to protect those fragile ties. Gayle had started her new life, and I could not be the person to hold her back from her dreams. I felt guilty for being a little jealous of her life. She had a Yale degree, a career, a husband, and God. My sister seemed to have it all. I could not understand why my life had to take a rockier path than hers.

While we were driving home, Dad turned around and smiled at me. "I knew you would come back to me, Cheryl. You vowed that you would never leave me."

I started to cry because I knew Dad would try to resurrect my surrogate wife role with him. I did not want to let go of my perfect dreams of how God would deliver me. Going back to Houston never factored into my dreams of deliverance. I started asking God what good could possibly come from living with my parents. I prayed, "Dear God, I'm happy for Gayle's new life and don't wish her any harm. I'm sorry for feeling jealous, but I don't understand why my dreams won't come true too. What about me? When will it be my turn for a better life?"

My dear child, you must keep your eyes on me. It is not your concern what I do in Gayle's life. She is my child, too, and I have special plans for

her life. You must trust and follow me. I know you are afraid that I will pun-
ish you or scold you for what you are feeling, but I am your Daddy. I will
not crush you in your sorrow, and I will comfort you when you mourn. I will
remind you that only I can satisfy your hunger and thirst. I am working out
your future perfectly. My ways and thoughts are not like yours, so do not
concern yourself with trying to figure me out or how I will deliver you. You
would not believe me even if I told you. Come to me and rest in my arms.

THE BLACK HOLE

I began to recognize that God was more interested in maturing my faith than he was in my employment status. When I returned to Houston, I tried unsuccessfully to secure a job as a receptionist or secretary. After three attempts, I gave up. Each interviewer told me that I was overqualified because of my Yale education. I knew they were lying. I had been at Yale for only one year but knew how to type sixty words per minute. I was not overqualified; these employers were scared by my disability and did not want to admit it. I reached my limit of rejection and stopped interviewing.

Over the course of the summer, I began to withdraw from everyone. To cope with living with people I did not want to see, I spent most of my time behind the closed doors of my room. I passed the hours by learning how to cross-stitch. I stopped eating and going to church. I did not realize it at the time, but I had slipped into a deep depression. When summer was over, I did not want to return to college and took a medical leave of absence instead. My summer of hell would turn into a year, and I did not even care anymore.

In my depression, I stopped praying consciously, but my heart desperately wanted a sign from God. I could not understand how anything good could come out of wasting away in my parents' apartment. "Dear God, where are you? Why are you so far away from me? I'm tired of these emotional swings. I'm tired of living a life that looks like it has no purpose. I know you said that my life matters, but when will I feel the peace from that promise?"

Within twenty minutes of that prayer, I saw a commercial on television for paralegal training, and I felt like I needed a skill in a field that would care more about my mind than my disability. I started to think about becoming a lawyer so I could sue anyone who discriminated against me. I thought a paralegal degree would give me more self-confidence. So I signed up. During my training, my self-confidence returned. My depression lifted as well, so that I was emotionally ready to return to Yale. I was set to learn another lesson from God: that I was still searching for happiness in things incapable of producing it.

It was time to return to Yale, but I knew I could not physically handle the terrain. My body was too weak from the slips and falls I had my first year trying to negotiate the hills, broken flagstone, uneven pavements, and ice and snow. My sister would not be there to help me. Even with Gayle there, my grades slipped to Cs during the winter semester because I could not get to many classes over the ice and snow. My academic dean told me to return to college and he would figure out how to get me to class. The first option was to live off campus and take a shuttle bus to class. When I told Mom and Dad my plans, Dad said that Mom could go to Yale with me and help me get to my classes. I was shocked, wondering why he wanted to push Mom on me.

"She could go up there and get her life back together. A change of venue would do her some good," Dad said.

"I would love to get my life off hold. This is exciting," Mom said.

I was frustrated with my parents. They were incapable of thinking of anyone other than themselves. Why would any young adult want her parents to go with her to college? College is supposed to be the time when young people break away from their parents. Mom had not held a job in more than ten years. I could not understand how she would be able to take care of herself, and I did not want to baby-sit her.

When I looked at Mom, my heart melted to see the excitement in her eyes. Despite my attempts to suppress my emotions, I felt compassion. I could almost feel Mom trying to get away from Dad. I was suspicious of Dad's motives and wondered if he had found another love interest. Pushing the thoughts from my mind, I told myself that I could not preoccupy myself with things I could not change. Although I felt sorry for my mom, I wanted to live by myself. I grew more confused, wondering if what I felt was dishonoring my parents. I prayed for a couple of days for guidance from God, but I could not hear a clear answer.

Mom and I packed our car and drove to New Haven. I received a full scholarship to Yale and arranged to pick up a rebate check for the housing and board allowance in my scholarship budget. The housing rebate was not enough to cover the cost of off-campus housing. The money was designed for one person, but it would have to support Mom and me in a motel near campus, Hanford Inn. This was the local trucker hangout. Although it was clean, I felt humiliated that I lived in a trucker motel while attending Yale University. I calculated that Mom needed to find a job within several months after our arrival. I began to pray toward that end because I could never depend on Mom for my livelihood. Periodically, I would wake up in a panic over the thought of being homeless again.

Mom began to feel the financial pressures and started to fall apart emotionally. I made her résumé look appealing, but Mom blew every interview. To make matters worse, Yale did not live up to its promise to help me get around campus. The one wheelchair-accessible van was unreliable. Drivers were frequently late or no-shows, and the hours of operation were severely limited.

To circumvent the unreliable transportation and my weakened physical state, Mom began pushing me around campus in a wheelchair. A bad situation had gotten worse. I was so ashamed that my mother was constantly with me that I refused to make friends with anyone.

Just when I thought things were unbearable, I heard a knock at our motel door. It was Dad. "Dad, what are you doing here?"

"Your mom called and said that you guys were running out of money and she couldn't find work. She asked for money, and I couldn't afford to send money and keep my bills going. So I decided to move here and find work."

"You drove all the way up here to live in here with us? In this one room?"

"Yes. I'm sure I will find work soon."

"How can we afford this? Now no one has a job!" I cried.

"I got hurt on my last job and I'm on worker's compensation, so we will have some weekly income. It won't be much, but we can get by until I find work," he assured me.

Since there was only one bed, we purchased a rollaway cot for me. When the days turned into months, I grew so tired of my father's thunderous snoring that I pulled my cot into the bathroom to sleep with a closed door. Several times during the night, my mother would come in to use the bathroom while I was sleeping. My father used a portable urinal and never used the bathroom while I was in there. However, by morning the stench of standing urine would fill the room and drive me to vomit. We had to open the doors and windows every morning so we could breathe. My mother would fumigate the room with Lysol.

I was attending one of the richest schools in the country while living like a pauper. The irony stung. I felt the same resentment as when the three of us were living in the car and storage facility and camping out in our foreclosed house. Months passed, and neither of my parents found jobs. I could not take sleeping in the bathroom and eating meals off a hot plate anymore. I was irritated that my parents had to push me around campus as if I were a baby. I was tired of being ashamed of where I lived and going through my Yale years without any friends. I thought camping out in our house after we were evicted was embarrassing. I thought living in the crack house was embarrassing. But my current living situation and having my parents push me in a wheelchair were more humiliating than all the other situations. My souring attitude and avoidance of everyone on campus nearly caused me to miss one of my best gifts from God—my friendship with Todd. Although we had different religions (he was Jewish) and his family was healthy, he and I shared the common bond of disability. Todd had diabetes since childhood and experienced similar instances of rejection and avoidance each time he pulled out his insulin. Although I was too embarrassed to make friends and pushed him away, Todd persisted. Nothing about my past repulsed him. He saw the beauty of faith that God saw in me. God, through Todd, tried to help me cast aside the shame.

I began to channel my growing frustration with my living situation toward the inaccessible campus. I now wanted to live on campus and not worry about the expensive off-campus rent. However, there were no wheelchair-accessible dorms available. Although I could not physically push myself in a wheelchair over Yale's tough terrain, I did not want to depend on my parents for another year. Help from my parents came with a price. I overheard them telling one of my professors that they had put their lives on hold to help ensure my future. My professor replied that she admired their act of selflessness.

Hearing that, I wanted to storm into the room to set the record straight. I was the one taking care of *them*. I wanted to scream that I made it to Yale despite all the hell my parents had put me through. When I met them at the door, I took one look at my mother and decided to keep silent. My parents' lives were broken, possibly beyond repair. They were grasping for anything to prove that they had accomplished something of worth in their lives. I lost interest in correcting the story. I knew the truth and somehow that was enough.

My dean suggested I apply for services at the Department of Vocational Rehabilitation. That would prove a good move. Through my rehabilitation counselor, I received confirmation that Yale needed to do more to accommodate my disability and reduce the barriers on campus. I was told that my health insurance should pay for the rental of an electric scooter or wheelchair while the state purchased one for me. I applied for Social Security disability income.

By summer I had income from Social Security, food stamps, supplemental welfare payments for disabled residents of Connecticut, and a subsidized one-bedroom apartment. My parents and I moved into the apartment. They still had not secured employment. I was supporting three people on welfare for one person. I wanted out. I wanted to live away from my parents. I wanted my own life. I decided the only way I could escape their pulling me down into their black hole was by living on campus.

SECTION 504

By my junior year in college, I learned a valuable lesson in the temporal nature of happiness apart from God. I decided that I wanted to return to campus for the last two years. Yale wanted to place me in one of the few wheelchair-accessible dorms on campus. I, however, wanted to live in the same dorm for upperclassmen that my sister had once occupied. She had started a legacy, or family tradition, at Yale, and legacies normally are lived out in the same dorms. The dorm my sister lived in was not wheelchair-accessible, and Yale did not want to renovate it. I asked my dean to plead my case with the administrators, but I could not rest my hopes on his actions. Having been burned before, I decided to search the law for myself.

I spent most of my free time researching disability law. I wanted to know if I could force Yale to renovate my dorm. Living on campus was part of the famous "Yale experience," which I was being unjustly denied. After writing a formal request to Yale and being turned down, I filed a charge of disability discrimination against the university with the Department of Education Office of Civil Rights.

Although Yale was a private institution, it still received millions in federal funds, so according to Section 504 of the Rehabilitation Act of 1973, the university was under contractual obligation not to discriminate because of disability. With one telephone call threatening an investigation, the Department of Education's civil rights officer initiated a chain of events that would improve the quality of life for students, employees, and visitors with disabilities for years to come. I learned that, over the summer, Yale would make my residential college and other areas on campus wheelchair-accessible. I had made a difference and had never been more proud of myself.

By my junior year, I was finally living on campus and feeling that I belonged at Yale. I had an electric scooter and loved my independence. I still had some problems getting around, especially when elevators broke or blizzards came. Nevertheless, I was independent. I had hopes that Mom and Dad would find jobs and support themselves so that I could go off welfare. During the summer I was selected by Senator Robert Dole's foundation as its scholar intern. Through my work at the foundation, I was immersed in the world of disability politics.

When I returned to Yale, I graduated with distinction in my major of psychology. I also continued working for the Dole Foundation as a consultant. The Equal Employment Opportunity Commission selected me to be a part of the Americans with Disabilities Act training and implementation network. In this capacity I began training businesses and people with disabilities on the rights and responsibilities under the new law. I was a vocal disability rights activist on campus, challenging anyone who saw ramps and wheelchair lifts as anything other than civil rights.

"Cheryl, how can you deny that these ugly ramps around campus detract from the aesthetic beauty of the buildings?" a student asked.

"It's not the ramps per se that detract from the beauty. It is how Yale chooses to build them. They could do a better job of blending them in with the architecture. But beauty aside, the ramps provide access to people in wheelchairs who pay the same tuition as everyone else, so we should have the same access to every building on campus."

"I know, but there aren't many people in wheelchairs on campus, and when you calculate the cost-benefit ratio, it doesn't make sound economic sense."

"We are talking about civil rights, not economic theory. Get your head out of the ivory tower for a second and see that I'm not talking about something that people with disabilities want Yale to give to us. I'm talking about a law with which we expect Yale to comply. If you carry that same type of thinking to the workplace, you will discriminate against people with disabilities and get yourself hauled into court."

I started challenging every instance of discrimination I could find on campus. I demanded the transportation system be more accessible so that people with disabilities would have the same access as nondisabled people. I even served as the student representative to the university's Disability Policy Committee.

When I graduated, I was pleasantly surprised to see a wheelchair ramp constructed for the main speaker's area. While listening to actress Jodie Foster deliver the commencement speech, I was satisfied that I had made a difference at Yale and would continue to make a difference once I was out in the "real world." I was happy. At least, I thought I was happy.

"Now we will move on to honors," the dean of Yale University said. "And for the Everett Chandler Prize for character and high moral purpose . . ."

As I was looking around at the other graduates, I never heard my name being called. "This honor is awarded to a graduating senior who has exemplified character and high moral purpose throughout his or her Yale career. Cheryl has done just that. She has many academic honors. While here at Yale, working on her degree in psychology, she was awarded the Andrew Mellon Undergraduate Minority Fellowship. She was also honored with a National Science Foundation Fellowship for graduate school. Additionally, the foundation has awarded Yale University an undergraduate scholarship for a minority undergraduate in her honor. She was selected by the Dole Foundation to work on helping implement the Americans with Disabilities Act, and in this role she has been tireless in her efforts to educate lawmakers, leaders, and society about the rights of the disabled. And we know how hard it is to get lawmakers to listen. She has also worked at improving access for the disabled here at Yale. For her efforts in promoting civil rights to all people, we award her this high honor."

I accepted the award, posed for pictures, and made my way back to my seat. I felt all my hard work had paid off and I had made enough of a difference that I was being honored for my character in front of thousands of people. I felt a deep happiness that was, unfortunately, short-lived. The intoxication of self-made success was addictive. I was on the same path my parents followed for happiness—education, career success, and accolades from people. Nothing I did, however, could revive that fleeting happiness I felt during graduation. My heart was whispering to me that I was off track for true happiness, but it would take three years for me to hear.

LET DOWN

Within three years after I graduated from Ohio State with my master's degree, I developed some compassion for Dad. Similar to my father, I had begun basing my happiness on my effort and intellect. Dad taught us that as African-Americans we had to be twice as good to be considered equal to whites. As an African-American woman with a disability, I felt I had to be three times better to be considered equal to anyone, regardless of ethnicity. I had taken perfectionism to a new level. I would work long hours, create dazzling reports, tackle assignments no one else wanted, all in an effort to be viewed as merely equal.

When I fell and broke my back and needed two spinal surgeries, I learned that everything I did to earn favor from people was meaningless. All my life I wondered how Mom and Dad could lose their jobs and never be able to recover. I soon learned the devastating aftermath of basing one's happiness and future on good standing among humankind. Human beings are fickle and unreliable.

After graduate school at Ohio State and a stint in Washington, D.C., I returned to Texas and started working at the Day Foundation. I was happy because I was helping hundreds of nonprofit organizations with their programs and fund-raising. I worked long hours, demonstrating my passion for perfectionism. After a year at the foundation, I fell and broke two vertebrae and needed surgery.

"Cheryl, look, we have a situation here," my boss, Greg, said.

These words signaled the end of my career at Day. My boss told me that when I interviewed, I did not need much to accommodate my disability. Once I was hired, they felt I began demanding rest rooms be renovated, ramps installed, and more. He went on to tell me that the company had invested all this money in me, but now I was out of pocket on medical leave.

Shocked at his bluntness, I did not know how to respond. I tried to explain that I did not purposefully break my back and that accommodating my disability was not an entitlement but the law. But Greg was intent on protecting the bottom line.

I sensed that my job was in jeopardy, so I offered to work from home while I was recuperating. My unusual work arrangement meant that I had to negotiate with the director of operations, Ted. He was an insensitive, power-hungry person who would fire people and then walk around joking how "another one bit the dust" or "just got rid of another one." Ted called me to express the foundation's concern about my ability to do my job.

"Are you trying to get rid of me, Ted, just because I hurt my back?"

"I'm not trying to get rid of you, Cheryl. I am simply protecting the foundation's interests. We are having concerns about you being able to perform the essential functions of the job."

I began to wonder if I was heading down the same path as Dad when he lost his job and was blacklisted. Mom would always say that Dad knew the signs that his boss was out to get him, but Dad did not play it smart. Mom said that he allowed his mouth and pride to get himself fired. I knew I needed to play this game carefully. I needed to stay far away from claiming discrimination despite clear violations of the law.

To show the foundation that I was willing to work around my new medical limitations, I arranged to work from home. During a month of that arrangement, I excelled in all the work standards for my position. I knew I now needed to be four or five times better than any of the nondisabled workers. Even after I was released from medical leave and returned to work, I continued my high level of achievement. I spent long hours in the office, worked on weekends, and sought more responsibilities.

After a year, I thought I would be promoted. But Greg told me that since I had missed more than three months with my surgeries, I needed more time in my position to justify a promotion. When I reminded him that I worked while I was out on medical leave, Greg told me his decision was final. He needed to see me in action to justify a promotion.

I sensed the foundation no longer wanted me there, and I needed to start networking fast to find another job. I accepted invitations to serve on other nonprofit boards that would expose me to more job opportunities. Greg and Ted told me that if I wanted to stay with the foundation, I would have to stop serving on one of my most important boards. Since my position at Day was so tenuous, I negotiated with the president of the foundation for terms on which I could continue to serve on the national board that was so important to me. I agreed that I would pay my own expenses and attend meetings using my vacation time. Greg told me that I would have to live with the consequences of my decision to pursue the matter.

The first consequence was the denial of my request for assistance when I traveled on business. My surgeries had left me with even more severe physical limitations than before, and I needed help transporting my scooter and negotiating inaccessible terrain during travel. Ted and Greg refused my request.

The employer-employee relationship soured further when Greg began threatening to assign me cases that did not require travel. Without traveling, I would not obtain the skills I needed to justify a promotion. I could not take these further violations of my employment rights and decided to make an official complaint with Ted, who also was the foundation's equal opportunity officer.

Because of my complaint, I was placed under greater scrutiny. Greg constantly asked my secretary of my whereabouts. He scrutinized all my receipts and expense reports from my trips. Personal leaves or vacation days were not approved unless I explicitly outlined where I was going. Greg began asking coworkers questions about me and gathering information for his file.

"Cheryl, what in the world did you do to Greg and Ted?" asked my coworker, Pat.

"What's going on?"

"They are asking everyone questions about you—where you go, who you talk to, how long you take for lunch, if we have ever seen you travel without help. They are out to get you, girl. You better watch your back."

"Are you serious?"

"Yes. I've seen this type of behavior in them before," Pat said. "They either find some reason to fire you or they make your life miserable and force you out."

"That's discrimination. They can't do that."

"It's hard to prove. That's the unfortunate thing about the law. Discrimination is hard to prove."

I had heard that statement before, when I was a freshman in college and trying to get placement through participating in the minority internship program. I could not understand why things had not changed. It had been six years since my first experience with employment discrimination because of my disability; it had been four years since the implementation of the Americans with Disabilities Act, and I was still facing the same song and dance. Nothing had changed. Money still ruled, thinking itself exempt from obeying the law.

I was proud, like my father, and my first reaction was to stand up to the foundation. I had documented clear violations of the law. If I did not stand up for my rights, I knew I could not look myself in the mirror. I was an activist, and it was time to protest.

It was ironic that I had conducted many workshops with managers on how to work with people with disabilities and avoid employment discrimination. I had conducted other workshops for people with disabilities on how they could assert their rights in the workplace. Now I was facing the very situation that the law addressed. I felt awful. Advocating for myself was much different than advocating for others; it was more painful. The Day Foundation had more money and influence than me; it had many mean-spirited people in high levels of administration, and I was a peon. If I were blacklisted, I feared I would end up like Mom and Dad.

When other coworkers began warning me about the covert activity by my boss and Ted, I knew I needed to look for another job. I tried to tell myself that God would take care of them and I did not need to concern myself with revenge. I struggled to contain my anger when I was passed up for another promotion.

The dreaded confrontation was soon in coming. Greg pulled out his folder and started a rapid-fire succession of questions about specific decisions I had made. His undercover investigation provided him with a list of minor problems. After each question, I asked him if I was the only one who had ever made a mistake. Greg admitted that others had made the same mistake when they first arrived at the foundation, but considering the current problems with my disability, he was having serious doubts about me.

When I appealed his decision to the president of the foundation, I was further disappointed that he supported Ted's assessment. Knowing that I had a good case for discrimination, I let my pride fuel my desire for retaliation.

I talked with a coworker, Rose, about Greg's behavior. I told Rose that I could no longer work in a hostile environment. She told me to start looking for another job and to take steps to protect myself. Everyone knew the corporate culture. If the administrators did not like a person's attitude, the person was usually gone by the end of the day.

"Why am I starting to feel like a house slave?" I asked. "You live a better life inside the house working for Massa, but you still aren't equal. If you step out of line, Massa will remind you that you are still a slave. Even if they abuse you, they still expect loyalty."

With that statement, I knew I had to leave quickly. My attitude was souring, and I could not keep a godly attitude in such a hostile environment. Rose asked me if I would sue. I paused and told her that it depended on what my heart told me. I made a few calls to friends at the Equal Employment Opportunity Commission, who unofficially verified I had a case.

After many years of blaming Dad's pride for his boss's firing and blacklisting him, I was facing the same situation. I knew I had to think about my future despite the bruises to my pride. I tried to tell myself that my anger was justified, and if I sued, I would be helping many people with disabilities by highlighting the discriminatory attitudes I had experienced.

Despite my attempts to persuade myself of noble intentions, my heart revealed the truth: all I wanted was revenge. I was also afraid that if I acted in revenge, the consequence of my sinful action would mean being blacklisted from my profession. I would suffer the same fate as my parents. I would wander in the wilderness and suffocate in the quicksand of poverty for the rest of my life.

My child, do not lose your focus. I will deal with those who harm you, just as I will help you in your troubles. I know when and how I will deliver my justice. Revenge has no place in the heart of one of my children. Check your heart before you act, and act only in faith in me. I am creating in you an overflow of love and good actions, not fear and vengeance. By my power, I will complete the good purpose I have for your life. Trust me. Your Daddy knows what he is doing.

CHAPTER TEN

Kindred Spirit

Lord, I couldn't hear nobody pray.
Oh, way down yonder by myself,
And I couldn't hear nobody pray.

NEGRO SPIRITUAL

I was twenty-two when I realized there was a difference between alone-ness and loneliness. I have always been comfortable with my alone-ness, for during those times I dreamed my greatest dreams, sang my most powerful songs, and felt safety in the silence. I spent many years preferring being alone, where no one could hurt or disappoint me. When alone, I could drop the pretenses and masks and be myself. As an introvert, I drew energy and strength from the times that allowed only my thoughts and God.

I was terrified, however, of loneliness. Feeling lonely was rooted in my fears of rejection. Loneliness came on when I could not find a sense of belonging among people I valued. Whenever I was driven by loneliness, I became desperate to find ways to be accepted. I grew up telling myself that all I needed to make me happy and complete was one good friend who accepted me, disability and all.

The first time I felt I belonged happened in the third grade. I was tired of being singled out, harassed, and ridiculed because of my disability. As soon as I wanted to give up, a new girl named Tiffany transferred to my school. Tiffany had a more unusual disability than mine. Her head was enormous and shaped like a balloon. Tubes bulged through her skin down her neck. She told me the tubes drained the fluid that tended to accumulate on her brain. My disability looked almost unnoticeable compared to hers. Whenever she would walk down the hall, kids would call her "Watermelonhead." I asked Tiffany if she felt bad by how they treated her. She gave me the pat adult answer, "Yeah, but I can't do anything to change stuff. God made me this way."

I told her that I thought God was mean for creating us so different from others. Tiffany said her mother told her that God made her special. I never felt special. Disability only invited ridicule and ostracism, not a sense of being special. I asked Tiffany, "Do you feel special? I don't." We sat together in silence. We could not understand how special people could be the targets of so much hatred.

I suppose misery does love company because Tiffany and I became best friends. When we walked down the hall, we were a sight to see. For once the kids harassed someone else more than they harassed me, but together, we seemed to diffuse the impact of the insults. I could have avoided her and allowed her to take it all alone, but I felt a powerful bond between us. We understood each other and drew strength from our common bond. We needed each other. We enjoyed the dignity and love we brought to each other's life. When I was with Tiffany, I felt a liberating feeling of normalcy.

After we graduated, I never saw Tiffany again. It would take over fifteen years before I found another friend with a disability. My desire to feel totally accepted, however, would not die. Even being a Christian did not impart that same feeling of complete understanding and belonging that I shared with Tiffany.

BELONGING

During my junior year in college, Senator Robert Dole's foundation selected me as its scholar intern. So the summer of 1992 I made my way to Washington, D.C. Congress had passed the Americans with Disabilities Act of 1990 (ADA), which guaranteed protection against discrimination in many sectors of society for forty-three million people with disabilities. When I arrived in Washington, I was plunged into the middle of an aggressive grass-roots campaign to implement the new law successfully. I had never heard of the ADA. I did not know that Senator Dole, having a disability himself, was a strong proponent of the law. I was also surprised to learn that the Dole Foundation had a mission to promote employment of people with disabilities, which had been a major obstacle in my life.

Many people with disabilities staffed the Dole Foundation; some of them had more severe disabilities than mine. It was exciting to see so many people like myself with powerful positions in Washington. My supervisor, Jeanne, quickly became my second mother and most influential mentor. In me, she seemed to see a young person full of potential. When I told her that I knew nothing about the ADA or disability politics, she began educating me about the disability community. Jeanne immersed me in the disability political scene on Capitol Hill and throughout Washington. She told me that the Dole Foundation was committed to helping implement the new law and educate people with disabilities about their new civil rights.

I became a woman on the move. If I was not representing the foundation in important meetings, I was at parties and mixers on Capitol Hill with foundation staff. For the first time in my life, my disability did not hinder me at all. In fact, my disability became an asset. Representing the Dole Foundation, I spoke at conferences and activist meetings and met hundreds of people with diverse disabilities. However, instead of feeling relieved or excited about meeting so many people like myself, I was uncomfortable.

I had grown up avoiding groups of people with disabilities. Jeanne asked if my avoidance was because I feared further stigmatization. My parents wanted to discount my disability so that everyone would notice my abilities. However, hanging around nondisabled people all the time only made me stick out more. I always felt I bore a stigma—African-American, female, disabled, or poor. I often said, "People will pick out any reason to exclude you. I just tend to keep to myself. I tried to tell myself that no one could hurt me if I didn't want to belong to any group. But to be honest, it does hurt to have so many different types of people excluding me for one reason or another."

Because I grew up never considering myself disabled, the disability community was a strange new world to me. People proudly called themselves disabled; some even jokingly called themselves "crips." Although I longed for another friend with a disability like Tiffany, I did not feel comfortable being around masses of people with disabilities.

The sheer number and different types of disabilities astonished me. I read everything I could find about the disability movement and disability politics. I discovered that 43 million people in America have disabilities, making it the largest minority group. Jeanne taught me that disability takes different forms. Some are visible, such as polio, other paralysis, or cerebral palsy, but the term also includes people who have hidden disabilities, such as psychiatric disabilities, hearing loss, or diabetes. Other people have cognitive disabilities such as mental retardation. I was meeting people who demanded to be recognized as viable and whole human beings. They rejected the societal stigmas and discrimination.

I could identify with the discomfort many nondisabled people feel when interacting with people with disabilities because I was meeting people with disabilities I had never seen or heard of. I did not know how to interact with them. When I met a woman with severe cerebral palsy, I could not understand her speech. I felt stupid and rude asking her to repeat herself three times. I finally gave up and pretended that I understood her.

Jeanne told me that was the worst thing to do. I needed to be honest with people with speech disabilities and explain that I was having trouble understanding them. She said that the person probably had developed a strategy for us to communicate better. I was afraid that I would offend the person, but Jeanne told me that risking offense was better than faking a conversation.

When I met a deaf person for the first time, I did not know how to interact with the interpreter. Jeanne taught me that although the interpreter was the one using voice, the deaf person was actually speaking, and I needed to focus my attention on that person. She told me that it was rude to look at the interpreter. I sighed in frustration. There were so many new rules and terms that I felt overwhelmed. Just because I had a disability, I did not automatically know how to interact with people with different disabilities.

Whenever Jeanne introduced me to people with disabilities, they would hug me as if they were welcoming a lost sister. Jeanne told me that most people with disabilities were taught to avoid further stigmatization by shunning relationships with other people with disabilities. She said that despite this ostracism, a new movement is growing to recognize the disability community as a cultural group, like ethnic groups. She told me, "No matter what type or severity of disability, people with disabilities all share a common experience with discrimination. There is a common history—some argue a common culture." I heard many women openly talk about being abused when they were children. I felt relieved that I was not the only one with a history of abuse. Soon I began to feel a sense of home.

I was ambivalent about embracing the disability culture even though I enjoyed the feeling of community. I found a people who wanted me to be a part of them, who constantly affirmed my worth each time I was in their presence. Members of the disability community welcomed me with open arms. I was simply one of them. For a short time I felt a peaceful sense of belonging. But when the euphoria of meeting people who shared my experiences with disability

discrimination wore off, the emptiness returned. During one of my
prayers, I asked God why the feeling of belonging had dissipated. I
would receive my answer later.

After several weeks of mingling with people with disabilities, I
found it harder to feel a total sense of belonging in the disability community. I was struck by the lack of minorities in the powerful circles
of disability politics. Political rhetoric stressed that disability was the
most inclusive minority group because it cut across race, gender, religion, culture, and social and economic status. Nevertheless, I still saw
white people in most positions of power within the community. I
asked Jeanne why there were not more minorities in leadership positions within the community. She brainstormed about possible reasons,
but I stopped her upon hearing "racism."

"Racism? But everyone seems so friendly. They have welcomed
me," I said.

"Yes, and I believe they are genuine, but they are people, too, and
many still carry baggage from the larger society. Many of us are working to change this because we need all people with disabilities to be
fully integrated within the community; we need everyone if we are to
remain politically powerful."

I was disappointed. I thought things would be different in the disability community. I always hoped that people who had experienced
oppression firsthand would not discriminate against other people. I
felt the same way about the African-American community. Then I
realized how naive I had been. I told Jeanne that power was relative. I
knew many minorities who were powerless in the context of the larger
society, but they acted oppressively toward others with even less status
and power. I had experienced discrimination from other women and
African-Americans. Although I had hoped discrimination would not
happen in the disability community, it was still a collection of people,
flaws and all.

Jeanne told me that I needed to commit myself to the larger goal of
inclusion of all people with disabilities in society and work to eradi-

cate racism within the community. But the expectations associated with carrying the torch after several years became overwhelming. Each time I heard about racism within the community, it diminished my sense of belonging.

To remedy my growing sense of racial isolation within the disability movement, Jeanne arranged for me to meet Diedre, a disabled African-American woman. Diedre was in charge of enforcing the ADA at the Equal Employment Opportunity Commission. When I saw her, I thought, *I want to be just like her one day.* She was smart, successful, and disabled. Diedre represented to me that it was possible for an African-American woman with a disability to make it in society.

Another factor eroding my sense of belonging to the disability community was my difficulty in embracing the idea of a disability culture. I grew up believing that culture was reserved for my ethnic identity. My parents taught me pride as an African American in a racist society. I understood my identity as primarily African-American. I felt loyal to an unwritten rule that I was supposed to identify first with people of my race.

Despite the strength of my ethnic identity, I felt alienated from the African-American community also because of my disability. The boys who most often beat me up and ridiculed me were African-American. I even could not find support from a minority internship program. I felt that my disability made me less of a "sister" in the community of my people. I felt as if they were telling me that because of my disability, I could not possibly uphold the glorious image of the strong African-American woman.

Even though I felt excluded by the African-American community, I loved my ethnic identity. I never stopped celebrating its rich heritage and strength. I told Jeanne that although I loved the disability community, there was room for only one master identity in my heart, and I believed a disability identity was not rich or powerful enough to fill the void if I abandoned my primary identity as African-American. My ethnic identity, however, had yet to fill the void either.

My head started to hurt. I was experiencing the effects of identity politics. I had highly politicized identities—female, disabled, and African-American. Each one of these identities demanded strong in-group loyalty, but none of them could make me feel whole. I had to find my master identity.

"I can tell you are religious too. What does your religion say about disability?" Jeanne asked.

The full theological impact of Jeanne's question escaped me at the time, but I now realize that God was gently telling me I already had a master identity as his child. The choice I would have to make would become clear later.

FREEDOM RIDERS

Later I told people that I had a Rosa Parks moment during the one year I worked for the Dole Foundation. One of the hallmarks of the ADA is its mandate that public transportation be accessible to people with disabilities. For people like me, it boiled down to having wheelchair lifts on buses and specially equipped vans to supplement the regular fleet of buses.

In trying to use public transportation, I quickly discovered that bus drivers hated dealing with wheelchair lifts or people in wheelchairs or on scooters. Operating the lifts meant delays and disruptions in the normal routine. Most of the time, the lifts did not work due to improper maintenance. Sometimes they would work long enough to get a person in a wheelchair on the bus but would break down so that someone else would have to carry the person off the bus. Because the lifts were broken regularly, I often waited for hours to get on a bus. I discovered that civil rights were only as good as the enforcement of them.

"I noticed you have been sitting on this corner for a while waiting on the bus. What's going on? I've seen so many buses stop," a woman in a wheelchair asked me.

"The lifts of those buses didn't work so I have to wait. I'm so angry and frustrated. I'm thinking about scooting my way to work and forgetting the bus all together."

"Did you make the driver try the lift, or did you take his word for it?" she asked.

I stared at her. "Took his word."

"Big mistake. These drivers lie all the time. Make them prove to you that the lift doesn't work. And make sure you are the first one to get on board when the bus stops because when all those other people get on, you won't have room to get to your area. The driver can then tell you the bus is too full for you and can legally prevent you from boarding."

When the next bus arrived, the displayed symbol verified it had a wheelchair lift. Fifteen other people were waiting to board, and the bus was full of passengers. I maneuvered myself to be first in line. I had a right to ride the bus and I would stand my ground.

"You need to get to the back of the line," the driver barked at me.

"Why? If I do that, the bus will be too full for me to get on."

"I said, get to the back of the line!" His order reminded me of images I remembered from the Civil Rights era. For a brief moment, I felt as if I were back in the 1960s when white drivers refused to serve African-Americans. However, this driver was African-American. To him I was not a sister—I was simply disabled.

"I will not. Let the lift down so I can get on this bus."

"The lift is broken."

"I don't believe you. Try it. If it is broken, I'll gladly step out of line."

We were at a standstill. The driver stared at me with contempt, cursing under his breath.

"Just let down the —— lift!" a man yelled from the line of riders behind me.

The driver bolted off the bus toward the man. The two of them exchanged curses and shoves. The driver stood next to me and told everyone to walk past me to get on board. But I said, "I know my rights here, and you are violating them. It is the law for you to let me board this bus."

I felt empowered by asserting my knowledge of the law. None of the other riders walked past me to board the bus. I was taking a stand, and these people were helping by not boarding the bus. Cursing, the driver moved to push me out of the way.

"If you touch me or my scooter, I'll call the police and have you arrested for assault."

The driver cursed again, got back on the bus, and lowered the lift. "Wow, it works after all. Must be a miracle," I said as I boarded.

When I boarded the bus, everyone on board and outside started clapping.

Later, everyone in the disability community to whom I related this experience had similar stories. Despite the common experience, I was still searching for something that political protest could not satisfy.

ACROSS THE WORLD

I should have been excited. It had been over five months since I left Washington to pursue a Ph.D. at Ohio State University when Jeanne called me and told me that the Dole Foundation wanted me to represent women with disabilities at the Nongovernmental Forum on Women at the United Nations Fourth World Conference on Women in Beijing, China. I had been coping with a series of health crises and was struggling with depression, but Jeanne was firm in telling me that the trip would be good for me. I would be traveling with a group of women with disabilities and would have a once-in-a-lifetime opportunity to see another part of the world. While I would represent the interests of young women with disabilities, she also wanted me to gain a better understanding of the plight of women with disabilities across the world.

My deteriorating health and depression had left me weak, but I wanted to seize the opportunity. I laughed to myself that not many African-Americans or people with disabilities had ever been to China. The poor, disabled, African-American girl would be traveling across the world for an important worldwide conference. First, I had to get permission from my doctor to travel to China.

I had recently undergone surgery to remove benign tumors from my arm, but the stitches had come apart, and I was nursing an open wound. My doctor would allow me to travel to China only if I agreed to abide by strict medical precautions. I had to take my own medical supplies and keep my wound covered at all times. I had to receive shots for polio, diphtheria, tetanus, smallpox, and yellow fever. I contacted five hundred Yale alumni to raise ten thousand dollars to cover the costs for a travel attendant who would push me in a wheelchair and help me negotiate other physical barriers in Beijing.

The travel organizer called me a week before the trip, telling me to leave my scooter and anything else mechanical behind because the roads in China were not accessible. She told me that I needed a strong attendant who could carry me because there would be many flights of stairs. I needed to take written prescriptions for all my medication. She explained Eastern rest rooms—the toilets were holes in the ground. We laughed at the graphic description, but I decided to seek out Western-style hotels along the way if I needed to use the rest room. Finally, I was ready for my adventure. I flew to San Francisco to join seasoned travelers with disabilities.

Overseas travel was a nightmare. It was a sixteen-hour flight to Beijing. We were delayed more than five hours in San Francisco because of mechanical problems. We arrived late in Tokyo and missed our connecting flight. The closer we got to China, the more explicit our travel coordinator became: China did not want the women activists in the country but was swayed by the money the conference generated. We were warned that we would see police officers lining the streets and watching us closely. They might stop and search us at any time.

I was shocked when I arrived in Beijing. The airport was small and primitive. Thousands of delegates to the conference filed off planes until travelers clogged every open spot in the terminals. I was concerned that those like myself in wheelchairs would not have room to get out of the airport. It took us over two hours to find everyone in our group and make it to our bus.

After we settled into our hotel rooms, we made our first sightseeing trip to the Great Wall of China. I sat on the curb laughing to myself as I watched the preparations. Our travel attendants were stuffing wheelchairs in the back of the bus. Women were being lifted out of their wheelchairs and carried onto the bus. The hotel workers stared; they had never seen so many people with disabilities before.

It took an hour to load the bus, but when we arrived at the Great Wall, all the waiting was worth it. Everywhere I turned, I saw nothing but majestic mountains. The Great Wall trailed along the tops of the mountains for miles. I had to pinch myself to prove that what I was seeing was real. I was really in China. I was really looking at the Great Wall. Attendants began carrying people in wheelchairs up the flights of steps leading to the Great Wall. I chose to use my crutches to walk up the steps myself.

Once I was on top of the wall, I marveled at the human accomplishment. I was standing on something that was begun more than a thousand years ago. I stopped following the group when my legs started to hurt from the many stair steps on the wall. I sat down and prayed as I stared at the majesty of God's mountains. One of the women in my group turned to me. Smiling and crying at the same time, she said, "You made it, Cheryl. How do you feel?" I had made it, and although I felt a degree of happiness, I still felt empty. I asked God why.

On our fourth day in Beijing, it was time to conduct business. I attended the International Symposium on Issues of Women with Disabilities. I sat in the company of hundreds of women representing fifty countries, only to be shocked and saddened by what I heard. Delegate after delegate described the horrors of being a disabled woman in countries across the world.

"In most countries, only 1 to 2 percent of disabled children have any education, and most of the precious few who do . . . are boys."

"In most countries, disabled women and girls have an exceedingly higher mortality rate than do disabled males."

"Involuntary sterilization, contraceptives, and abortion continue to be forced upon women with disabilities."

"Disabled women are nearly always excluded from economic development programs, regardless of whether the programs target disabled people or women in general."

"There are over three hundred million women with disabilities worldwide, most of whom are excluded from mainstream society."

"Many countries have eugenic protection laws that prevent the increase of 'inferior descendants.' That means that it is legal to kill or forcibly sterilize people with disabilities."

"Every day, women with disabilities are given hysterectomies because caregivers decided that these women should never have children."

"Millions of disabled women and girls are raped and abused. . . ."

I could not listen anymore to the worldwide cruelty toward women with disabilities. I could not understand how people could treat other human beings as if they were less than human. I began to feel overwhelmed by a worldwide problem. It hit me that here I was, in the midst of a search to belong, willingly sitting in a meeting and being told that I would not belong fully anywhere in the world. The delegates broke down into smaller working groups to develop a Disabled Women's Bill of Rights. When it was time to ratify the document, a representative from each group rose to proclaim a resolution.

"Disabled women can and should contribute to their nations' productivity and have equal opportunities to earn a decent wage. They should have adequate education and training as well as guarantees against workplace discrimination because of disability and gender."

"Women with disabilities need sensitive, reliable health care services in which clinics are free of physical barriers and workers are not biased toward preventing or hindering the right to become a mother."

"Women with disabilities who want to bear, adopt, and/or raise children should have that opportunity."

"Women and girls with disabilities belong in their own homes and neighborhoods, not in institutions."

"All human beings have the right to live free of the fear of violence. Women and girls with disabilities are all too frequently violated in their homes, in institutions, and on the streets. Criminal justice systems should recognize the rights and needs of victims with disabilities. Battered women's shelters, rape crisis centers, and other victim services should be accessible and sensitive to disabled women."

I started crying when I heard the last one. Too many people in my life had violated that right. We adjourned after the delegates approved the rights and issues we would promote throughout the conference. The U.S. contingency of women with disabilities was ready to start lobbying the hundreds of thousands of nondisabled delegates at the women's conference to embrace the issues of women with disabilities

When the conference started, it was a nightmare trying to get around. The Chinese version of wheelchair-accessible transportation made me appreciate even my worst experiences in the United States. Although the bus had a mechanical lift, there were no straps to keep the wheelchairs secured inside. The attendants spent most of their time helping the person in the wheelchair stay upright while the bus was in motion.

All the nongovernmental organizations met in a rural site outside Beijing. Although the entrance to the site was impressive, dirt roads and lack of pavement made using a wheelchair nearly impossible. I was not prepared for the emotional strain of trying to negotiate the hostile terrain; my depression and poor health had left me too weak to cope.

When the first day at the conference ended, I noticed that most of my fellow delegates were also tired, frustrated, and irritated. It rained all day, turning the unpaved pathways into quicksand for our wheelchairs. Some of the women missed the rendezvous time for taking the bus back to the hotel. After waiting for two hours, tempers began to flare. People began yelling and screaming at each other. Others started to cry.

I could not take it anymore. I thought my head would explode. I wanted to be left alone or run away. When I returned to the hotel, I slept for ten hours, missing the next day's meeting. When I showed up at the conference the following day, one of my fellow delegates pulled me aside to gently remind me that I was there to represent the interests of young people with disabilities. She began listing all the meetings I needed to attend. When I told her that my depression and health had worsened, she told me that I just had to force myself to attend to business.

Everything made more sense to me after that conversation. I began to understand why I felt incomplete in the disability, African-American, or women's communities. These groups were primarily focused on political change. The active members, having chosen the political group as their master identities, immersed themselves in the politics of their identity. I supported many political causes within each group, but none of them could understand that my passionate search had less to do with politics and more to do with finding peace. Although I believed deeply in the fight for equality for all people, I could not work anymore for the political cause. My soul felt too restless and empty. I was searching in the wrong place for my master identity. Before I could be of any use to social causes, I needed to address my past.

"Dear God, I don't understand why I feel empty and restless after becoming your child. I now realize that I was searching for my meaning and purpose apart from you. What do I do now?"

MASTER IDENTITY

Religion and disability politics often collided. I had spent so many years fighting disability stereotypes and discrimination that it was hard not to scrutinize the church. I heard many disability activists complain that religion further stigmatized people with disabilities. They said the Bible was full of accounts in which the ancient people thought sin caused disability. They further complained that religious people regularly used words that disability activists rejected as stig-matizing, like *lame* and *cripple*. They cited many religious stories that emphasized the wretchedness of the life of a person with a disability, thus perpetuating the stereotype that without healing, a person with a disability could not be a whole person.

I understood their arguments. I remember how uncomfortable I felt when listening to a sermon or Bible class lesson in which the speaker used a person with disability as the subject of a lesson in gratitude. Speakers would typically say, "I used to complain about not having new shoes until I met a man with no legs. . . ." I also did not like Christians using my supposedly pitiful life to make them feel better about themselves or more grateful to God.

Many disability activists, however, rejected the concept of over-coming. Many of them wanted to be considered as regular, whole people and not poster children for inspiration. They so did not want to be pitied that some of them felt that comments about their being "courageous," "brave," or "unfortunate" emphasized a pathetic, less-than-whole state.

This argument placed me in direct conflict with my steadfast belief in John 9. I was not ashamed of my belief that God had allowed me to be born with a disability so that he could display his power in my life. I did not believe that he would demonstrate that power by healing my disability; I felt that God's power was revealed in how dignified a man-ner I lived my life despite the obstacles. Disability was but one of my many obstacles, along with poverty, mental illness, race, and gender.

· I would have many more disagreements with members of the politicized disability community about religion and disability. I would always defend God's love, but I could not defend some of the responses of his other children to disability. I could not defend the existence of inaccessible churches. It had been a circuitous journey, but I finally understood that I was searching for an identity in other people and groups mostly because I could not feel at peace in the church.

I started to feel an emptiness that none of the meetings, galas, or parties on Capitol Hill could fill. I was learning that fame, status, and praise were addictive but never satisfying. I was looking for spiritual bonds that I could not obtain from any of my identities. I was deeply committed to helping in the fight for equal rights for people with disabilities. But before I could benefit the movement, I needed to deal with the soul wounds driving me on the insatiable search for love and total acceptance. God had allowed me to wander aimlessly so that I could understand that the belonging I desired could only come from my relationship with him. I had to decide that his love was enough to fill my soul completely and give me identity.

Being so enlightened about my new civil rights and becoming immersed in disability politics had weakened my desire to go to church. It bothered me greatly whenever I noticed that many churches were inaccessible to people in wheelchairs. Even if the front door was accessible, many churches did not have elevators. I was also not satisfied that many people in the religious community were not active in the push for civil rights for people with disabilities. I saw them distributing wheelchairs, but I knew firsthand that stereotypes and stigmas were more of a barrier to people with disabilities. A wheelchair meant less if nondisabled people saw no need to remove attitudinal barriers.

I scrambled to reestablish the bonds I felt with members of the church by searching for a wheelchair-accessible church. Many of the churches I called had steps but offered to carry me inside the building—a notion I found offensive. To many disability-rights activists, such an action should be avoided because it perpetuates a stereotype of helplessness. The movement was about interdependence and independence. Being carried was a glaring symbol of powerlessness, besides being undignified.

In my souring attitude, I began noticing the other ways churches excluded people with disabilities. Few churches had sign language interpreters. Most churches did not offer large-print material for the visually impaired. When I looked around, people with disabilities were invisible in most churches. Yet I began to recognize that the real battle had begun in my spirit. I could not stop my descent into cataloguing perceived injustice and acts of exclusion; I was growing away from fellow Christians.

One of the ministers at my previous church noticed that I had stopped attending and called me. I told him that I was having trouble with churches because I did not see many people with disabilities there. Why weren't they accommodated?

"Well, we don't have enough people in wheelchairs to justify making extensive renovations."

"But the physical barriers are the main cause for not having many people with disabilities. I can't even bring my friends to this church because there are no ramps."

"We could carry you in just like the story in the Bible where the friends lifted the man paralyzed on the mat and lowered him through the roof to see Jesus," he offered.

"Yeah, but they didn't have wheelchairs back then. If that guy had a wheelchair, he could have made it through the crowd by himself. I'm struggling because people with disabilities don't want people to carry them around like an invalid. I know I don't. I want to remain independent and move around my church with dignity."

"Well, Cheryl, we all need one another, and you can just look at being carried up the steps as being served by your brothers and sisters in Christ."

"Being carried will turn off many people with disabilities. And for those who aren't Christian, I just see it as a needless barrier to someone who wants to come into the building. It's just one more thing to repel people with disabilities who may be looking for God."

"Cheryl, I don't know what to say. Just don't let these issues separate you from your family in Christ."

"I feel like a huge part of who I am is being rejected when I can't get into a building and there is nothing I can do about it."

"No one is rejecting you because of your handicap. Why do you believe that? I think Satan is trying to trick you into thinking we are your enemies."

I did not feel the church was my enemy; I was just having trouble integrating my newfound acceptance as a person with a disability with my identity as a Christian. I wanted people to be able to honor God by giving themselves to service to others. However, I did not want other people's acts of service to be at the expense of the dignity of the person being served. I told my minister that there were many affordable options for churches to make their buildings more accessible to disabled people. I said, "With such an action, the church would be telling the world that it was truly welcoming all people."

My minister cautioned me about allowing the thinking of the world to erode the bonds I had with fellow Christians. He challenged me to make a better choice. Instead of pulling away from church, I should work to improve access and inclusion. He said, "Many churches just don't have a clue how they can be more accessible. Educate us instead of running away."

His words cut my heart like a knife. I was running away again. My typical response to the possibility of being hurt was to run away. I wanted to feel most at home with fellow Christians. I wanted to feel the satisfying sense of community within the church, but I was afraid that my longings made me vulnerable to rejection by the people I loved the most. It was possible that everything I suggested would be dismissed. What would be my response if churches told me that disability was a nonissue? How could I ever feel a sense of belonging in a group that did nothing to make itself fully inclusive?

My dear child, you are spinning your wheels going down the wrong path. The cries of your soul have nothing to do with feeling community with other people. You have yet to feel the full peace and security of my love. You are seeking an identity apart from me. I am your master identity. No other identity can offer you the promises I can. I am here to patiently love and guide you. I have given you my Spirit to fill the depths of your soul and comfort your aching heart. Daddy is telling you to be still and look in my face. I will tell you who you are. I want you to see that your identity comes through your relationship with me.

You are a new person because of my power to free you from your past. My Spirit lives inside you and tells you constantly that you are mine. I have brought you out of the bonds of your past to be with me. I am calling you to stand in my strength. I have called you to live a life of hope and faith. Because of my Son, you will have a life of victory, not one of shame and sorrow. You are alive and growing because of your relationship with me. Be thankful. You are mine forever. Be secure.

Your purpose is to remain with me. I want you to show the world that because you are my child, you have overcome the shackles of your past. You are not helpless. You are not unworthy. You are not defeated. Because of me, you can stand firm and know I am all that you need.

CHAPTER ELEVEN

Soulmate

I believe I'll go back home
And acknowledge that I done wrong.
When I was in my Father's house,
I was well supplied.
I made a mistake in a-doin' well,
Now I'm dissatisfied.
I believe I'll go back home.

NEGRO SPIRITUAL

It had been a tough six years since I had become a Christian. When I was seventeen, I thought that becoming a child of God would some how make all of my earthly problems disappear. I thought that after I was baptized, I would automatically feel complete and soul-satisfied. I thought that knowing God loved me would be enough to make up for the many years I considered him distant and aloof. I thought that wearing the "Christian" label would miraculously erase the years of abuse and doubt. My soul wounds were deep but not impossible for God to heal.

However, I was the biggest obstacle to my own healing. I was incapable of being still long enough to feel the depth of God's Spirit in my heart and soul. Moreover, healing was painful, and I tended to run away from pain.

In the fall of 1993, I moved to Columbus, Ohio, for graduate school. At this point, I needed to leave Washington and distance myself from disability politics, inaccessible churches, and the spiritual malaise that had engulfed me. I was waiting for God to tell me what I was doing wrong; I had been his child for seven years and still felt empty.

After five months in my new city, loneliness crept in again. I was attending a large, wealthy, primarily white church in Columbus. I was one of only three African-Americans in the congregation. I could not figure out why I felt disconnected despite trying to feel like part of the family. I immersed myself in all things Christian. Whenever the doors of the church were open, I was there. Although the church was accessible, again, I was not comfortable with my difference.

Instead of wallowing in my negative emotions about the racial composition of the church, I plunged into church work with great fervor. The busier I became, the less lonely I felt. I was working myself numb. After five months of frenzy, I had many good acquaintances but no intimate friends.

My church instituted an adopt-a-college-student program in which couples from the congregation became surrogate families for students. Paul and Kathy were my surrogate parents, but since they were close to my own age, they felt more like a brother and sister than parents. They were a fun-loving couple who invited me to their house for several dinners each month.

Kathy and I would talk for hours about marriage and family. The more I heard Kathy's love-at-first-sight stories, the more dissatisfied I became with my single status. I wanted my own family so that I could escape being lonely. Kathy asked me, as married couples always did, why I was single. I told her that I had not found the right man. In reality, I had never even had a date. When Paul walked into the room, Kathy said, "Honey, do you know any African-American men? Cheryl needs to get married. I want her to be happy like us."

Paul and Kathy did not know any African-American men. I told them I was open to dating men of other races. Paul shifted in his chair and told me, "I don't know of any interracial couples around here. I'm not saying anything is wrong with it or anything. I just don't see any couples like that around here." Kathy nodded and said that it would be easier to find someone in my own race than to attempt an interracial relationship.

I tried to lighten the tone of the conversation by joking, "Well, when you are desperate, you tend not to close yourself off to any one race. Gotta increase my odds." Everyone laughed at my half-joke, half-truth.

Paul suggested I start attending an African-American congregation. I balked. I had not been part of an African-American congregation since my freshman year at Yale. I was still too afraid that I would have to pass a litmus test of blackness to be accepted. I would rather remain apart from other African-Americans and preserve my love for my culture than be rejected again. I told Paul that I did not prefer all-white congregations either. I wanted a mixed race congregation.

Paul and Kathy told me that Sunday morning was the most segregated hour in the week—there were no mixed congregations in the city. Kathy turned to me and said, "Cheryl, I believe in prayer. I'm going to pray every day that God sends you a brother as wonderful as my Paul. You need someone to take care of you."

While the months dragged on without an answer to that prayer, my loneliness grew and my attitude toward my congregation soured. I struggled to make it to Sunday morning worship, let alone singles classes or events. My focus had again bounced back to only my needs. Kathy had vocalized one of my deepest desires: I wanted someone to take care of me. I was tired of facing the world alone. As soon as I admitted my feelings, I felt guilty. I tried telling God that I was not saying our relationship was not enough, but I wanted a human being with whom I could share my life. I wanted a family like my sister had.

"What's wrong with feeling this way, God? What is wrong with needing to be needed?"

When New Year's Eve approached, the singles in my congregation began preparing for the area-wide singles fellowship, in which all the local churches got together for fun and Bible study. Theoretically, all congregations were invited, but only white churches participated. I was tired of going to events at which I was the only African-American in a sea of hundreds. Instead of disability access as the barrier between other Christians and me, it was now race. I did not yet understand that my dissatisfaction had little to do with disability or race. These issues reflected a deeper issue within my soul.

I did not want to go to the singles fellowship but reluctantly went anyway. I went mostly because I was afraid that I could lose my "chance" and miss the one man who would fall in love with me. When I drove to the church, I began to fight the negative thoughts in my head telling me that I was ugly, that no one would ever be interested in me romantically.

Everything in me seemed to want to skip the event, stay home, and protect my heart. I would have turned around if the singles minister had not spotted me as I pulled into the church parking lot. When I walked into the building, I was shocked at the large turnout. However, in the midst of two hundred singles, I was, again, the only African-American. I sighed, put on my happy mask, and began to mingle.

Within twenty minutes, another caravan of cars pulled up to the building, and more people started filing through the door—African-American and white singles. Hope returned. Then I saw him.

Gregory, an African-American, stood at six feet, five inches. He strode through the doors of the church with an air of strong self-confidence. He had a commanding presence as he began to scan the room and mingle effortlessly. I knew I had to muster enough courage to talk with him.

When he walked further through the crowd, our eyes met. My first thought was the story Paul and Kathy told me of their first encounter: Paul saw Kathy across the room, their eyes met, and within two weeks, Paul knew he wanted to marry her. I began to wonder if this new man was my Paul.

Gregory sat on the table next to me so that we were talking at eye level. I began to block out everyone else around me as Gregory and I talked. Originally from the South, he was in graduate school at Ohio State University. He had been a Christian for over seven years. Mostly, Gregory asked questions about me—where I lived, my background, my field of study at Ohio State, my reasons for choosing my current congregation, and a host of other questions. When I talked, he gave me his undivided attention.

"You have a beautiful smile, Cheryl." I was hooked. No man had ever given me a compliment before.

When Gregory asked for my telephone number, I was sure that it signaled his interest. I began to feel better about everything. That someone was interested in me romantically made me feel good about myself. I even got a better attitude about being at the fellowship. I mingled with other people with more confidence. My sour attitude had disappeared; suddenly I wanted to be there. I made sure I was nearby when the Bible study started so that Gregory could invite me to sit next to him. It was difficult to focus on the study when I was so consumed with my newfound love interest.

I had never been in a dating relationship before so I did not know what to do with the new emotions I felt. I did not know what indicated a dating relationship or how desires for such a relationship were interfering with my relationship with God. It would be years before I could recognize that I started my relationship with Gregory with an unhealthy focus. Thinking about him and the possibility of marriage began to consume me—and I had just met him!

THE HOOK

Several days passed, during which time Gregory did not call me. I would look at my answering machine and feel depressed to see no messages. I felt worse when there were messages but not from him. I was consumed by fearful thoughts—"Does he still like me? Should I call him? What should I do?"

When Gregory finally called, we scheduled our first real date. We met at a restaurant and continued our remarkably comfortable conversation. We laughed as we discussed our personal and spiritual lives. I told him portions of my life story as a test. I felt that if he was still around after hearing my story, then maybe we had a chance.

"Wow, Cheryl. I'm blown away by how God protected you throughout everything. You are obviously a woman of great faith. You make my God more real."

"Well, I don't know if I feel comfortable with being called 'a woman of great faith.' Despite everything, I still feel like sometimes he's not going to intervene—particularly when a situation goes on for a long time."

"Ah yeah, but even the apostles doubted. You know who to stick with."

"Yeah, I'm not going anywhere. I just don't know where God is leading me. I don't know what he would like me to do with my life, but I feel optimistic that he has a plan for me."

Gregory replied, "Oh, I'm excited about meeting you. I see you being a powerful sister in the world and in the church."

"I just want to be stronger in my faith. I wish I could feel more confident about my personal relationship with God. I wish I could feel him more. I don't like being insecure." I do not believe I heard myself or understood the depth of my confession to Gregory. I had verbalized the core problem of my soul: I felt insecure in my relationship with God.

Although my eyes were open, I could not see the cliff ahead. I continued down the ill-fated path of pursuing Gregory. I marveled at his knowledge of life, the world, and the Bible. He spoke with eloquence and confidence about everything. He told me about his hopes and dreams. It had been seven years since he last dated someone, and he had never dated a Christian.

When we finally looked at our watches, we discovered we'd been in the restaurant for seven hours. Gregory began to exclaim how much he enjoyed himself—how quickly the time had passed! He told me that we needed to find more time to spend together on campus. When we walked to our cars, he invited me to visit his church that next Sunday. Gregory prayed for us before we left.

"Dear God, I feel something about Gregory," I prayed later. "Is he going to be the one for me? I know it is too soon for him to fall in love with me, and I know I shouldn't expect it. I know he stepped into my life at the time I needed him the most. I was at my breaking point, feeling so ugly. You knew how miserable I was. You knew I was lonely. Lord, I feel something in this relationship. He has everything I have asked for in a husband. Gregory understands me and listens to me. Lord, Gregory spent his prayer time thanking you for our relationship and me. Lord, if that is not a sign of his interest in me, then will you make it more clear to me?"

Looking back on this prayer, I am saddened to see how easy it was to tell God that he was not enough to complete me. I was looking to Gregory to rescue me from my loneliness.

As months passed, Gregory and I began to spend more time together. I began to worship at his church and spend time with the singles there. I loved that the congregation was mixed racially. I also began to fall in love with Gregory. He told me how his feelings for me deepened and that I began to consume his prayers.

However, once I decided to become a permanent member of the church, Gregory began to ignore me when we were at church functions. He never sat next to me. He rarely talked to me before or after services. I began to panic, wondering if he had lost interest in me. He was treating me like a stranger in public but like a girlfriend in private.

When I could not stand the pain of being ignored anymore, I cornered Gregory after worship services. "What is going on, Gregory? Why do you ignore me when we are around your church friends? It hurts."

"I didn't mean to hurt you, Cheryl. It's just a matter of considering the needs of others. Many single sisters in this congregation desire to be in a dating relationship. Many of them would envy the depth of the relationship you and I share. I think we should not be consumed with ourselves and always hang around each other. I think it will cause more problems for others."

"I don't understand. If we enjoy each other's company, why would anyone be mad at us for being together?"

"I always look forward to spending time with you, Cheryl. You have so much to offer, and God wants you to spend the time at church getting into the lives of other sisters here."

I dropped the subject because it became clear to me that Gregory wanted to get as close as possible to dating without officially being a couple. Because he was pushing me away and pulling me close simultaneously, I was confused. It seemed that every word he spoke held a double meaning, and I would spend hours after our conversations trying to understand his real intent. The ambiguity of our relationship had me hooked. Gregory treated me like a girlfriend, and, despite the uncertainty, his words were sweet to me.

Foreign Language

I should have run away from Gregory, but I could not leave. He told his friends that I was his best friend and he could depend on me for anything. I overheard him telling one of his friends that he was deeply satisfied in our relationship—our conversation, laughter, and prayer. Gregory, however, was the only one satisfied in our relationship. I was miserable. I felt used. I felt the same paralysis as I did when Dad used me to fulfill his emotional needs. Although I was now an independent adult, I could not walk away.

"Gregory, where is this relationship going?"

"What do you mean?"

"You know what I mean. Are we dating? Just friends? What?"

"Oh, I don't date."

I looked up, puzzled. Gregory and I had been spending time together for months. We were *dating*. Nevertheless, he told me that he did not have the time and energy needed to keep a romantic relationship going. He did not want to spend energy trying to maintain the romance in a dating relationship.

I said, "I don't understand how you can *not* consider what you and I have been doing as dating."

"We are going out and are very close spiritual friends. You are my soulmate."

I had no clue what he meant by "soulmate." I had only heard the term in reference to a spouse or dating partner. Gregory was muddying the waters. To him, being a soulmate meant two souls connected in a spiritual bond of Christ. A soulmate represented a depth of relationship that all Christians should have. He told me that he and I were bonded together in our souls. Gregory used other romantic terms to describe our relationship. When he told me he was committed to me, I was further confused.

"What does that mean?"

He said, "It means that I am making a choice to stick with our relationship no matter what."

"And how is that different from dating?"

"Cheryl, it is not a romantic thing. I'm talking about choices, not romance."

I was confused, so I asked one of my friends if I was reading the relationship wrong. My friend called Gregory a Christian gigolo because his words about dating did not match his actions. She said he had a pattern of similar relationships with other women where he lived previously. I did not want to believe her, but I could not dismiss the way his words were stringing me along. He would initiate one-on-one dinners and outings with me. He would tell me that I made his God more real, that I was number one in his life, and that I had the qualities he wanted in a wife. I had been waiting all my life to hear those romantic words, and now that I had fallen in love with the man saying them, I could not accept that there was no future in the relationship.

I began to focus my prayers on winning Gregory's love. My time at the church building was spent looking for Gregory and noticing to whom he was talking. The more I fell for him, the more jealous I was at the time he spent with other women at church. I did not realize that God was no longer first in my life; the desire for a romantic relationship was now paramount. Although I was pursuing my doctorate in psychology, I did not notice how unhealthy my one-way relationship with Gregory had become.

My sense of self-worth was now tied to Gregory's love. Despite the growing pain of unrequited love, I continued the relationship. I spent hours thinking about him, devising plans for how he and I could meet and be together. Whenever I saw Gregory with another woman at church, I became jealous and depressed. I would start to plan how I could spend time with him immediately after he finished talking to the woman. I began to be preoccupied with how I looked to Gregory whenever I sang, prayed, spoke, or did anything at church.

I wanted to serve God completely and sincerely, but I also wanted Gregory to fall in love with my spiritual side. My past was not dormant; it had left me numb enough to tolerate Gregory's painful smooth talking and insecure enough to accept the pain as the best I could expect from a man. I was out of control.

PLAYING THE FIELD

Toward the fourth month of our relationship, I began to hear more about Gregory's other close female friendships. His two other soulmates were women from his congregation back home. He expressed obvious respect for Tina and Kelly, who had known him for seven years. I was hurt because I thought I was his only soulmate. Then he described Kelly as his number one. I looked at him and asked how two people could be tops in his life.

Gregory rose to the occasion by explaining that he and Kelly went way back. She always cooked for him and sent him care packages. Apparently, Kelly was in the same boat as me. She was a godly woman who thought she was in a developing relationship with Gregory that would one day lead to marriage. Gregory looked at me and said that I was special to him because I was number one in depth and sincerity in our relationship.

I should have slapped him right then because he admitted he was playing the field, but I felt better knowing that I was special in some way to a man. After a year with Gregory, I accepted the cruel fact that we were dating by my standards, but not by his. We had grown closer. We went out often and spent time together talking and laughing. We also worked together closely organizing the singles ministry at church. Many people at our church speculated that we were dating; some told me that they were praying for our relationship. We looked good together and worked well together.

Gregory had baptized another single woman at our church, Teresa, who later became one of my dearest friends. She was a beautiful business executive. After her baptism, Gregory told me that he had developed romantic feelings for her. His words knocked the wind out of me. I was speechless. I always thought I was competing with his two other soulmates, not with a stranger. I vowed I would not cry in front of him. I struggled to keep my emotions in check, refusing to talk until I had collected myself. I made up an excuse to leave and cried all the way home.

At that time, I felt Teresa was more beautiful than me. She was tall, thin, and wealthy. She was also white. The first African-American man I had been close to was not attracted to me, but to a white woman. When the emotions subsided, I realized that the most hurtful part of Gregory's confession was not that he was attracted to a white woman; after all, I was open to interracial relationships too. What hurt was his rejecting me after all my time and emotional investment in him. He didn't know anything about Teresa, but I had told him my entire life story. I had shared my innermost secrets with him. I had given him my heart. Although he thought I was beautiful and fun to be with, he was not in love with me. He had romantic feelings for someone he had just met.

When I got home, I told myself that I needed to get out of the relationship. Then Gregory called to apologize for hurting my feelings. He told me that he thought he could tell me anything, but he was not going to date or marry her. He said that he got more out of our relationship than I realized. I was his soulmate, and he was committed to me. He depended on me to challenge him in his relationship with God. "So many people are out there feeding my pride and ego, but you always point out things that I need to change to be a better person and follower of Christ. I am a better person because of you."

"But it's not enough for you to marry me."

"I'm just not ready to get married. I want a graduate degree. I'm not saying I won't ever fall in love. Actually, I told someone before coming to Ohio State that graduate school would probably be the best or most likely time to get married. If I ever get married, it would be at that time because the woman would probably help me get through school. Isn't that interesting?"

Gregory's ambiguous words trapped me again. I had been helping and encouraging him to finish his degree. If I meant so much to him, I could not understand why we were not married by now. I could hear echoes of my cousin John telling me that I was ugly and crippled and would never find anyone to love me as he did. I had a strong, paralyzing fear that if I walked away I would never get another chance at marriage. Gregory was my only chance.

I knew what I was feeling was wrong. I knew God would not answer my prayers for Gregory. But I had invested so much of myself in the relationship that I was terrified of the final rejection. I could not leave, and I could not stay. I was taken to a new level of misery.

"Dear God, I've gotten myself in a mess and I can't let go. I'm afraid of being alone, and I know I'm doing something wrong because it just hurts so much."

Gregory was the sole focus in life. My entire life—emotional, physical, and spiritual—was wrapped up in him becoming my husband. I was trying to please him instead of God. Everything I did, I did for fear of losing Gregory or pushing him away from marriage. My primary motivation for helping him was to fulfill my need to be needed. Therefore, I could not create any healthy boundaries in the relationship. I was physically unable to set any limits to how much pain I would take. My entire self-worth was tied up in pleasing Gregory. I was helpless to save myself.

Escape Plan

There were many opportunities to escape the bondage of my relationship with Gregory, but I could not seize them. Since I was the closest person to him, I began to feel guilty about wanting to leave him. The unhealthy patterns I had developed in my relationship with my father had crept into my adult life. Gregory was exactly like my father. He had a strong, authoritative presence. He was an eloquent and persuasive speaker who used the Bible to justify many questionable actions.

Gregory was also selfish like my father; both of them used emotionally weak women to satisfy their needs. Gregory and my father knew the language that would trigger my panic and ultimate dependence on them. Gregory also shared my father's impulsiveness and poor decision-making. Gregory neglected his studies to the point of being expelled from graduate school, then turned to me for financial and emotional help. He told me, "Cheryl, you are the only one I can depend on."

I had been a victim for so many years that I forgot that I was now an adult with the power to choose to leave. I had learned to be helpless, so I carried this destructive pattern into adulthood. When I told

Gregory that our relationship was out of balance because I loved him more than he loved me, he told me we needed to take a time-out.

The fears of rejection and abandonment surfaced, and I promised myself to check my feelings and continue in the relationship. My motives were wrong—I was sacrificing my heart so I wouldn't be alone. I was sacrificing my feelings just to make Gregory more comfortable in the relationship. He was enjoying all the benefits of dating without any work. I was left with the lonely task of trying to contain my intense feelings of one-sided love. The spin I placed on the situation was that I valued our relationship so much that I was willing to fight for it. I thought surely Gregory would fall in love with someone who placed such a high priority on a relationship and was willing to suffer for it.

After a year and a half with Gregory, I grew numb—still trapped, but emotionally numb. I was tired. The time had come to push Gregory away, since I couldn't walk away on my own. So I tried to anger him by blasting his behavior and ambiguous language. Gregory never raised his voice as he reiterated the sincerity of his feelings for me.

FIZZLE

I wasted almost three years consumed with Gregory and the desire for marriage. I had forgotten the passion I once had for God—the love I once had for him. I sought to put a man's love in a place in my soul that only God could occupy. Just like my involvement in the disability community in D.C., my self-worth was inextricably tied to esteem, importance, and love from other people. I was basing my entire life on the wrong emotional plane. I did not know that as long as I searched for belonging and happiness in people rather than God, I would remain hopelessly unhappy.

"Oh, dear God, how do I change this about myself? How do I start over again? I want to change, but I don't know how. I've been this way all my life, and I feel so powerless to change. Please help me."

My relationship with Gregory came to an emotionally anticlimatic end when we met Ann. She had been visiting our church for several weeks. In spending time with her, Gregory learned about her history of child abuse and domestic violence. He asked me to allow her to live with me until she sorted out her life.

I passively agreed. As I had become preoccupied with my sudden health problems, I failed to notice or care about the time Ann and Gregory were spending together in my house. I spent most of the day in bed. I had no energy and no desire to talk with them. I also lost my appetite. I did not realize it at the time, but I was clinically depressed.

Ann had her own mental health problems. She had a volatile temper that reminded me of my mother. One moment Ann was fine, then something would set her off. When she was enraged, she would slam doors, scream obscenities, and break things. One evening, slamming doors and screaming woke me.

When I reached her room, I found her screaming, cursing, and crying over the telephone at Gregory. I could not understand why they were fighting. I just wanted her out of my house. She saw me standing at the doorway and ran away. I picked up the telephone to hear Gregory's voice on the other end. "Gregory, what is going on? Why is she so angry?"

"We had a disagreement. I'm sorry about her screaming like that."

"I want her out of here. She has a mental illness. I think she may be bipolar. She needs help, and right now I can't take that kind of behavior here. Her mood swings remind me of living with my mother."

Gregory sighed and agreed that I needed my space to heal. When Ann returned, I told her that she had to find another place to live because I could not recover with a roommate who had such a volatile temper. She nodded and began to pack.

Gregory came to pick her up in the morning. I did not come out of my room. And that was the last time I talked to him. Several weeks passed, and during that time he did not return my calls. I knew he was physically fine because other friends had seen him.

The time apart was surprisingly liberating. I was tired of the hurtful relationship, and I did not panic at the distance. Then I received a card in the mail from him, telling me that he was busy doing some things but we would hang out for my birthday, which was coming up in several days.

My birthday came and went with no sign of Gregory. I was irritated that he stood me up but accepted it as one more sign that it was time to move on. At midnight the next day, I went to the store for my favorite ice cream. When I returned home, I found a message on my answering machine from him. He told me he was returning from Montana with Ann, his new wife.

I dropped the bags I was holding and sat on the couch in disbelief. Gregory had married my former roommate who did not have any of the qualities he said he wanted in a wife. After hearing the rest of his message, that he still wanted to celebrate my birthday when he returned, I erased it. The blinders I had worn for years fell off. I was hurt and angry but clearsighted enough to see the whole fiasco.

I was ashamed to have wasted so much time on someone unworthy of my attention. Gregory's choice was disappointing. I probably would have been depressed if he had married one of his other close girlfriends because all of us shared similar traits. But he married someone totally different from his professed ideal, someone with emotional needs he could never fill. He even told me once that whoever married Ann would be miserable.

With Gregory's choice, I immediately felt free. I called Teresa and told her about his sudden marriage. She confessed that she and Gregory dated briefly, but she ended the relationship because she felt as if she was cheating on me by being with him. I reassured Teresa that I did not hate her. I was happy to discover that I was not the only person Gregory had wooed. When the story of his marriage reached the congregation, a handful of other women came forward with similar stories. Although my ego felt better that I was not the only person he duped, I was ashamed of my behavior toward God. For more than two years I had neglected him. My prayers and thoughts were consumed with begging for marriage to Gregory.

Listening to a sermon the following Sunday, I learned that I was an idolater. I had given more love, attention, and trust to something other than God. I didn't realize how hurt God was by my actions until I went to a friend's home for Sunday lunch. Laura had three children whom she waited on day and night. She sacrificed her budding career in real estate to be a stay-at-home mother. Laura's children had everything they needed.

This particular Sunday, Laura was recovering from the flu but managed to make an elaborate meal because she was excited that her husband, her children, and friends would be at the house. Jarred, her middle son, came inside from playing and asked for a drink. Laura gave him punch that she made from scratch, but Jarred pushed it away, saying it tasted nasty.

When we ate dinner, Jarred pushed everything away—it all tasted yucky. Laura left the room in tears. Martin, Laura's husband, chastised Jarred, "Your mother has spent all your life showering you with love. She anticipates your needs and provides for them. She rushes to your side when you are hurt. She makes sure that everything she says to you builds you up and makes you a better person. Your mother never does anything to harm you. Yet, with all that she does for you out of love, you have the gall to disrespect her like you did. What you did was selfish. It boils down to telling her that you don't love her."

It was as if Martin was chastising me. I finally understood the impact of idolatry. I was hurting my heavenly Father when all he ever did was shower me with love. I was ashamed and afraid of God's punishment, which I deserved. I deserved no mercy for rejecting God and replacing him with Gregory. I could not hide behind being a victim forever. I knew on many levels that my behavior with Gregory was wrong, yet I chose to stay; I tried to force my own way. With this insight, I begged God for forgiveness.

Years later I discovered how miserable my life would have been with Gregory. He and Ann divorced within one year, and he drifted along alienating people with one poor decision after another. During this misguided episode in my life, God revealed his mercy by not answering my prayers as I had requested. God's "no" demonstrated his love and protection. He had more to teach me about healthy love. Tough love hurts, but I never forgot the lessons I learned; now I can spot unhealthy people and unhealthy relationships from miles away. I do not try to change people anymore. Instead, I choose to walk away from anyone who impairs my relationship with God.

My dear child, do not be afraid. I love you and forgive you. Perfect love like I have for you does not keep a record of wrongs. I am celebrating that you have returned to my arms. It hurt me to watch this situation unfold, but I knew you would return. I love you with a mercy and compassion unmatched by any other. I search hearts and know yours intimately. My precious, busy child, you must be still and get to know me. You are scrambling to fill spots in your heart and soul that are reserved only for me.

You have much to learn about perfect love, my dear child. To understand love, you must first come to know me, for I am the love that is patient, unselfish, and not easily angered. The love I want for you is one that always protects, trusts, hopes, and perseveres. The love you thought you had did not measure up to true love.

I need you to leave your past with me so that I can heal your soul. Be still long enough to feel me at work in your life. I have called you to be my child. When you accepted me as your Father, I made you victorious over your past. You have yet to realize that through your relationship with me you are an overcomer. I will help you to live a life that reflects your victory.

I am your patient and loving Father. Do not worry that I will grow tired of your cries or weary of showing you mercy and compassion. I will never crush your bruised heart. Trust me. I have you in the palm of my hand. I know your future, how to mold you to perfection. Fight hard to protect your faith in me. My promises to you are eternal and irrevocable. You must know that you, my child, are never alone.

PART FOUR

Up from the Depths

I wish I knew how it would feel to be
 free.
I wish I could break all the chains
 holding me.
I wish I could say all the things that I
 should say.
Say 'em loud. Say 'em clear
For the whole wide world to hear.
I wish I could share all the love that's
 in my heart.
Remove all the bars that keep us
 apart.
I wish you could know what it means
 to be me.
Then you'd see and agree that every-
 one should be free.

I wish I could give all the love to give.
I wish I could live like I'm longing to
    live.
I wish I could do all the things that I
    can do.
Though I'm way overdue, I'd be strong
    and new.
I wish I could be like a bird in the sky.
How sweet it would be if I found I
    could fly.
I'd soar to the sun and look down at
    the sea.
Then I'd sing because I'd know how it
    would feel to be free.

B. TAYLOR, DUANE MUSIC INC. (ASCAP)

CHAPTER TWELVE

Soul Processing

I was born by the river in a little old tent,
And just like the river I've been running ever since.
It's been a long time coming, but I know
A change is gonna come.

SAM COOKE, ABKCO MUSIC INC. (BMI)

I was like a deer caught in the headlights. I saw it coming but could not escape the collision. I had only two more years left in my doctoral training in psychology, so I knew the signs of emotional deterioration. The heavy sorrow would not go away. I could not feel happiness in anything I once loved. I slept more than sixteen hours a day and still felt tired. My feet felt like bricks, and breathing made me tired. For several weeks, I had no interest in eating.

Once a person who had excelled in school, I was having trouble reading, thinking, and forming complete sentences. When I looked in the mirror, I was staring at my mother. Years of running away from my past and my fears had created a frightened girl on a collision course with a killer.

When I was twenty-five, major depression caught up with me and pulled me into the same abyss of hopelessness that had trapped my mother. For almost five years, I came to know how a person with a brilliant future could lose it all in the suffocating black hole of mental illness.

I had been struggling with depression most of my life and never realized it. Depression hit me when I was in the hospital facing surgery, when my cousin molested me, when I was homeless, when my parents became my dependents at Yale, and during my relationship with Gregory. Depression has many causes. In my case, there was strong evidence for a genetic risk, as schizophrenia and depression plagued my parents and many in my extended family. Extreme stress and trauma could have triggered or exacerbated my depression. I had experienced twenty-five years of stress and trauma.

I always felt I was in crisis mode. I did not believe I had the luxury of working through the past and grieving losses; I spent my emotional energies preparing for the next crisis. After each I would numb my feelings, tuck the problem away, and brace for the next trauma. I did not know how to leave my burdens with God, and I was too afraid of working through my past. I was too afraid to thaw my frozen feelings because if I started to cry, I knew I would not be able to stop.

In 1995 while struggling with the last throes of my bad relationship with Gregory, I could no longer carry the burdens of my soul or handle one more crisis. I had come to terms with my disability. Through my work with the disability community, I saw the possibilities of a life worth living with a disability. Through my studies of the Bible and prayers, I was confident that somehow God would use the disability to achieve his purposes. In the big picture of my past, the physical limitations of my disability were less traumatic than abuse and poverty.

When the relative importance of my disability receded into the background, I assumed the physical trauma in my life would be over. I never thought about the possibility that I could contract another major illness or disease—or have an accident and break a bone. I erroneously thought that my lot of physical suffering was over and I would have to merely live with accommodating my childhood disability.

Before I became a Christian, my life seemed to have no purpose, so I wanted to escape the emotional pain by committing suicide. Monica and Denise helped me to know hope again in God. But I expected instant emotional healing. I hoped that God would show me mercy and stop major problems from intruding into my life. I wanted God to agree that my quota of misfortune was filled. I wanted a peace on earth that would materialize according to my dreams and expectations. All those expectations of a trauma-free life caved in when, in 1995, my body buckled under the constant stress and began to fall apart.

It was supposed to be a routine physical. I was supposed to be in and out of the doctor's office in thirty minutes. Instead, I was there for more than two hours. Each word my doctor said stunned me: "I'm feeling a significant mass spanning across your right breast toward your underarm." I could not hear her voice anymore. My mind immediately jumped to the obvious: cancer. The dreaded *C* word that strikes fear in the most powerful and elite of the world.

Dr. Anderson tried in vain to convince me that the mass did not necessarily mean I had cancer. "Don't worry. I'm sure it is nothing, but we need to rule out things." Dazed, I left with her mammogram referral. I began to obsess about cancer and death. Had I accomplished God's purpose for my life? If so, what was that purpose?

I arrived at the cancer hospital in tears. I wanted my sister with me. I wanted someone to hold my hand and give me a hug. I began longing for a boyfriend or husband by my side. I felt alone and lonely. I sat frozen in my car, too afraid to take my hands off the steering wheel.

I tried calling Gregory and some girlfriends from church, but no one was home. It was as if God wanted me to lean on him alone, to recognize that I needed to look to him and not anyone else for my strength. After several minutes of praying and crying, I had mustered enough resolve to move toward the doctor's office.

After the mammogram, the technician never returned with the results, but the nurse told me that I needed a biopsy to check for cancerous cells. When I returned home, Dr. Anderson called to tell me that other tests revealed at least one part of the mass might have been linked to problems with my lymph system. The following day another doctor diagnosed a disease of the sweat glands. The glands under my arm needed to be surgically removed. Within a week, my preoperative laboratory tests revealed a host of deficiencies and abnormalities, such as an underactive thyroid, anemia, and vitamin deficiencies.

I began a cocktail of twelve different medicines. Within two days, I broke out in hives all over my body. Doctors speculated that I was either panicking about the impending surgery or experiencing side effects from the medication. They prescribed a tranquilizer and antihistamine, both sedating. I became a zombie, engulfed in a fog that created a distant, vacant, and droopy look on my face. I began vomiting uncontrollably and awoke one morning lying on the bathroom floor where I had collapsed in exhaustion from dehydration.

After meeting with the doctor, I received more medicine. I knew the medicine was making me sicker, but I was too emotionally drained to advocate for myself. I became childlike. I had stopped caring.

CUTTING AND CRYING

The doctors decided to perform the breast biopsy before removing my diseased sweat glands. A needle biopsy was the quickest, easiest procedure to check for cancerous cells. The doctor began telling me that he found many of these masses to be fluid-filled, and a needle could sometimes pop the fluid sacs, taking care of the problem. I dismissed his statement because the radiologists and Dr. Anderson both said the mass looked solid. Furthermore, I was depressed and thought nothing good could ever happen to me.

Dr. Weiss plunged the needle deep into twenty different spots of the tumor. There were no fluid pockets—my tumor was solid. Dr. Weiss immediately tried to reassure me that the tumor could still be benign, but I would not know the results for a week. Instead of obsessing about cancer, however, I had to prepare for the arm surgery.

The surgery was a nightmare. In the middle of the procedure, the anesthesia began to wear off, and I became conscious of my surroundings. Although I did not feel pain, I felt the doctor tugging and pulling. I was afraid, disoriented, and panic-stricken. Despite my strong desire to run away, I could not move because of the powerful muscle relaxant I had been given before surgery. I was terrified. I tried to scream, but my mouth would not open. My eyes felt as if someone had cemented them closed. I could hear classical music playing in the background as the surgeon worked. I remember hearing someone yell, and then everything went blank.

Later, I drifted in and out of consciousness under the morphine drip. No one believed me when I said that I awoke during the surgery. After I arrived home to recuperate, the church had arranged for several people to come by throughout the day to help me with meals, clothes, baths, and wound care.

On the third day, I woke at 2:00 A.M. feeling that something was wrong with the surgical site. I went to the bathroom and found the bandage was soaked with blood. When I peeled the bandage back, I saw that the stitches in the entire area had come apart. I was looking at a gaping crater in my arm. When it registered in my brain that I was looking at my pinkish-white flesh through the bloody ooze dripping down my body, I began to throw up. I called Ann, but she was not at home. So I called Gregory to take me to the emergency room.

Arriving at the hospital, I was an emotional wreck. I could not think. I could not talk. I could not do anything except cry. The doctor numbed the area and began to clean the fleshy crater by scraping off the dead skin and encrusted blood. To prevent an abscess or infection, the doctor decided against resuturing the surgical site. The nurse taught me how to clean and care for the wound while I waited many months for my body to fill the area with tissue.

Within several days, Dr. Anderson called with the results of my breast biopsy. The test was inconclusive, so I agreed to have surgery to remove the tumor so they could test it for cancer. Dr. Anderson wanted me in surgery the following week, but I refused. I could not face another surgery when I was still recuperating from this one. I promised her I would have the surgery, but I needed more time to heal.

When I hung up the telephone, an overwhelming sensation of dread swept over me. No matter how hard I tried to push my fears down, they refused to remain dormant. Seeing that my old coping style was failing, I picked up the telephone to admit to someone else that I was powerless to save myself.

I called the crisis center at school, begging to see someone right away. After telling the intake counselor about my sudden health crisis and depressive symptoms, I had an appointment with a counselor, Jackie, for that same day. I liked her immediately. She was a motherly figure who showered me with love and acceptance. She immediately recognized my depressive symptoms and arranged an appointment for me to see the psychiatrist for antidepressant medication.

Jackie and I talked about my fears over the upcoming breast surgery. I also told her about the other health problems in my life, including my childhood disability. She patted my hand and told me that the stress I had endured would drive most people to depression. Jackie told me that I needed to start preparing my family and friends for how my depression might worsen before the medication could take effect. I had to give them a picture of what the worst would look like. She handed me a mound of pamphlets on depression. Once I returned home, I began calling my sister and closest friends.

I postponed the breast surgery for several weeks while I traveled to the U.N. Conference on Women in Beijing, China. I tried to convince myself that I could handle traveling to another part of the world to represent women with disabilities, but I was really running away from finding out if I had cancer. I was also at the depth of my unhealthy relationship with Gregory. When I returned from the stressful trip to China, I was stretched to the breaking point.

But I could not run from the breast surgery any longer. If I had cancer, any delay would allow the disease to spread so it would be my fault if I died. I called my doctor, and within a week I was scheduled for surgery. I told my sister and close friends that I did not know what form my depression would take after the surgery. I had told a friend that my life felt like a rubber band. Trauma had stretched me to the breaking point repeatedly and one day I would snap. She told me to rejoice because life could be worse. Obviously, that did not help much. I always hated it when Christians gave pat, simplistic answers to the profound question of pain and suffering.

Upon arriving at the surgery floor and registering, I began to break out in hives. My heart beat rapidly, and I started to hyperventilate. I was having a panic attack. I prayed constantly for strength while I went through the preoperative procedures. Dr. Weiss was going to conduct the biopsy under local anesthesia, despite my preference for general. He felt I would recover better. I did not have the energy to explain to him that, suffering from depression as I was, I did not think I could handle being awake during the procedure. A nurse held my hand as Dr. Weiss numbed the area. Although I did not feel his slicing the area open, I felt the tugging and pulling as he searched for the suspicious tumor in my breast.

Halfway through the procedure, something went wrong. Dr. Weiss moved farther from the numbed area and began to cut into sensitive flesh. A lightening bolt of pain seared through my body, and I screamed. My eyes rolled back, and I tried to leap off the table. The nurse held my hand as I started to wail.

Well, my emotional rubber band broke when I felt the knife cutting nonanesthetized tissue. I was taken by surprise, lost my grip on hope, and fell backward into a pit of hell that suffocated the life out of me.

Hell on Earth

I know what hell feels like. It is the soul-wrenching, agonizing feeling of profound hopelessness and abandonment. The feeling of being permanently separated from God slowly, brutally ripped my heart apart. Major depression was a hideous beast that gnawed at my soul, devouring all hope and faith and leaving behind an empty, shattered shell that was once a vibrant person.

In my depression, I understood the agony David and Jesus felt when they cried out, "My God, why have you forsaken me?" I felt God had closed his ears to my soul cries for rescue. As the beast of depression carried me down into its lair of gloom, I seemed to see God turn his back on me. I could see my arms flailing wildly trying to grasp him. Many times I would feel the stir of faint whispers in my soul: *My dear child, I am still with you. I am carrying you. Despite what you feel, I have never left your side.* The whispers would be engulfed quickly by a wave of anguish. My prayers were reduced to, "Lord, please help me hold out. I want to believe."

Life after the surgery grew darker. Although the pathology tests on the tumor came back negative for cancer, I was not happy. When I heard the wonderful news about the test, I felt nothing. I did not feel relieved or happy. I was simply numb. I lost interest in everything I once found pleasurable. I lost my appetite. I could sleep eighteen hours a day straight. I had no energy to shower, change clothes, or change the linens on my bed. Everything and everyone zapped my energy. All I wanted was to be left alone; nevertheless, I felt an intense, painful loneliness.

My psychiatrist prescribed the antidepressant Zoloft, and Jackie and I continued our therapy sessions. Life consisted of sleeping and therapy. For the first time in more than two years, I did not care about my education, career, or relationship with Gregory. I did not care about anything. My days were a rigid routine: I would struggle to fall asleep, sleep for more than fourteen hours, wake to take my medication, and struggle to fall asleep again. I was biding time until the medication and therapy began to work. I began to pray, "God, please make the medicine work. Please take this pain away from me. Please help me. I can't live anymore if you turn away from me."

I will never leave you. Keep fighting. I am your Daddy, and I am here comforting you as you mourn.

I did feel God briefly. For a two-week period, I mustered enough energy to analyze the data I had collected for my master's degree and to write my 250-page thesis. After I submitted it, my advisor returned it with only minor revisions. One week later I defended my thesis and passed. Although it was not the Ph.D., I had achieved one of the most important goals of my life and I felt nothing—no joy, no satisfaction. I went back home, collapsed in my bed, and slept for three days.

Friends from church began calling, but I never returned telephone calls. I received get-well cards but never opened them. My depression sank to a new low when I began to experience hallucinations. I saw a dark man hiding behind my bushes waiting to attack me. I had to turn on every light in my house because I feared a man was hiding in the dark waiting to jump me. I opened every closet door for fear of the man hiding within. I could see the faceless man vividly.

Walking to my car to make my doctor's appointment was an ordeal. I saw the dark man leaping from one tree to another. When I locked myself inside my car, I saw him in my back seat ready to strangle me from behind. I was paralyzed with fear. I did not realize that the faceless man represented all the sexual predators who had abused me.

When I made it to therapy and finally confronted more of my past with Jackie, it became clear to me that God was using my depression to heal the other injuries I was carrying within my heart and soul. It was time to thaw my frozen feelings and begin the long process of healing.

My psychiatrist increased my medication. After six weeks I began to feel more energy as the grip of the beast loosened; I also felt a rush of painful emotions. Memories of each crisis in my life surfaced all at once so that I could barely handle the pain. In many ways, emotional pain is worse than physical pain. Emotional pain has a way of eroding self-confidence, self-worth, faith, and hope.

For the first time, I began to feel the emotions I had suppressed during each trial in my life. I wanted to run away but felt as if God was holding me down, forcing me to face my fears. I still equated pain with punishment, so for the first time in my Christian life, I admitted that I was angry with God. My friends at church told me that it was irreverent to be angry with God. I disagreed; I would rather be honest with God than fake it. I silenced them with examples of Jeremiah and David who cried out in frustration and anger at God during their suffering. I did not want to be afraid or angry; I wanted to be real with him.

GOING HOME

The nightmares of my past began invading my sleep, and "daymares" consumed my waking moments. I wanted the emotional pain to stop, but I did not want to cry—tears frightened me. My friend Teresa came over to take me for a ride along a trail by the river. I sobbed the entire trip, unable to explain why I was so sad. I had lost hope again and wanted to die. I had grown passively suicidal. I would not take my life intentionally, but I did not care if someone killed me or if God decided not to wake me in the morning. I knew heaven was a better place, and I wanted to go where I would not have to cry anymore. I was ready to go home.

I became quietly preoccupied with death images. Each time I drove through an intersection, I visualized what it would be like if a car slammed into me. Whenever I drove over a bridge, I visualized its collapsing. When I was home, I visualized the apartment walls falling down around me. When I was in my bed, I visualized someone suffocating me.

An incident that happened when I was driving to my therapy session with Jackie demonstrates God's mercy during that time of incapacitation. I was waiting at a red light. Without planning, I gently lifted my foot off the brake pedal and coasted into the middle of oncoming traffic. I wanted to close my eyes and welcome the relief death would bring, but I could not. It was as if my eyes were forced to stay open. I was about to witness the majesty of God.

One by one, every car that should have hit mine swerved to avoid me. There were no accidents in that intersection despite my attempts to hasten death. Every car was led safely through. People did not blow their horns or curse me. It was as if I had never pulled out in the intersection at all. No one stopped to check on me. No police arrived. People continued on their way. My depression even muted my concern for the person who would slam into me.

My dear child, your life is in my hands. I have plans for your life. What I want to accomplish in your life will bring you hope and a future. You must trust me. You must be still and trust that I am healing you.

Although I did not realize it at the time, God had spoken: I was to remain alive. My life was not mine to take away. When I told Jackie about the incident, she wanted me to check myself into the psychiatric hospital for a crisis observation. But I was determined not to go to the hospital. I was not going to allow myself to be committed. I was not like my mother. I could not be like my mother. I sighed—I was turning into my mother.

"Are you afraid you will be committed involuntarily?" Jackie asked.

I buried my head in my hands and began to cry as the images of my mother's being committed to the hospital filled my mind. My life was falling apart, and I was helpless. Jackie tried to reassure me that I could leave the next morning if I felt like it, but I told her that I needed to talk with my family.

When I left Jackie's office, I realized that I did not have any family in Columbus. Although I knew I would not be committed for life in the psychiatric hospital, I was terrified. In my mind, one night there would prove I had become my mother. I drove around until I found myself at Gregory's apartment. He called Jackie, and they agreed that I needed to sleep in a safe place that night. The last thing I told Gregory as we drove toward the hospital was to make sure that no one forgot about me and kept me there against my will.

I felt nothing as we walked through the doors and toured the area. Some patients made me nervous, however. Everywhere I turned, I saw faces full of hopelessness. On some faces I saw death. By nightfall I knew who had already attempted suicide—I could tell by their faces. I did not belong there. I thought I had no hope, but when I saw true hopelessness, I could feel the fragile flicker of hope I still had within my soul.

I began telling myself not to give up on God because as long as I was still breathing, there was hope that he would change my life. I knew I needed to rebuild my trust in him again. So I began to talk to him honestly about my fears, frustrations, and anger. The more I talked with him that evening, the less I wanted to die. By midnight I wanted to go to my apartment.

When I walked into the patient lounge, I sat at a table to drink herbal tea. One of the therapists on call that night saw me and sat down next to me. The first thing he asked me was why I was in the hospital.

I told him, "My therapist thinks I'm passively suicidal."

"Are you?"

"I was but not anymore."

"Why did you want to die?" he asked.

"I lost hope in God. I lost hope that he has a plan and a purpose for my life. I was just so tired, I wanted to go to heaven to be with God."

I expected the therapist to be surprised at my religious talk, but he nodded his head in reassurance. He asked me more questions about my faith. He looked into my eyes and asked if I had regained my hope.

"I do feel a flicker of hope. I know it is fragile though. I know I'm still weak, but I don't belong in here."

"No, you don't belong in here. You have so much going for you. You are too high functioning to be in here. Too many girls in here have given up on life. They don't have any hope. At least, not yet."

"Yeah, I can tell. It depresses me more being here," I admitted.

"I understand. Well, I'm impressed that you decided to come despite the stigma of mental illness."

"Well, I don't care about stigma anymore in my life. Look at me. I'm a walking stigma. I'm African-American, female, and disabled. Adding mental illness to this mix can't make life any worse."

"You have a wonderful sense of humor," he chuckled.

"Thank you. I haven't laughed in a very long time. I forgot how good it felt."

"You have a beautiful smile and laugh. They sure light up a room. Your smile brightens everything around like a rainbow after a storm."

I felt uncomfortable by the compliments, but I appreciated his reminding me that God had given me a sign that he was still with me: my smile. When I started to look back over my life, I began to see how much I was able to smile despite the hardship. Common nicknames for me included "Sunshine" and "Smiley Face." I still had a pleasant personality and was not embittered by life. I still loved people and wanted to work to better others' lives. My ability to love and to smile despite my past was direct evidence that God had not abandoned me, but it was still too hard to accept that his promises were true. I was still too insecure.

"Having a hard time taking compliments? I see you squirming over there," the therapist said.

"Yeah. Not too many people in my life have complimented me on anything. Abused me is more like it. I have had plenty of that."

"Well, you just need to hang around the right people now that you are an adult. You have power now to control some of the negative influences in your life."

"You are right. I guess I've never learned how to live a nonvictimized life. I guess I just expect to be a victim all the time. That is all I know," I said.

"Well, it's time to shed that baggage. You seem like a very spiritual person. Tap into that source of strength. Fight hard to reclaim the source of the power you have held all your life. Life should have broken you a long time ago. You should have given up long before now, but you did not. Once you become confident in the source of your strength, I have no doubt that you won't be in this type of place ever again. Stay strong."

With his last statement, I was shocked into silence. I knew I had been in the presence of an angel. I could hear God talk to my heart through the therapist. God had sent someone to encourage me to stay strong. I could hear him tell me to fight hard to trust him more. When I went to my room to sleep, I honestly told God that I wanted to trust him more, but I was weak. As I slept, I could feel him whisper that I needed to finally face my past. It was time to stop running away. Too tired to run, I had no choice but to remain still.

That is right, my child, I want you to be still and come to know that I, God, am your Father. Let go and fall into my arms. I will heal your soul. Continue to tell me everything about what you feel. I will never grow tired of listening to you and comforting you as you grieve. I have so much for you to see, my precious child. First, I want you to climb onto my lap and see your Father's face. I want you to know all about the source of your strength. I want you to be confident in my love for you. A time is coming when you will be mature enough to move on to a deeper relationship with me. Since I am a patient Father, I will help you grow. I will teach you my ways, and you will be my child for all eternity. Now, my dear one, give me all the fears, anguish, frustration, and anger associated with your past—I promise to comfort you and give you peace.

SHOOTING THE WOUNDED

When I left the hospital the next morning, I began the journey through recovery. Jackie told me that I would have to wrestle with my doubts and fears. She wanted me to write down my prayers so that I could marvel at how God would heal me. In a couple of weeks, I began to notice the heavy cloud of despair lifting. I began to sleep better. I picked up my Bible and could concentrate for five minutes at a time. God, Jackie, and I began the healing process by listing everything I had lost in my life. I listed everything that was taken away from me or had been destroyed. There was no turning back now—I had already passed the point of no return on the road to wholeness.

I told God that I was scared of the concept of grieving—it was foreign to me. I could not understand how thinking about the past or crying about it could aid in healing. I was scared to unleash the memories and relive the pain. I was shocked when I looked at my list and saw how long it was. I would be grieving for my lost childhood, my mentally ill parents, and each instance of abuse and injustice.

When I next saw Jackie after making my list, I told her that I could not see how I could ever be healthy again with a list that long. Before Jackie spoke, I could feel God telling me that faith is based on believing in his promises and not on what I could see, feel, or understand. Jackie told me that recovery is a miracle because out of the ashes of death and destruction, I would rise to be a new person—stronger, wiser, and healthier than before.

The first obstacle to recovery involved my friends in the church. I knew all about the general stigma of depression, but I was to learn that the stigma was worse in Christian circles. The antidepressants were reducing chemical imbalances within my brain, and my work with Jackie and honest prayers to God were dealing with my soul cries. I wanted to go back to church and be around other Christians again. Being ashamed of nothing, I rose to make a statement during Bible class.

"I'm glad to be back after the many months of healing from my various health problems. Thank you for your prayers. Although I'm back, I'm still healing. I'm recovering from major depression and I'm going to ask your help."

I continued by stressing that I did not need anyone to preach at me or make me feel guilty about my depression. I addressed each Christian stigma I knew about depression. I told my classmates that my depression was caused by many factors, which God and I were dealing with. I wanted people to think twice before they opened their mouths to speak to someone who was emotionally fragile, still undergoing God's healing. I was setting healthy boundaries for the first time in my life in protecting my fragile flicker of hope. Opening the Bible to Job, I told them that the best way to help me was to be like Job's friends were at first: they comforted him with their silent presence.

"I'm not asking for anyone to come up with profound statements. I don't need anyone to try to figure out my problem and try to fix me. I don't need a rebuke. God is healing me, and all my family needs to do is to stay out of the way. The most profound thing you can do for me is to pray for me."

To my close friends I strengthened the boundaries. I told each of them that if they wanted to remain close to me during the healing process, they would hear me talk about fears, doubts, and frustrations about God as I wrestled with my faith. I invited them to speak their hearts when they felt moved by God to speak to me, but when in doubt, they should keep their thoughts to themselves. I was going to be honest with God in processing some painful admissions about my feelings toward him.

All of my friends told me that they wanted to stand with me, but of my six closest friends, not one of them would remain with me throughout the healing process. All of us became impatient with each other.

The first acquaintances I had to distance myself from were those who felt that taking antidepressant medication was a sin or a sign of weak faith. One of them told me that taking "happy pills" was not authorized in the Bible. Another friend asked me nicely if I really needed to take the medicine, or was it just a crutch I was using to avoid standing on my own faith?

Although I was angry with them, I replied that none of the medicines or medical procedures we rely upon today are mentioned in the Bible. Mental illness is as genuine a disease as heart disease or diabetes. Furthermore, if I did not have a chemical imbalance in my brain, then the medicine would not do anything for me—they were not "happy pills."

After giving my friends another chance to remain supportive while I was recovering, I decided I was spending too much energy protecting myself. I stopped leaning on these friends for support because they did not understand what I was going through, and I was too weak to be a teacher.

Another friend and I began a discussion about my need for more faith. She said, "Cheryl, life is not easy, and you just have to get used to that. I'm sure God is telling you to increase your faith." I could accept the statement at face value because I agreed that I had to accept living in an imperfect world where bad things happened to good people. I also agreed that I needed to grow more in my faith.

My friend, however, would not let it be. She wanted me to admit that my depression may have been punishment for my lack of faith. I told her that she did not know my heart well enough to make such a judgment. I disregarded her accusation because I was close enough to God to know that he was proud of my tenacious desire to hold on to my mustard seed of faith. I was offended because she had crossed the line that Job's friends had crossed: she was trying to speak for God.

A couple of other friends distanced themselves when they could not see any improvement in my life after their many months of prayer. Many days I was upbeat and other days I was downcast—my mood depended on the pain I was dealing with in therapy. Some would ask me, "Are you getting any better? I've been praying for you."

I would thank them for their prayers and tell them that recovery was a long process. I felt as if some people wanted me to put on a false face and pretend I was happy so that they could see an instant answer to their prayers. I remember commenting in Bible class that Christians were good at encouraging those with acute illnesses, but many tend to grow tired of serving those with chronic illnesses.

I began to feel guilty for seeing my name on the prayer list each week and then have people call or come up to me after worship to ask if God had answered their prayers. The lack of patience by my fellow church members began to rub off on me—I was tired of the slow pace of therapy. When I began to worry that I was not healing fast enough, I quickly told myself to stand firm, wait on God's timing, and not allow myself to be swayed by others' impatience. When other friends started questioning my faith and spirituality, I grew tired of going to church. I was tired of having to protect myself from people who should have accepted me as I was.

A turning point came when my sister had her first baby. After I first held baby Anne in my arms, I knew I wanted to leave Columbus and finish recovery in Dallas. I wanted to be with my sister again. Within a couple of weeks after returning to Columbus from visiting my niece, I learned that Gregory had eloped with my former roommate. Having obtained my master's degree, I lost interest in continuing with the program toward the doctorate. I wanted to go home and help my sister raise baby Anne. I wanted a fresh start. Within two days, a friend helped me pack my car, and I drove one thousand miles to Dallas.

SLIP AND FALL

Within several months of relocating to Dallas, I slipped and fell. X rays showed that I had fractured a vertebra in my lower back. In addition to being fractured, it was slipping out of the spinal column. If I did not have a spinal fusion operation, I could be paralyzed. Before that happened, I was beginning to see daylight from the pit of despair. I had been climbing out of the black hole, but the news of my need for major surgery knocked me backward again. I was devastated. I took a test for depression and anxiety, and both scores were extremely high. The beast had come back to life.

While I prepared for surgery, I felt all my energy draining away. I began to sleep for fourteen hours again. I became sluggish, losing interest in the things I once enjoyed. I also stopped eating. The nightmares of death came back. I had reached the dosage limit for Zoloft, so my psychiatrist added another antidepressant. I did not want to go backward in my faith and start to fear God was abandoning me again, so I called the church I had been attending and began talking with the minister about my fears.

Friends from my new church organized a prayer and praise devotional at my house the night before surgery. I would be in the operating room for eight hours. When I arrived at the hospital at 7:00 A.M., one of the elders of my church was there to pray over me. A steady stream of friends from church popped by for hugs and prayer. The surgery was delayed for four hours because my neurosurgeon was called to an emergency. When it was time for surgery, I was spiritually and emotionally ready.

Afterward, when I awoke in my room, Gayle and Mom were by my bedside. I had never been happier to see two people. Unlike the loneliness I felt during the surgeries in Columbus, I felt a peace that I finally had family by my side.

But they could not protect me from the intense physical pain I would soon experience. Physical therapists came to force me out of bed. I had to sit up and walk less than twenty-four hours after spinal surgery. I complained but gave in when they told me that I would develop pneumonia if I did not move around. I now knew why I always heard moaning, crying, and screams in the hospital. The physical therapists lifted me to secure my back brace and began to push and pull me toward an upright position. I do not know if it was the anesthesia, the morphine, or pain, but the more I became upright, the dizzier I became.

I left the hospital in two weeks for recovery at home with in-home health care. I was to remain mostly on my back and in my back brace for months. I had a walker and orders to use it at least twice a day during physical therapy. Mostly I watched television and visited with friends who stopped by my house. Within three months, my boss at the Day Foundation began to pressure me to return to work. That would not happen.

All hopes of a speedy recovery were dashed after a routine spine check. Every rod and screw that my doctor had inserted in the verte-bra had broken, and the vertebra above that one was now broken.

I was in shock. My spinal fusion had failed. I needed to have the same eight-hour surgery again. My neurosurgeon would insert more rods and screws to repair my vertebrae. Nevertheless, I had to cope with the reality that I would have a more pronounced disability. Again, the unexpected news kicked me back into the arms of depression.

"Lord, I just don't know if I can accept a life that won't ever change. Isn't this abnormal for one person to bear? Each time I try to recover, something else comes along and knocks me back down. I'm tired and I don't feel like forcing myself to be happy while I'm suffering. I really want to stay around and help raise baby Anne, but, Lord, if my lot in life is to suffer to this extent, I would rather just go home to heaven."

As soon as I admitted I wanted to go to heaven, I knew I couldn't go back to being passively suicidal. I was not going to allow the beast of depression to plunge me back into believing these distorted images of God were real. I was disappointed that God had allowed the newest trauma; I somehow knew, however, that he would not allow the crisis to crush me. I knew God had the power to do any-thing, but I struggled with his desire to deliver to me a less traumatic life on earth.

I know the desires of your heart. I am using this period of trials to teach you that I am all you need. I will see you through so that you emerge vic-torious and strong.

When I started having problems at the Day Foundation, I knew I was in a battle for my hope and faith. My psychiatrist added another antidepressant, but the medication was no longer working for me; my spiritual anguish had outweighed my chemical imbalance. I was fight-ing God. I did not want to accept the cruel fact that pain and suffering were the inevitable result of living in a fallen world.

God did not design the world to be full of chaos, injustice, and oppression. Humankind's selfish free will chose something less than perfection. I would not experience the utopia I craved until I rested in

God's arms in heaven. The longer I fought against accepting reality, the worse I would become. I was tired of the recurring battle with depression. I had heard that God brought his children a peace during times of suffering. I wanted that peace. I told God, "I give up. How can I accept the hardships of the world and not allow it to plunge me back in the depths of depression again?"

Someone once told me that I needed to stop longing for a better past. There was nothing I could do to turn back time. I could do nothing to force the people in my life to make better decisions. I could not go back and make better choices. I told myself that if I remained mired in the past, I would allow it to destroy my present and future.

I was not concerned about losing my eternal relationship with God, but I always wanted to make a difference on earth. I wanted my life to be worth something in the end. I wanted to see God's purpose for my life. I could feel God reaching out to me, asking me to trust him enough to keep my eyes on him rather than on the raging storms around me. It was time to fight each negative thought that dominated my mind.

Finally, I realized that I was contributing to my depression by enter taining false images of God and his love. I decided that I could not trust my emotions anymore until they stopped projecting lies. Tired of living like a victim, I begged God to infuse me with the spirit of an overcomer. I wanted to be free from the enslavement of depression and my past.

Be still and know that I am God. I am your Father. I will direct your steps and teach you how to become more like your Daddy. I long for the time when you see yourself as I see you. You will see more clearly in time. Be patient. You are like clay in my hands, and I am molding you into something more beautiful than you are right now.

Always remember that I am all you need to accomplish the impossible in your life. You have found me, and we will remain together for eternity. I want you to be as happy about our relationship as I am. Get to know me better. The more you know me, the more you will trust my promises. I know that some of my other children have hurt you, but forgive them—they did not know what they were doing. Just as I extended you mercy when you failed me, I want you to show your love for me by extending mercy to those who failed you. Do not be afraid, discouraged, or anxious. I know what I am doing.

CHAPTER THIRTEEN

There Is a Balm in Gilead

Earth has no sorrow that heaven cannot heal.
THOMAS MOORE

One day I woke up tired of feeling like a victim. Lingering emotional pain and feelings of worthlessness began to frustrate me. However, sometimes frustration can motivate change. I was ready to learn how to live as an overcomer rather than a victim. Back in college, one of my friends called me a survivor, but I found no comfort in the compliment. Although I have always felt proud that I made it through the trauma, I wanted to do more than merely survive. I wanted to rise so far above my painful beginnings that the past no longer negatively impacted me. Only then could I consider myself an overcomer.

"Cheryl, one of your problems is that you aren't celebrating your victories along the way," one of my mentors told me. "You should rejoice in being a survivor. And to be honest, you are an overcomer too. Look at what you have accomplished—you graduated from Yale University with honors, you worked on Capitol Hill with former Senator Dole's foundation, you have achieved so much in your young life. You should be proud of yourself."

"I am proud of myself, but you have to understand that I'm defining 'overcoming' in a different way." I tried to explain my concept of overcoming to no avail. It has less to do with earthly success than with finding soul-satisfying peace and wholeness. I had seen too many survivors try to soothe the wounds of their souls by becoming addicted to perfectionism, acclaim from others, and the relentless pursuit of achievement. Although they had survived, they had not overcome the past. Overcoming meant that my past would not creep into my life to sabotage my future. I knew that I was not yet an overcomer; I had too many fears. Those fears were fueling a deep and recurring depression that threatened to consume me. I was too passive in my recovery, relying too much on medicine as the source of my healing. It was time to take drastic action.

PERSEVERANCE—A MATTER OF TRUST

I knew that God was ultimately to provide the peace and healing I desired. Nevertheless, I had work to do as well. I needed the resolve to fight the lies coming from my fears and insecurities. The hope began to swell within me that I was created for a purpose; there must have been some reason why I was still standing. I started to believe that God created me for a good purpose that I would soon discover. I repeatedly told myself that I was somebody, that God loved me. My insecurities were so vast, I had to brainwash myself with God's truth. There was no place in my life for fear or shame, and I needed to learn how to live accordingly.

At first I felt as if I were fighting a world war with pebbles. How could scrutinizing my thoughts help me overcome my past? I realized my mind was full of self-defeating lies that I heard or said about myself growing up. My relatives were no longer in my life, but their verbal abuse stayed in my mind. I was tearing myself down inside my mind by continuing to listen to them. The resulting discouragement was drowning out God's affirming voice. I heard God telling me that the maturation of my faith depended upon my learning how to be still and quiet. I needed to learn how to wait for God to answer me. By rooting out the distractions in my life, I believed I would hear him speak to my soul. Survivors are often restless, tending to scramble around in their search for peace. I was no exception. I overloaded my life with one project after another. My strategy was to avoid thinking about the future or mourning the past. Being still was painful because there were no distractions to protect me from my own mind.

I took one step in being still. I decided to take ten minutes to close my eyes and not say a word. As soon as the quietness engulfed me, the demons from my past swooped down in full force. I was assailed with thoughts of being ugly, worthless, and unloved. Immediately after each negative thought, I could feel a faint presence reassuring me that those thoughts were lies.

After several weeks of regular stillness, I began to hear God's voice more clearly. Whenever negative thoughts came into my mind, God seemed to refute them. I was developing the ability to discern what came from my Father and what were evil lies. God spoke to my heart constantly, yet my restlessness still tended to drown out his voice.

This restlessness became the first barrier to fall. After years of treating my depression with medication, the beast still would not go away. I was grateful that the medication had cleared up most of the malevolent black fog from my mind, but my issues could not be broken down into simple biological or chemical components. Medication helped me reach the point where I had the physical and emotional strength to address my spiritual wounds. I had spent years in pastoral counseling grappling with the lingering spiritual questions about God's love and mercy in light of pain, suffering, and injustice. I recognized that in several areas of my life, I had extremely low self-esteem. Sometimes I felt a sense of worthlessness or a wave of dread about the future. Although

I could not prove it, I began to sense that the main culprit behind my persistent depression seemed to be spiritual rather than chemical.

One of the most difficult challenges in being a Christian psychologist is determining the boundary between what is medical and what is spiritual, while still appreciating the interactions between the two. I was trained to look at things scientifically. The scientific evidence clearly showed that antidepressants increased my chances of successfully treating depression. I never regretted my choice to use medication. I have defended that choice in some Christian circles that criticize the use of it. Those who tell me that using antidepressants indicate weak faith offend me. I typically respond that antidepressants are not "happy pills"—they did not have the power to create false happiness. In many people, the medication is powerful enough to correct chemical imbalances that could result in unnecessary death or mental suffering. I also value the courageous battles of many people with mental illness. I believe that it takes a deep and tenacious faith to find and remain with God despite feeling like a prisoner in your own mind. In my case, medication was powerful but unable to destroy the slave master.

My psychiatrist, Dr. Ford, is an excellent doctor and an expert in treating victims of childhood trauma. It was hard trying to find a doctor who shared my religious beliefs. Therefore, I compartmentalized my life: my psychiatrist handled my medical and psychological concerns, and my minister addressed my spiritual needs. Dr. Ford and I realized that my spiritual wounds impacted my emotional health. She listened to me without imposing her religious beliefs on me and always knew when to defer issues to my minister. Despite my respect for her, I grew concerned by her emphasis on medication in my recovery. Whenever I mentioned that my depression was lingering, she immediately increased my medication.

At first I was a "good little patient" and acquiesced without protesting, even if I did not agree. Medication could only make me less sad; it could not make me happy. I was no longer satisfied with being less sad. I wanted to know what was missing in my life that impeded lasting peace, but I was too weak to voice my concerns. It was easier to defer to her authority. I did not feel like a professional equal to my psychiatrist, so I began to sink into the mode of a stereotypical patient—silent, cooperative, and deferent to her superior judgment.

Dr. Ford had prescribed three different antidepressants along with antianxiety medication. I knew that I was on the wrong path for healing. Those four little pills only made me nauseated and irritated. They would never be powerful enough to heal my soul. Frustrated, I wanted to stop medication entirely, even though I understood the scientific evidence supporting long-term treatment for people with recurring major depression.

Despite all the proof, I woke up one morning with a radical resolve: to stop all medication, at least for a short period. I had been struggling with recurring bouts of severe nausea ever since I had been on the cocktail of antidepression and antianxiety medicines. Each time I swallowed a pill, my stomach would revolt. The scientist in me said that side effects were normal and I would be irresponsible to my profession if I decided to stop taking my medications because of the transient side effects. The spiritual side of me questioned whether I had put too much faith in the power of a pill to heal my soul.

I was nervous when I told my psychiatrist that I wanted to stop taking the medicine. How could I explain taking a leap of faith without appearing irresponsible, irrational, and self-destructive? I had spent years putting my faith in people and things other than God. I felt I needed to make a statement to myself that if I fell back into the slimy pit of depression again, it would not be because I had unresolved spiritual issues.

"Cheryl, you know better than discontinuing medication for those reasons. You are a psychologist yourself. I think you are a strong candidate for long-term use of antidepressants because of your chronic history with depression," Dr. Ford said.

In this clash of science and faith, I had to determine which course to take. I agreed that I could possibly have to fight depression for the rest of my life. Everything within me, however, was telling me that my depression was lingering mostly because of a wounded soul. In my case, I felt the medication was now causing more problems than it was solving.

"Cheryl, if you end your medication right now, your depression may return," she warned.

I replied, "My depression returned in the past even when I was on medication."

Dr. Ford asked me if I felt religious guilt about taking medication. The answer was no. "I hear what you are saying, Cheryl, but I want you to know that you are making a decision against my counsel. I do not want to dismiss your faith, but I just don't think it is wise to stop medication at this point."

"Well, I think it is time for me to try another approach. I understand your hesitation. I'm not advocating that everyone should stop taking medication and focus solely on prayer and spiritual counseling either. I'm not trying to stigmatize the use of medication. I have been thankful for it, but other therapies have a place in treating depression too."

I was not asking for permission to take my bold step. I did promise to monitor my moods and, at the first sign of my depression worsening, return to medication. There are those times, however, when it is best to act on your own faith and stop trying to convince others to believe or support you. I had reached one of those moments. I could have spent hours trying to convince my doctor that I was making a rational choice that was best for me. I chose, instead, to state my position, listen and consider her arguments, and then stand by my final decision, fully accepting any consequences. I believed in God's power to heal in any means he chose. It was time to allow him to work on my soul in other ways.

"What will you do if the depression returns? We can prevent it with the medicine. Or, at the very least, we can prolong the time between your next battle with it," she said.

"I'm not afraid of the depression returning. I know the signs, and I know how to act quickly to prevent it from degenerating as it has before. If it does return, and I have to get back on medication, it won't be the result of my spiritual issues that I'm working on right now. I won't be ashamed if I have to take medication again. Dr. Ford, I know that you don't understand what I'm doing. I can't really explain what I'm trying to accomplish. I think the medication has reached its limit to help me."

"I think this just might be your depression talking, Cheryl."

I shook my head vigorously in disagreement. When people know you battle depression, they tend to attribute everything you say to the illness. I also knew that it is impossible to prove sanity—the more you protest, the more insane you look. I rose to leave, thanking Dr. Ford for her help. When I closed the door to her office, I knew I had done the right thing. I knew myself better than anyone else. I had spent my entire life seeking salvation and wholeness from everything other than God. Now he had brought me to an exciting time in my life when I was about to see his power over a foe I thought was unconquerable. Medication had brought me to a point at which I had mental clarity to see God's love within my life. I was beginning to accept that God could love me. When you grow up believing that every person you see hates you, it is hard to fathom that someone you cannot see loves you. I felt that if I could believe God loved me, I would find peace.

I was agitated for the first several weeks after discontinuing the medication. I thought I would not be afraid, but negative thoughts assailed me, telling me that the beast of depression was bigger than God and me and would return to take over my life.

One day my four-year-old niece came to me with excitement on her face. She had been afraid of "the blue eye" that she saw in her bedroom, but after watching a Christian children's video, she came up to me singing, "God is bigger than the bogey man. He's watching out for you and me." Her beautiful brown eyes were shining at the most profound realization in her short life.

"Aunt Cheryl, did you know that God is *huge* and beats up bogey men?" Her little arms were flailing while she shouted in excitement. I laughed and told her that God was indeed more powerful than anything on, above, or below the earth.

As soon as the words left my mouth, my heart fluttered. Did I really believe what I had just told my niece? Did I believe that God was all-powerful and that there was nothing too big or hard for him? If I believed, then why was I afraid that depression was bigger than God? Why was I terrified that he would abandon me when I began to fight the beast? God may not intervene to stop depression from returning, but I had to believe that never again would depression be my slave master. I could accept battling the beast but not being enslaved again. Here I was, choosing to do battle with an enemy that might be bigger than me if I were standing alone. But God promised to never leave me.

It has been more than three years since I discontinued the antidepressant medication. In that time, I have undergone trials that showed me how much I have healed from the past. Mom had to be committed several times to a psychiatric hospital, and my father died unexpectedly in his sleep. There were a couple of occasions when I thought my depression had returned—I felt despair, lethargy, and the familiar cloud of gloom engulfing me. I was terrified and contemplated returning to medication. When I spoke to Dr. Ford, I was pleasantly surprised that she did not automatically reach for her prescription pad; instead, she helped me understand the difference between depression and normal grief.

I had been anxious about any form of sadness. After experiencing the hell of depression, I did not want to start a chain of events that would plunge me back into the dark pit. I wanted to freeze my emotions and never experience sadness again, but those desires are unrealistic. One paradox of life is that you must experience the pain of mourning a loss before you can heal. Cliches can sometimes be profound when you hear them at just the right time. I had walled up my emotions all of my life and ended up struggling with depression.

Under the guidance of Dr. Ford and my minister, I dismantled the walls and gave myself permission to cry. After I cried, the sadness did not linger and the depression did not return.

CHARACTER—A PRODUCT OF FORGIVENESS

I have never been a bitter person. By most standards, I have justification to lash out and hurt people who have harmed me over the years. Yet even before I knew God, I decided to focus on succeeding in life rather than pursuing vengeance. I was no saint; I wanted my abusers to be punished harshly. I believed, however, that if I preoccupied myself with punishing them, the hatred would swell and consume and destroy me. I had seen that type of destructive spirit throughout my family, and I wanted no part of it. I mostly wanted people to leave me alone. I wanted to be free of harm. Although I was afraid of rejection, I forced myself to conceal my fear and make friends. I would tell myself, "I know you don't want to do this, Cheryl, but do it anyway." I always considered a network of reliable friends crucial to a healthy life. I knew many victims were so embittered by their traumas that they pushed everyone away and never developed intimate relation ships. Although I understood their fears and hurts, I did not want to be like them.

When I was thirteen, I told myself that I would never be anything in life if I allowed other people to make me a bitter, hateful, or resentful person. At that time, my mother had her first mental breakdown, and I saw how, because of her paranoia, she had no friends or loved ones from whom to draw strength. She had no one by her side during any of her breakdowns. I did not want to be like her—all alone in the world.

When depression oppressed me, I began to panic. I was heading down the same path as Mom's. The illness was sucking the hope out of me. I immersed myself in therapy and bought volumes of books on depression and child abuse. I wanted to be free, but I was nursing many wounds. I asked God how I could accept what had happened and move on with my life. I knew I needed to forgive, but I rejected the mechanical exercise of a "forgive and struggle to forget" approach, particularly after I realized how much pain my parents caused.

I had forgiven Mom years ago; she and I are now kindred spirits. I understand her deeply because she and I share similar battles with mental illness. Despite that, I did not dismiss or minimize her actions. I told her what she did that hurt me, and in her broken state, she cried. She said that she never wanted to hurt any of her kids—she did not realize the damage she was doing. For my part, I always regretted the time when I was sixteen that I kicked Mom out of the house because she could not keep a job. I felt guilty for that for years. I felt even more so after I discovered that she immediately checked herself into a mental facility after I cursed at her and told her to leave the house. When I developed my relationship with God, I knew I needed to apologize for my behavior and ask her for forgiveness.

Since our mutual forgiveness, our relationship has been unusual yet satisfying. Her battles with mental illness have been more severe than mine, forcing her on permanent psychiatric disability. As a result of her condition, I have assumed the role of her guardian. I manage her finances, health care, and living expenses. Mom trusts me completely. When she is having a psychotic attack, she may not remember anyone—except me. In return for her trust, I give Mom unconditional love and treat her with dignity. She cannot offer me the strength and guidance that I always wanted in a mother, but I have learned to appreciate whatever she does give me.

During her healthy days, we have vacationed together. I wanted to make sure that she saw the places she only dreamed about when she was a child. Mom, being proud, always offered to help carry luggage or handle other needs occasioned by my disability. Our relationship works most of the time. When she is in a psychotic state, however, I typically feel overwhelmed. During those moments, I always feel the stirrings of depression. I tell myself repeatedly that I cannot allow my mother's illness to pull me down. There is a dancelike quality to managing the effects of a loved one's mental illness. You learn when to move forward to help and when to step back for others to take the lead in the care. Forgiveness restored my relationship with Mom.

My relationship with my father, however, was never resolved before his death. Forgiving Mom was easy. She wanted a better relationship with her children and humbled herself enough to admit that her hands caused harm. But Dad was like all the other abusers—prideful, narcissistic, and selfish. He never saw the need to apologize or change his destructive pattern of behavior.

I first confronted Dad about his abusive behavior toward me when I was eighteen years old. Naively, I still held out hope that he would come to his senses and we could start a new, healthy relationship. Despite my anger at the harm he had inflicted, I wanted him in my life, but only if he could behave himself. My sister and my counselor thought it was a bad idea to establish a relationship with Dad. I, however, wanted to know if he would ever change. I knew that change was possible, but only if Dad could love someone more than himself. If I never confronted him or gave him an opportunity to ask for forgiveness, I feared I would be unable to heal. My resentment and anger toward him had grown so intense as to hold me back. I was frustrated in caring so much for someone who loved only himself. Nevertheless, I needed to know with certainty if Dad would have a place in my new life.

One Sunday, after hearing a sermon about forgiveness, I realized that my motives for reconciling with Dad were wrong. By focusing on my recovery, I had made forgiveness a tool solely to satisfy my needs. I wanted to heal, so I needed to take steps to achieve that goal. In that mindset, I really did not care much about Dad's relationship with God. Godly confrontation was supposed to be a way for me to prompt him into repairing his relationship with God. Still young in the faith, I could not honestly say that I loved my father enough to put the state of his soul before my need to heal. Being a Christian was going to be much harder than I thought.

Regardless of my mixed motives for wanting to forgive Dad, I started preparing for my confrontation with him. Gayle and I sat in our dorm room at college talking about our differing experiences growing up. I told her about being evicted, living in the car, doing my homework by hurricane lamp, and losing my friends to Dad's financial schemes. I told her about his pawning my violin and piano, plotting to rob a store, and his acts of adultery. Gayle was incensed when I told her how he shared intimate secrets with me about his marriage and affairs. I confessed my role in contributing to Mom's mental breakdown when I kicked her out the house as a result of one of his visions. Gayle called him a selfish child abuser. My therapist called it emotional incest. All of us were angry with him. Gayle wanted to confront him immediately, so she and I called home.

Both of us were emotionally charged. Dad quickly became defensive when we started with rapid-fire questions about his past decisions, motives, and love for us. The conversation disintegrated with Dad's growing more defensive and telling us that he did not have any regrets—none whatsoever. He said that everything he did was because he loved his family. After I poured out my heart to him, Dad said that if he had to do it all over again, he would do the exact same thing. Gayle, outraged, started quoting Bible verses condemning some of his actions. I was silent. The same father who said that he would give his life for me could not humble himself enough to apologize for anything.

"I'm not going to justify anything to you kids. I told you that I love you guys more than life itself. I told you that I would give my life for you. I'm not about to prove anything by dragging up the past," Dad said.

"Dad, if you love us so much, why can't you just accept our pain and apologize? All we are asking is for you to do something short of giving your life," I replied.

"Yeah, I find it hard to believe that you would give your life for us when you can't even say you are sorry," Gayle said.

Dad hung up the telephone. Gayle said that she did not care anymore. She would not waste her energy on someone who could not love anyone other than himself. It was as if Gayle flipped a switch off because she never mentioned Dad again.

I was not satisfied. I prayed that night asking God how forgiveness is possible when the offender does not ask for forgiveness and continues to offend. What if the offender is your parent—someone you are commanded to honor? I felt that God was asking me to do something that did not make sense.

When I relocated to Dallas almost seven years later, I faced Dad again. He had left Mom on the streets of Dallas in the dilapidated 1977 Volare and eloped with one of his former mistresses. In her fragile emotional state, Mom signed divorce papers that left Dad and his new wife with most of the money from a personal injury case he settled. After twenty-five years of a tumultuous marriage, Mom was left on Gayle's doorstep with a worthless car and a pocket of petty cash. The next time I saw Dad, he was driving a brand new Lincoln Continental. Nevertheless, Gayle caught him sneaking in her house stealing jewelry from her. He said he needed to pawn it to purchase medicine. Gayle was furious enough to tell him that she would call the police next time. I felt ashamed that such a dysfunctional person could be my father.

One day Dad caught up with me while I was heading home from work. He wanted to explain about the divorce, remarriage, and attempted theft. When he started to talk, I discovered that he mostly wanted my blessing for his marriage because it was holy (according to him). However, he said the situation did not concern me. God had told him that he did not condone Dad's first marriage, but Dad stayed with Mom for the sake of Gayle and me. Now God had led Dad back to the woman he was supposed to marry, and they were copastors of a church.

"I've been running away from my true calling in life," Dad said. "I made a pact with God that I would do whatever he wanted me to do with my life. When I finally obeyed God, he opened the heavenly realm to me. I can hear divine voices and I see divine things. I share these visions with my church, and they receive the blessings. Your Mom did not support me and that is why I divorced her. If she were from God, then she would have supported my ministry. Do you believe what I'm saying?"

I looked at Dad with a blank, impatient stare. Shaking my head, I told him that he needed to get some help. There was no sense in talking to him. There was nothing I could say that would convince him to change his ways. Dad continued to talk about how he wanted the "good old days" back when his daughters honored and respected him. When I reminded him that the "good old days" for me were full of abuse, neglect, and trauma, he became silent.

Then he said, "What do you want from me? What do you want me to say? I can't change the past."

"You could take responsibility for what your choices did to my life."

"OK, OK, if I hurt you, I'm sorry. OK? Can you let this die? I'm sick of revisiting this every time I talk to you or Gayle. You guys are supposed to be Christians and forgive."

I told Dad that forgiveness did not mean that I would not hold him accountable for his actions. He did not want to hear that he was in a destructive cycle of selfish behavior that hurt everyone in his path. God wanted more than lip service; he wanted to change Dad's heart. I sternly told him that I would not allow anyone in my life who acted as he did. His pride had encrusted his heart, and he was using God to justify unholy, selfish, and hurtful behavior.

Dad said that most of the damage I claimed was all in my mind. When he began quoting Bible verses about not being shown the proper honor as my father, I decided to leave. He started to tell me about having a vision that his service as God's messenger would divide his family. This was one point I was not willing to debate with Dad. Having my own relationship with God, I knew enough about God's nature to know what came from him and what was an evil lie. I would not—could not—change Dad, and I knew it was time to let go. Unless he changed, I would have to keep my distance.

"This is not honoring your father. Or did you conveniently forget that command while you look down on me?"

I was tired of his beating me over the head with that commandment. God also expects parents not to physically, emotionally, or spiritually harm their children. I told Dad that honoring him had nothing to do with condoning his lifestyle or choices, nor did it require me to automatically wipe the slate clean and never bring up his offenses. He thought that anything short of letting him off the hook was dishonoring him. When he started to question my relationship with God, I knew it was time to leave.

"I will always be your father."

"Yes, you will."

"You are supposed to—"

"Dad, I've had enough, OK? I'm tired and I have simply had enough." I gave him my phone number and told him that when he was serious about restoring a relationship with me, he knew what he needed to do. I walked away.

Although I never called my father, I kept the door open for reconciliation by accepting his calls, most of which were solicitations for money. Once he asked me for almost five thousand dollars to cover a bounced check he wrote for lumber to build his new church. He told me that God would bless me if I helped him and curse me if I turned my back on his prophet. When I refused to bail him out of his irresponsible predicament, he started to berate me. I hung up.

Whenever Dad called, I hoped that I would see a sign of change. However, he never would change—he loved himself too much. The last time I heard from him was a letter he wrote several weeks before his death. The letter was similar to his telephone calls; he condemned Gayle and me for being disrespectful. I will never know if his heart was changed right before he died; I will not speculate about whether he ever fixed his relationship with God.

Dad's death brought some relief because he was incapable of stopping himself from offending. Each time he and I interacted, he added insult to my injuries. After confronting him and giving him the opportunity to make things right between us, I knew I had done all I could do, and I felt a sense of peace when he died. He would always say that Gayle and I should "give him his flowers while he was still alive" because he could not hear "I love you" from his grave. Unfortunately, when I heard that he died, I had no flowers or expressions of love for him. I was not surprised that he died estranged from his family. It was a sad ending to a sad saga, but Dad chose his own path. After his death, I stopped thinking about what life could have been like if he had been a better father.

Once Dad died, I saw no need to confront any of my other abusers. Dad had caused the greatest damage. I had not seen my grandparents, uncle, or cousin in over ten years. I heard that my uncle was in jail on drug-related charges and my cousin had moved to Alaska. My grandfather was dead, and my grandmother was in failing health. These people were set in their ways, and I never had a relationship with them. I would not gain anything by confronting them about the past. Since they did not care about me, I decided not to allow my past encounters with them ruin my new life.

At this point, I could feel myself on the threshold of God revealing his purpose for my life, and I was finally ready to let go. I used to think that there was a magical or mystical spirit that would come and take away the burdens from the past. When I grew up and began to trust God more, I realized that I needed to choose to let go of the burdens before God could take them away. Once I was finished mourning my losses, I needed to ask God to help me drop the burden and walk away from it, never to pick it up again. It is a daily struggle to leave the past in the past. Dad's death was a turning point in my life; I wanted to choose to let go. I was ready. I looked up to heaven and told God that although I did not fully understand what I was doing, I was releasing my past into his hands. It was time to sing a new song.

CHAPTER FOURTEEN

Life Purpose

If I can help somebody as I travel along,
If I can help somebody in a word or a song,
If I can help somebody from doom and wrong,
Lord, my living shall not be in vain.

A. B. ANDROZZO, ARRANGED BY M. PAICH

This song was another of Martin Luther King's favorites. When I first heard Mahalia Jackson sing it, I immediately fell in love with it. I have heard variations of the sentiment in this song over the years from many survivors of trauma. I have said it as well—"If I can help one person from my experiences, then what I have gone through will have been worth it."

One of my friends asked me if I really believed what I said. How could helping one person make experiencing abuse, rejection, and pain worthwhile? I simply told her that when someone suffers, I have to know that in the end something good will come out of it all. Otherwise, I will remain bitter or hopeless, and the perpetrator wins.

Overcoming meant I was allowing God to transform what was intended to destroy me into something that would help me by bringing me closer to him and enabling me to help others.

Life has been full of demoralization and despair, but in the midst of it all, there were rays of hope that one day I would find purpose. In the back of my mind, I felt that if I took the pills or ran into a busy intersection, I would die when my purpose might have been revealed to me that same day, had I just held on a little longer. "Maybe tomorrow will be better," was my mantra. As long as I rose each morning, there was hope that the day would be different from yesterday.

The history of the African-American people told me that there was power in the struggle, despite what my emotions were telling me. I began to draw power from knowing that not everyone could have endured what I went through. During the times when I was especially weak and ready to give up, God sent angels in the form of friends and strangers to say or do something to lift my spirits until I found the heart to carry on by myself. Being an "angel" to someone else is what makes my living worthwhile. God calls each one of us to comfort others just as each of us has been comforted. Instinctively, many survivors become passionate about comforting those who suffer as they have suffered. There is healing power within the touch, empathy, and acceptance of someone who understands from direct experience a particular sorrow.

One of my angels told me, "Cheryl, despite what you feel, you have made it through. It is now your responsibility and privilege to reach down and help lift others to where you are." I have chosen many methods of reaching out to fellow strugglers, but four have been most meaningful in using my past to influence what I do with my life today.

MUSIC—A POWERFUL SOOTHER OF THE SOUL

I have been a musician since I began learning voice, piano, and violin at my third-grade magnet school for music. Music lessons kept me physically away from the school bullies. But, more importantly, music gave me a sense of power and accomplishment. With my hands and mouth I was able to produce something beautiful. When I performed, it made someone else smile. When my classmates and I sang at hospitals, we brightened the lives of many people in pain. When my parents began to argue, I always ran to my piano or violin to escape the hostility.

Dad's pawning my piano and violin when I was fifteen stripped me of two major therapeutic instruments in my life. It crushed my spirit so that I never played the piano or violin again. However, no one ever stole my voice. I drew strength from singing spirituals, hymns, and other songs for inspiration. I also participated in choir through junior and senior high school. At church, I sing in our praise and worship group dedicated to bringing people closer to God through song.

I have learned that music protects, heals, and comforts the soul. Through music, I am able to express my emotions in ways more powerful than merely speaking. When I am down, music always lifts my troubled spirits. I am no brilliant soloist like Mahalia Jackson or Whitney Houston, but I do have the spiritual gift of music through which God brings comfort to myself and others.

One of my favorite instances of the healing power of music happened when I was in the hospital recuperating from spinal fusion surgery. It had been less than twenty-four hours since the procedure, and I was in intense pain. I could hear fellow patients throughout the orthopedic floor moaning, crying, and screaming as the physical therapists made their rounds.

Around midday, my church's praise and worship group came to visit me. Twenty people packed into my tiny room and started to sing my favorite songs. I tried to sing, but I was too weak. Within five minutes the cries from people on my floor stopped. Nurses and therapists squeezed their way to the door of my crowded room to listen. When the group started to sing about God's power to heal, one of the nurses was overcome with emotion and left the room crying. When she returned, she talked about how much she needed to know that God loved her and that he had touched her heart through the singing.

News of the free concert on the orthopedic floor spread throughout the hospital. Whenever the staff stopped by to work on me, they commented how much they wished they could have been there to hear the music. The therapists told me that no patient cried while my praise group was singing. I could understand this. Whenever I sang or listened to music, my pain also seemed to vanish.

CENTRAL DALLAS MINISTRIES—OFFERING HOPE TO URBAN COMMUNITIES

When I was homeless in Houston, I wish a ministry like Central Dallas Ministries (CDM) had existed to help my family. CDM is a model, faith-based community-building organization in the urban areas of Dallas. Because CDM believes in the ability of people to transform their own lives, it dedicates staff and volunteer resources to strengthen homes, churches, and schools by addressing each person's total needs—mind, body, and spirit. I serve on the board of directors of CDM to set policy and direction for the $1.5 million organization that has over forty staff members. CDM is a dynamic organization that operates many programs such as a food pantry, job/life skills training, medical and legal assistance, and spiritual counseling. CDM's aim is to connect marginalized people to the resources that will encourage them to change their own lives.

My heart connects with the residents of the communities where Central Dallas Ministries operates its programs. When I see many of them, I see myself and how my life started. Some of these neighbors battle the same stresses I fought: mental illness, abuse, homelessness, poverty, and hopelessness. When I told my story to one neighbor, she asked me, "What would you have done if you weren't smart?" I understood that behind the question is the fear that one has to be a Yale graduate to overcome poverty. I always tell people that I am not really all that smart, but I work hard to overcome my limitations. I still believe in the creed of the Civil Rights movement: that education is a critical key to escaping poverty. My parents' lives and my personal struggles even after obtaining my Yale degree uncovered a caveat to the creed, however. Perseverance and a person's faith in God are the keys to overcome obstacles that schooling cannot address.

I know many well-educated people who struggle with undiagnosed mental illness, substance abuse, or physical illnesses. I have seen these obstacles stymie educated individuals, stripping them of their college accomplishments. As my parents' lives illustrate, without faith and perseverance, no amount of education or financial success will bring about true peace and wholeness. Sometimes education is not enough. Mental illness and spiritual bankruptcy can place people on the path toward profound despair and destruction.

Comforting others through Central Dallas Ministries mostly involves the ability to relate intimately to the trauma many of the neighbors experience daily. I have met some survivors of child abuse and rape, some with mental illness, some who are physically disabled, and some looking intensely for hope. One young woman, Kay, asked me with tears in her eyes, "How can you believe that God loves you when you live like I do? I mean, nothing good ever happens to me. I got beat by my father, and now I get beat by my husband." Because my background was filled with similar tragedy, Kay and I could relate to each other. She could not say that I did not understand her because I did. She could not dismiss my encouragement because I suffered a similar past full of abuse. I also unknowingly made some bad choices as an adult that set me up for further trauma. As an example, I told Kay about my relationship with Gregory. I confessed that I was so insecure and wounded, I would have probably married an abusive man just so I would not be alone. I could not love myself or believe that God could love me either.

Kay told me her story; she saw God as a bully who took joy in punishing her forever. She saw him as someone who did not listen to her because he never stopped her father from sexually abusing her. In listening to her, I could feel God's reassurance that one of my purposes in life is to use my past to comfort others and bring them into a clearer understanding of his love for them.

I let Kay talk freely without preaching at her. I simply shared with her how hard it was for me to accept that God did not cause the abuse to happen. Because of everyone's free will, sometimes people disobey God and harm other people. Regardless of the evil actions of others, my most difficult choice was to fight the urge to remain a victim and thus allow the perpetrators to triumph. Kay and I talked honestly about how survivors can fight the fear, isolation, bitterness, rage, self-hatred, and depression. I reassured her that there was power in the struggle.

I further confessed that my private thoughts used to be consumed with asking God why he was punishing me or why he would not answer me. I always heard that God's reasons are above what we can understand. Such explanations, however, never really brought me comfort. When you are hurting, your entire being is screaming out for immediate and clear answers. Many people like Kay are looking for answers to the cries of their souls. I did not tell her that the real issue was trust in God. When I was down, I was already defensive and Christian clichés only angered me. I simply told Kay to keep asking God tough questions about the nature of his love and why he seems so distant. I told her that it was OK to cry and yell because for some people, life on earth seems more painful that anything one can comprehend about hell.

"Kay, it is OK to struggle. God does not love you any less because your heart struggles to believe that he loves you. The power you'll receive from your traumas does not come from making it, but from what you learn about yourself, others, and God along the way. You are stronger than you think. You just have to learn how to live in a healthy way."

As soon as the words came from my mouth, I realized that they did not come from me but from God to benefit both Kay and me. Life is all about fighting—fighting to hold on to hope, love, and faith despite the evils that plague human existence.

Each time I meet people at CDM, the beauty of perseverance strikes me. No one enjoys suffering or abuse. No one relishes homelessness and poverty. However, the dignity and faith that I have seen on many of their faces always make me feel less alone. These are my people— people who struggle to realize God's purpose for their lives. I do not romanticize the horrors of poverty or the host of ills that some people battle, like chemical dependency or domestic violence. Since CDM is a faith-based organization, people are open about their faith, and I am encouraged to see others who know that perseverance has little to do with finishing the earthly race glamorously. Perseverance is about finishing with stronger faith and love than what you started out with, regardless of how beat up you are in the end. Victory will still be victory for those who can only crawl across the finish line.

At CDM, I see other people getting up after each life blow. I am not the only one holding on ferociously to the hope that one day life will be better—that God will make it better in the end. I laugh sometimes when I imagine the number of people who will finish the race crawling, in last place. Only a merciful and loving God would equally reward the first- and last-place finishers. It is my privilege to be intimately associated with Central Dallas Ministries and all the last-place runners like me. CDM allows me the opportunity to fulfill another charge a mentor gave me. She told me that I was to become in someone else's life the person I wish I had in my life as I grew up. This charge is a variation of the unspoken expectation placed on many people in the African-American community: when a person makes it up the ladder of success, he has the responsibility to reach down and pull up someone else.

HEART OF A CHAMPION FOUNDATION—BUILDING CHARACTER IN TODAY'S YOUTH

I have always wondered how one finds his or her purpose in life. Why was I created? What does God want me to do with my life? I have always been a restless soul, never at any organization for longer than two years. After my troubles with the Day Foundation and my battle with lingering depression, I had no more energy to run away.

The restlessness can be destructive; I was never content with life in a perpetual state of emptiness. But at times restlessness is God's voice gently leading me to another level of living out my faith. I remember hearing the older people in my life saying, "God's got ahold of you, baby. You better sit and listen to him." Whenever I feel anxious or restless, I always stop to hear if God is trying to tell me something. I was at that point when I met Blake.

Although Blake was the deacon of evangelism at my church, we had never had the opportunity to talk much. Several members of the church constantly told each of us that we needed to meet because both of us had tender hearts for hurting people, but the timing never worked out. He had a wife and four young children, and I had my mother.

When we finally arranged a meeting, I left knowing that God had revealed a little bit more about his purpose for my life. Blake and two of his business partners were interested in starting a nonprofit foundation for youth and needed advice on how to build their programs, governing board, and operational procedures. I routinely give nonprofit management advice in my career, so I initially thought this meeting would be nothing more than consultation. After our meeting, however, I knew that God had given me a path away from the problems I was having with Day Foundation and toward a position for which I was uniquely prepared.

Heart of a Champion Foundation appealed to me because of its commitment to fostering character in young people through the schools. Most of my trauma at school occurred at the hands of kids without character. These youths had no respect nor compassion for others and terrorized anyone who was different. Whenever I told adults about teasing, taunts, and assaults at the hands of fellow students, most of them dismissed bullying as a fact of life that I must accept and deal with. I rolled my eyes each time I heard, "Cheryl, kids can be cruel." I wanted to know what adults were going to do about the situation. Unfortunately, adults are now forced to deal with the culture of apathy that allows school violence, harassment, and bullying.

Today many victims of school-based trauma are resorting to suicide or violence to deal with their problems.

At the time I was consulting with the foundation about how to develop its programs, the board of directors asked me to lead the organization as executive director. I felt there was more here than an opportunity to escape my problems with Day; I felt a rush of excitement and hope that I could be instrumental in developing something that could make a difference in someone's life. I had helped many nonprofit organizations serve their clients better through grants I supervised through both the Dole and Day foundations. I was dissatisfied at the Day Foundation because I was not directly involved in helping other people.

Because I am an idealist, I also discovered that I did not function at my best in the traditional, hands-off approach to philanthropy. I did not care about what name should be placed on a plaque for donor recognition or how a grant could ultimately make the granter look good. I wanted to be a part of something that encouraged its employees to get their hands dirty in making the world a better place. Some of my friends thought I was crazy to leave the comfort of a multimillion-dollar organization for a start-up.

All my friends were cautiously happy. I was exuberant because I was now in control of the philosophy and climate of my place of employment, and I could surround myself with fellow visionaries who wanted to do more than write a check to someone else to do the actual work. I knew that finding peace for myself meant I had to become involved in the lives of others. By helping young people develop the character necessary to stop the violence or despair they encounter in schools and in their communities, I knew I could find a sense of peace. The adrenaline of entrepreneurship overtook me as I immersed myself into developing a strong organization.

Within one year we had created a comprehensive, multimedia program that involved many athletes of character as messengers of hope. After consulting with educators, we crafted a character curriculum that used radio, television, the Internet, school assemblies, and peer counseling to attack the destructive apathy and hatred that plagues many schools.

Instead of touting the same tired messages in many violence prevention or character education programs, Heart of a Champion Foundation rests its programs on using the professional athlete of character as the messenger. While carefully selecting athletes and sports personalities, Heart of a Champion Foundation developed radio programs, a video character curriculum, a magazine, and book series designed to penetrate the hearts and minds of even the most apathetic kids. The foundation did not glorify athletes but used the power of sports to get past the walls many youngsters construct to block out character or violence prevention messages. Instead of providing one-shot school assembly programs in which an athlete goes into a school, preaches at the kids, and then leaves, Heart of a Champion Foundation created a comprehensive year-long program that provided motivation for young people to take the lessons learned into their homes, communities, and peer groups.

I loved my work, but after a year I began to feel the familiar restlessness. Building an organization had been more challenging than I thought. I wore many hats: fund-raising, program development, board development, marketing, accounting, and public relations. I lost some of my staff to more lucrative positions in the private sector. Some board members' interests changed, and they decided to withdraw from their director positions. It was hard work; some days I felt overwhelmed, but I always remembered that what I was doing mattered.

I was still restless. Something else was missing. I, the young woman in a never-ending search for identity, belonging, and purpose, was still not satisfied. I was months away from my doctorate in psychology, my mother had been committed to another psychiatric facility, and despite the work I was doing, the youth organization did not fulfill me as I thought it would. I had spent over seven years in grant-making, disability, and mental health. The foundation, despite its compelling mission and programs, did not satisfy my ultimate career and personal goals. I knew the restlessness I felt this time was not associated with baggage from my past; it felt more like a discomfort that caused me to pause and be vigilant. God was trying to tell me something or move me in another direction. Although I was not certain of the meaning of my uncertainty, I knew my time as executive director of the foundation would soon be over.

I was beginning to look like a job hopper. I asked God how long it should take to find my purpose. I was only thirty years old and growing impatient. Gayle had told me that people often search most of their lives for their purpose, and some never find it. After all that I had been through, however, I had found comfort in believing that I was special; therefore, God had something unique to accomplish in my life. I had believed that God would allow me to discover my purpose at a young age so that I would have a longer time to make meaningful contributions.

For three months I waited expectantly for some sign from God. I had an overwhelming feeling that my lifelong search would be over. Instead of my finding purpose and meaning, however, my mother slipped into another psychotic state. Doctors scrambled for answers when she began showing signs of severe dementia. She could not use eating utensils because she did not know what they were for. She could not draw a clock because she did not remember what one looked like. Speaking in complete sentences was impossible because she lost her train of thought and began to ramble incoherently. She began to faint periodically and fell in the bathroom, breaking several ribs.

One night I caught her wandering outside. She was fearless of a pack of coyotes charging toward her from a distance. That night, Mom had to be committed to a psychiatric facility again. She was admitted to a new hospital, one that would change both of our lives.

Green Oaks Foundation for Mental Health— Providing Hope for People in Despair

While Mom was in the hospital for two weeks, I began to function as her case manager. I talked with the psychiatrists every day to assess her progress and provide feedback on her condition from my perspective. In preparation for her return home, I began searching for an all-day outpatient program for severely mentally ill adults. Since I needed to return to work, I could not stay at home to look after Mom. She also needed more care than I was able to give. Mom would benefit from a structured program that involved group and individual therapy and close medical management of her psychiatric symptoms. If I waited too long, she would be discharged into an environment that would not help her recovery. We lived in the suburbs of Dallas in an isolated, countrylike residential community. There was no public transportation, and Mom could not drive. Therefore, if she returned home to drown in her misery all day, she would never recover.

Mom's physical health problems intensified despite psychiatric treatment. She had blurred vision, acute dementia, and uncontrolled hypertension and diabetes. I began speaking with the internal medicine physicians to ensure they understood how to treat the general medical needs of mental health patients. I challenged each assumption that some of her physical symptoms were merely manifestations of her psychotic state. I would not accept any blanket assumptions and continued pressing for the testing of her hormone levels, thyroid function, and heart function. With dementia and profound confusion, Mom functioned much like an Alzheimer's patient. I knew those symptoms could be caused by her psychosis, but I also knew that uncontrolled hypertension could cause confusion and deteriorated mental faculties.

After observing and talking with Mom each day, I came home to research her symptoms. Within several weeks, Mom was on a carefully balanced combination of medication for depression, schizophrenia, hypertension, and diabetes.

In Mom's case, there was no clear boundary separating what was mental from what was physical. She did not have the energy or mental clarity to advocate for herself or adequately describe her symptoms. She would either minimize or forget critical symptoms. Ironically, Mom was in the same position I had been in thirty years ago—helpless and confused, in the hospital, and at the mercy of others. The roles were now reversed; I was the guardian and she was the dependent.

Since I had become my mother's primary advocate, I began to realize how stressful being the primary caregiver is for someone with mental and physical illnesses. Unlike my mother, however, I had a strong network of people who offered me support and encouragement. When I was born, Mom had no one. I began to have a better understanding of how the needs of a family member's chronic illness could cause caregivers to experience such problems as divorce or depression.

I visited Mom in the hospital and listened to her incoherent rambling during lunch. My eyes began to swell at the anguish I felt about the state of her life. She had lost her way, and I began losing hope that she would ever be well again. As soon as the fatalistic thought entered my mind, another thought overpowered it: Mom should have been dead a long time ago, but she was still alive for a purpose. God promised her a hope and future as well.

"Mom, do you know why God created you?" I did not expect an answer, given her mental state, but she surprised me.

"I'm going to be somebody one day. You just wait and see. I may not be who I want to be, but I thank God that I'm not who I used to be." Then Mom began rambling again. Although I had heard her statement many times before, Mom's declaration was more profound. In the midst of insanity, she had a moment of radiant hope. Mom was holding on for the day that God would make her somebody.

"Mom, what will make you a somebody?" I did not know what to expect in answer. I wondered if she would talk about having the wealth and career she once had. Although she talked about God on one level, I wondered if she could comprehend how God defined a "somebody."

"I'm tired of living like this. I'm going to get out of here. I'm going to be somebody. You can't be nothing when you feel so thrown away. I feel like I've been thrown in a dumpster like a baby nobody wants, but the devil ain't going to get me. He better stop talking to me too."

Mom was hearing voices again. In her agitated state, she began repeating, "I am somebody." The nurses and other patients turned toward her as her voice grew louder. She looked as if she were trying to brainwash herself into believing that God did not make a mistake when he created her—that he did not abandon her in a dumpster.

I looked around, understanding the hopelessness I saw on the faces of people all around me. Each one of them was looking for hope and peace that none of them knew how to find. I always speculated that Mom was fighting suicidal thoughts by her constant repetition of "I am somebody." Therefore, she wouldn't think of how to kill herself. She would hold on until God made a way.

I stayed with Mom until she calmed down. When I returned home, I started thinking about whether I believed I was somebody. Did I know that I was somebody, regardless of what I may or may not achieve in the future? Did I know that God's definition of somebody does not rest on anything I do in service to him? Thinking this through, I realized that I had been in a holding pattern because God wanted me to dig deeper into my own soul. He wanted me to see that I was still in the performance trap. I continued to believe the lie that I needed to do big and great things for God just to be somebody. I was already a somebody because I was a child of God, and no amount of achievement would make me a better somebody.

After Mom was released from the hospital and began attending the outpatient program, I heard that the psychiatric hospital had started a new mental health foundation and was looking for an executive direc-tor. As I was still young, I did not expect to be selected, but within several weeks after sending my résumé and completing the interview, I received a job offer. After the new foundation incorporated, I became the president/CEO of the Green Oaks Foundation for Mental Health, which is still associated with the psychiatric hospital. Within one day I knew that I had found what I longed to do with my life experiences, education, and passion for mental health.

Green Oaks is a nonprofit public foundation that raises and distributes funds to assist people with mental illness and chemical dependency with short-term crisis grants to help them reduce or eliminate environmental and social barriers in their lives that undermine long-term recovery. Associated with the largest health care corporation in the country, the foundation is positioned to be a national leader in the mental health field.

Building such a foundation requires long hours and hard work. After building Heart of a Champion, I thought I would never lead another start-up organization. But when I found my dreams and purpose merged in one organization, I cast aside doubts and got to work. I have staff to hire, programs to develop and implement, and funds to raise, but I am not tired or anxious about anything. God has led me to an organization in which I can use all of my talents, interests, education, and experiences. I do not know what the future holds for me and the foundation. Regardless of the uncertainty, I am excited to be the dreamer with the opportunity to put into practice her own vision for serving those with mental illness. My personal experiences humanize my business dealings and fuel my passion to do all that I can to offer hope to those who struggle with hopelessness.

Promise—Breaking the Cycle of Abuse

Sometimes people have a way of asking you questions that linger in your mind forever. When I was struggling with depression, one of my friends asked me, "Cheryl, I know you said that you want peace and meaning, but it seems like something else is haunting you. What exactly are you searching for? Do you even know?"

I could not answer because I did not understand her question. Over the years, however, the question continued to pop into my mind. What am I searching for? Inherent in the young is the quest for identity, purpose, and meaning in one's life. I knew that I was searching to accomplish something deeper. I wanted to do something in my life that broke the cycle of abuse and pathology in my family. For generations, family members had perpetuated verbal, emotional, physical, and spiritual abuse on their children.

Mom and Dad tried to escape the past by attending college and moving hundreds of miles away from their families. They tried to start fresh but failed to recognize they had become abusers, until it was too late. I am sure they told themselves they would grow up to be different from their parents. Unable to escape their own pasts, they slipped into the same dysfunctional parenting style that their parents had used. Internally, I had placed a huge burden on myself: I wanted to be the person used by God to break the cycle of abuse permanently. Similarly, Gayle wanted her children to live in a healthy spiritual home. We both knew that only God could break the legacy of abuse.

Given that I did not have children, I began to focus my attention on my sister's growing family. Gayle had three children since the onset of depression in my life, and I wanted to play an integral part in their development. Each child had his share of trauma to endure upon entering the world. The oldest, Anne, is a healthy five-year-old at the writing of this book, after being born one month premature and weighing five pounds. Having asthma, she has been rushed to the emergency room several times. Jerome, nineteen months, had trouble during delivery when his blood pressure dropped dangerously. He was delivered via an emergency cesarean section. He later developed severe pneumonia and nearly died. Antoinette was born healthy despite having a knot in her umbilical cord. She was also delivered by cesarean, and during the procedure the doctors were shocked to see that my sister's uterus was about to rupture.

I used to take birth and raising children for granted. After all, millions of children are born each day. Millions are not, however, raised to be healthy, loving, and faithful. As I looked at the three precious angels in my life, I realized the challenge more clearly. My legacy would not be what I accomplished in academics, in the disability community, at church, or at work. The legacy I desired rested on doing what my parents were unable to do—raise up a generation far removed from abuse and trauma and directed to God.

I focused my time, love, and attention on my sister's children. I became like a second mother to Anne, Jerome, and Antoinette, providing supplemental discipline, educational opportunities, and fun activities. My sister and brother-in-law built a household of faith for their children and they have flourished. I am proud to have played a part in their healthy development. Unlike Gayle and me, these children do not have misery etched on their faces. They do not fear for their safety or well-being. Our extended family network surrounds the children with love, guidance, and security.

When I found God at seventeen, I unknowingly started a powerful chain reaction in my family. Through my intense search for God, meaning, and hope, my sister and brother-in-law were inspired to search for God themselves. Gayle was a nice person in general but struggled with her temper. She also needed God to heal her from her abusive past. Once she found God, she shared the good news of healing and hope with her fiancé. One of my friends described me as the spiritual matriarch of my family because my search for God started it all.

Adversity has taught me many lessons about life. I orient my life by a simple principle, although a cliché: the decisions I make today will shape my future. I realized early that if I did not want an abusive future I needed to root out every instance of abuse, hostility, and dysfunction in my present. But I did not know how to be healthy. At first I merely ran away from the past, hoping that the future would be better. God, however, began to show me through other people what *healthy* meant. I have seen some solid parent-child relationships and marriages.

Depression forced me to start working through the trauma before my nieces and nephew were born. The head start allowed me to see more clearly that through their lives, and the lives of any children I would have, the ultimate victory over the past would be manifest.

When Gayle and I first realized we were all that we had in the world, both of us made a pact to never grow up to be like our parents. Ordinary family moments took on sacred status. We vowed we would listen to our children and make sure we constantly told them that they were loved. We would never allow anyone to harm them physically or emotionally. We told each other we would be nothing like our parents. Many abused children say the same thing only to find themselves become abusers. Even before I discovered my faith in God, I knew Gayle and I would not physically abuse our children. I was not so certain about emotional abuse. She and I both had pent-up hostility that frightened even us. I was afraid that the past was bigger than me.

When I found God, I discovered that apart from him I was too weak and vulnerable to fight the impact of an abusive upbringing. With God, however, there was no fear because we had the power we needed to forge a new generation under the guiding protection of faith. Knowing the triggers and signs of abuse, I began to monitor the actions of my family, including myself. I was hypervigilant for several months after Anne was born. After examining our responses to daily hassles and stress, including crisis moments, I became convinced that Gayle and I were healthy. Instead of fearing whether we would become like our parents, I would look at the children and take pride in knowing that we finally made it out of bondage. Gayle and I broke the cycle of abuse when we decided to follow God and allow ourselves to be molded into the people he wanted us to be.

Although Mom did not escape the effects of her past, she is no longer abusive. Whether it was medication, therapy, or forgiveness from God, Gayle, and me, I do not know the source of her transformation. Mom told me that her grandchildren are three reasons for her to live. She wants to make sure they grow up to be anything they want

to be. Gayle and I have monitored her interactions with them and marvel at her loving kisses, hugs, and attention. When she is well, she
reads, sings, and teaches them with the maternal love that Gayle and I
always wanted.

I caught myself feeling envious once because Anne, Jerome, and
Antoinette were receiving everything I always wanted from my
mother. I laughed the feeling off when I realized that Mom was only
able to give love because it was showered on her by Gayle and me.
Unlike her life with Dad, Mom's living environment is now stable and
rooted in faith and love. On limited public assistance, she has health
care and Social Security disability income. Still, Mom has a long way
to go. She is still searching for purpose. I pray that she finds meaning
and wholeness. In the process of her quest, God is transforming her
heart and removing her burdens. My nieces and nephew now have
what I never had—a real "grandmommy" who is integral to their lives
and development.

When I look at Mom and my nieces and nephew, I see promise.
God is working out the impossible, realigning future generations
under him. One of the images I will never forget about the epic minis-
eries *Roots* is how each generation in slavery told its children detailed
accounts of its family history from Africa to bondage in America. The
goal of passing along the stories of the struggle was to ensure that
young people never forgot the power, love, and faithfulness of God.
When they remember God, they remain on the path laid out for them
through the blood, sweat, and tears of their ancestors. When they are
older, Anne, Jerome, and Antoinette will also know their roots. They
will hear of all the ways God carried Gayle and me to the real promised land, through faith, love, purpose, and hope. The children will
also be instructed to pass the stories of faith along to their children so
that no one ever forgets that God is love.

Epilogue

I still laugh at the responses I receive when I tell people that I have written my autobiography. The most common response is, "You haven't lived long enough to have one of those." To the contrary, I have lived a life full of tragedies and triumph, each giving rise to a deeper faith in God. Although I still have some lingering struggles and doubts, the trauma of the past is largely behind me, and I am excited about the future. I am a proud survivor and overcomer. Against the odds, I found God. Through our relationship, I am being healed from the legacy of my past. What I have written has been my present understanding and analysis of my past. I am sure God will teach me more as I mature.

My story reflects the common goal of youth: a search for identity, belonging, and purpose. My search took place in the shadows of despair and trauma. There is no "happily ever after" ending. I am not famous or wealthy. I am still looking for answers to my soul's deepest questions and longings. I am still healing, learning how to trust and let go of things I cannot change. I have not "arrived," if arriving means I will never again struggle or suffer. It is hard to accept the reality that life can be tough and unfair, that the world can be mean and heartless, and that many people will make selfish decisions that hurt others. This type of misery was never in God's perfect plan and does not mean that God is cruel, distant, or uncaring.

Although I still have struggles with feelings from the past, I know that my hope and faith are inextinguishable. God promised to give me hope and a future, and his purpose for my life is unfolding before me. Despite the tragedy of my childhood, I am proud of who I have become. Not many people blossom in adversity. As an overcomer, I am triumphant, not because I have achieved earthly success, but because abuse, loneliness, and despair were not powerful enough to destroy or embitter me. Nothing on earth can overpower God. He promised that nothing could ever separate me from his love. I am learning to accept his promises as fact, despite the whims of my feelings. My challenge is to keep hoping, believing, and trusting even when God seems distant or silent. I searched for God and found him. As a result, I know my family and I will never be the same again. In my long sojourn, I have discovered God was never far away. He whispered to my soul his promises to heal. Learning how to rest my weary soul in his hands and believing his promises have made all the difference.

> *My precious child,*
> *Don't be discouraged. Joy comes in the*
>   *morning.*
> *Know that I am near.*
> *Stand still and look up. I am going to show*
>   *up.*
> *I am standing by.*
> *There's healing for your sorrow. Healing for*
>   *your pain.*
> *Healing for your spirit. There's shelter from*
>   *the rain.*
> *I'll send My healing. For this you'll know,*
> *I am the Balm in Gilead to heal your soul.*

RICHARD SMALLWOOD, ADAPTED BY C. GREEN,
ZOMBA SONGS INC. (BMI)